WESTERN ISLES LIBRARIES

Readers are requested to take great care of the item while in their possession, and to point out any defects that they may notice in them to the Librarian.
This item should be returned on or before the latest date stamped below, but an extension of the period of loan may be granted when desired.

Mario
LANZA

Mario
LANZA

Sublime Serenade

DAVID BRET

BOOKS

Ten years on, this book is dedicated to the memory of Amália Rodrigues (23 July 1920–6 October 1999) and *Les Enfants de Novembre*. *N'oublie pas...la vie sans amis c'est comme un jardin sans fleurs.*

First published in Great Britain in 2009 by
JR Books, 10 Greenland Street,
London NW1 0ND
www.jrbooks.com

A catalogue record for this book is available from the British Library.

ISBN 978-1-906779-52-8

1 3 5 7 9 10 8 6 4 2

Printed by MPG Books, Bodmin, Cornwall

Contents

Acknowledgements

Writing this book would not have been possible had it not been for the inspiration, criticisms and love of that select group of individuals who, whether they be in this world or the next, I will always regard as my true family and *autre coeur*: Barbara, Irene Bevan, Marlene Dietrich, René Chevalier, Axel Dotti, Dorothy Squires and Roger Normand, *que vous dormez en paix*, Lucette Chevalier, Maria da Fé, Jacqueline Danno, Doris Day, Hélène Delavault, Tony Griffin, Betty and Gérard Garmain, Annick Roux, John and Anne Taylor, Terry Sanderson, Charley Marouani, David and Sally Bolt. Also a very special mention for Amália Rodrigues, Joey Stefano, those *hiboux*, *fadistas* and *amis de foutre* who happened along the way, and *mes enfants perdus*.

Thanks too to Mikey Blatin and Theo Morgan, and an especial thank you to Sam Samuelian and Roland Bessette, the roses among the poison ivy. And where would I be without Jeremy Robson and the munificent team at JR Books; my agent Guy Rose and his lovely wife, Alex; and also my wife, Jeanne, for putting up with my bad moods and for still being the keeper of my soul.

And finally a *grand chapeau bas* to Mario Lanza, for having lived.

David Bret

Introduction

They labelled him 'The American Caruso', although in fact the appellation came from himself and his obsession with a tenor, long dead when he came along, whom most Americans had never even heard of and only really got to know because of him! Also, to bestow such a title on him is almost offensive. Truthfully, they should never be compared at all because, artistically and vocally, they were a world and several generations apart. On stage, Caruso was in a class of his own, sailing through even the toughest of roles with consummate ease, whereas those supposedly in the know have said that Lanza may not have had the stamina – certainly in his later years, when his voice was in its prime, but he himself was in poor shape – to sustain a complete performance other than in the lighter Bellini or Verdi roles. The argument, of course, is that he was never given the right encouragement. Where Lanza triumphed over his alter ego was in the studio, for whereas Caruso's vocal flaws had often been camouflaged by the primeval recording techniques of the day, with Lanza – even when singing what others claimed to be badly (though there was actually no such thing as a bad Lanza performance) – these flaws were virtually non-existent. Technically, Lanza was far superior to Caruso; quite simply, Lanza had no vocal imperfections. Vocally, the man was a genius, and it was only his own laziness, coupled with studio greed, that prevented him from achieving what Caruso had accomplished on the legitimate opera stage.

Maria Callas, that most discerning of divas, who reigned supreme in an age when the word was used in its proper context – as opposed to being applied to any songstress of dubious vocal ability – called him 'the greatest tenor who ever lived', and regretted never having performed with him. Like hers, his was a monstrous talent complemented by an equally monstrous ego and a quite ferocious, almost at times dangerous, temper brought about by what might be diagnosed by today's doctors as bipolar disorder – or alternatively, as a side-effect of his indisputable genius. As an entertainer, from the fans' point of view on celluloid as well as in the recording studio and on the concert platform, he could do no wrong. On the film set, one saw a completely different Lanza from the fun-loving, copiously vulgar yet hilariously witty Lanza of the record-ing studio. Apart from the 'little people' – technicians, clapper-girls, cameramen and the like – the studio chiefs could be merciless in their demands, and some of his co-stars left much to be desired. Many of these people dismissed him as an extremely unpleasant individual and swore never to work with him again, yet his sometimes unsavoury behaviour was almost always in retaliation to their treatment of him, and a reaction to their lack of respect for him. When he died, virtually none of these people attended his funeral, and the event itself was deliberately turned into a farce. Yet would Lanza, despite his many flaws never a hypocrite, have wanted them there?

Though there have been many good and several great, if not over-hyped, tenors, there have only been two truly magnificent lyric tenors who have successfully made the opera-to-operetta transition by way of lieder, secular and popular song, to which can be added the category of Broadway hits: Fritz Wunderlich, and Mario Lanza. They were way ahead of their time. Indeed, Lanza's album, *A Cavalcade Of Show Tunes*, is quite possibly the best such album ever recorded. Both tenors left us way too soon, still in their thirties, having just reached their peak. Neither achieved their most heartfelt goal: to sing grand opera at major houses such as La Scala and the New York Met. Wunderlich (1930–66) failed because of his steadfast refusal to sing in any other language but his native Palatinate German. Lanza failed because the Hollywood powers who came to control him were interested only in personal appearances and making money – because he, despite the bravado of his persona, was nevertheless too weak-spirited to fight both these moguls and his personal demons which saw him deliriously happy one moment, and plunged into the darkest 'black dog' depression the next.

Like Callas and her infatuation with the bel canto repertoire, Lanza's insistence on recording just about every major tenor aria in the repertoire – stretching his voice sometimes beyond its already formidable limits –

resulted in him 'singing himself out' way too soon. Like her, at his peak he was unsurpassable. Even towards the end, when detractors declared that the voice that had made him millions was starting to let him down, he was still better than anyone else.

Lanza has often been labelled 'The Fourth Tenor' after Pavarotti, Domingo and Carreras, but truthfully he was the first, and the one whom every single one of today's tenors, whether authentic or publicity manufactured, should use as a yardstick to gauge their own performances, which frequently sound less than mediocre when compared to the blazing, lodestar talent that was Mario Lanza in his prime.

This is his story...

Chapter One

Vesti la giubba

It was a magnificent, moving spectacle . . . it chilled the blood
with awe and wonder, and warmed the heart with love.

*Bandleader Earl Denny on Mario Lanza's first known
public performance*

He was born Alfredo Arnoldo Cocozza, at 9.45am on 31 January 1921, at 636 Christian Street in Philadelphia's colourful Little Italy suburb. His father, 27-year-old Antonio, had emigrated here with his family in 1905 from Collemacchia, a small town in Italy's Molise region. His mother, Maria Lanza, originated from Tocco da Casauria, in Abruzzi, though she had left as a babe in arms with her mother to join her father, Salvatore, who had emigrated to America the previous year. The entire clan, including Salvatore Lanza, his wife Elisabetta and their eight children, lived and squabbled together in a small house, which doubled as a general store-cum-delicatessen. And from a very early age, strict disciplinarian Salvatore made sure that everyone mucked in with the running of his household and business.

Most of the family appear to have been musical, and passionate about the only Italian singer most people in Middle America had heard of: Enrico Caruso, who died suddenly when Alfredo, or Freddie, as his loved ones called him, was six months old. Lanza once said, never more seriously, that Caruso's spirit had moved on not to heaven, but to within him, and he may have been right. Unfortunately, the primeval recording techniques at the turn of the century when the great tenor was at his peak do not do him justice, so he and Lanza cannot justifiably be compared.

Lanza would spent his entire life absolutely obsessed by Caruso. He always maintained that the priest who baptised him had been called Father Caruso. He listened to recordings by the great tenor almost every day of his life, and when about to make a major decision he would ask himself, 'What would Caruso do if he were me?'

Maria Lanza claimed that her greatest desire had been to sing opera herself at La Scala – a combination of daydreaming and reflecting on what her famous son had achieved. In the same way, the mothers of his contemporaries Judy Garland and Montgomery Clift (Lanza would meet both) nurtured similar unachieved ambitions, without having a fraction of their offsprings' innate talent. The slight difference between Maria Lanza and Ethel Gumm (Judy's mother) or Sunny Clift (Montgomery's mother) was that Maria *could* sing, as private recordings reveal, and sing rather well in a light mezzo-soprano voice. The only reason she never tried to achieve her dream was because her martinet father would not allow her to spread her wings – as the eldest of the Lanzas' children, she had been expected to stay home and care for the younger siblings, seven of which lived. This dedication and inordinate pandering would later be transferred to her only son, who returned her affection by developing what some considered to be an unhealthy Oedipus complex, not just with Maria, but with the other women in his life. Maria was only a little over 16 years his senior, a narrow gap in those days, and throughout his youth he would find himself sexually attracted only to women who were of the same age as or older than his mother. Indeed, after Lanza's death, one incident was reported of how Maria had actually been mistaken for his lover. 'As he grew into his teens, the age span between them seemed less because Mary [sic] continued to retain her sweet sixteen figure and looks,' observed Terry Robinson in *Lanza: His Tragic Life*. His co-biographer, Raymond Strait, goes on to explain how they were strolling along the street one day when a group of young men hanging about outside a drugstore ogled Maria. When one of these made a dirty remark, Freddie laid him out on the pavement with the warning, 'That's my mother – next time I'll finish you for good!'

Maria's unyielding ambitions for her son were also a means of diverting attention from a husband who, though kind and supportive, was not the virile hunk her parents had hoped she might settle down with and raise a family as large as their own. Called up at the outbreak of World

War I, Antonio had been shipped off to France to serve at the front with 37th Division 145th Infantry. He was one of the 1,250,000 US soldiers who had outnumbered the Germans three to one in the Meuse–Argonne Offensive near Verdun, the Expeditionary Force's biggest operation. On 15 October 1918, towards the end of this particular conflict, he had been wounded by a dum-dum bullet which had almost severed his right arm below the elbow. He had also been gassed and suffered severe shell-shock, a condition which would affect him for the rest of his life.

It is not clear exactly when Antonio and Maria met for the first time – only that the encounter took place in her father's shop. Both claimed that it had been in 1919, after Antonio's discharge from the army, when Maria would have been 16, though it has been suggested that they were dating *before* he left for Europe, which of course means that had their union been consummated, under State law Antonio could have been arrested and charged with statutory rape. For his bravery on the field at Verdun, he was awarded the prestigious Purple Heart, and when he walked Maria down the aisle he was feted by the Lanzas not just as the latest addition to their extended family, but as a war hero. Many years later, MGM, that great fabricator of stars' biographies, would exaggerate by turning Antonio Cocozza into another d'Annunzio. How he earned his crust after demobilisation is also uncertain. At the time of his marriage he worked as a cabinet varnisher for the Victor Talking Machine Company (later RCA Victor), and later he worked as a lathe-turner in a factory, but much of his income appears to have come from his war pension, supplemented by scrounging from his family. And whilst he lounged around, Maria was expected to look after their son and work part-time at home, hooking peg-rugs and taking in sewing.

As with many of his contemporaries, little is known of Freddie Cocozza's childhood other than those anecdotes and reminiscences the singer chose to recount and mentally edit, as well as the reflections of those closest to him, peppered with exaggeration and invention. Thus we were led to believe that a miracle performed by St Theresa cured Edith Piaf of blindness, when doctors were actually treating her for conjunctivitis – and that Errol Flynn was a champion boxer, and not a Tasmanian hellraiser on the run from the police. Similarly, six-year-old Freddie is supposed to have listened to Caruso's crackly rendition of 'Vesti la giubba' thirty times on the trot on his grandfather's gramophone until he had learned the piece by heart, and at this point he decided to become an opera singer. It all makes for an interesting story, of course, bearing in mind that he would not just emulate but in some people's eyes surpass the greatest tenor of his generation, some years later, in one of his most celebrated films.

Perhaps equally far-fetched, one would imagine (though if true, it would confirm that the family did have links with the Mafia, something which has never been proved), is the story of how, in that same year of 1927, Freddie was witness to the shooting of his uncle, Vincente Cocozza, outside a restaurant near his home. He would excitedly recall how he had been standing on the pavement, minding his own business, when a car had zipped by and one of its occupants had opened fire, killing Vincente and the man with him. It seems rather incredible that a boy so young could have had such a vivid recollection of what appears to have been a gangland murder, let alone remember the name of the intended victim – Anthony 'Musky' Zanghi. When challenged about this once, he amended the story slightly: he had been nine years old, and the incident had taken place outside the family home on Christian Street. The truth is that almost certainly Freddie had been 'filled in' about the killing years later by a family member, or more than likely read about it on the front page of the *Philadelphia Enquirer*.

In 1930, following one argument too many with Maria's interfering parents, the Cocozzas moved out of Christian Street and into a six-roomed house at 2040 Mercy Street. Antonio and Maria still spent much of their leisure time with her warring family – they had little choice, for Salvatore Lanza had financed the move, and was still paying them a weekly allowance. Between the ages of seven and fourteen, Freddie had so many changes of school that he must have felt dizzy. Freddie's grandfather also decided which school he would attend. As Freddie had been baptised at St Mary Magdalene di Pazzi, Philadelphia's first all-Catholic church, Salvatore considered it appropriate that his grandson attend its school, on Montrose Street, yet no sooner had he settled in here than he was moved to the Edgar Allan Poe Elementary. By the end of 1932 Freddie had been enrolled at the Edwin Nare Junior High – and by the time he left here in the summer of 1935 he had changed his mind about an operatic career, telling friends that he wanted to be the next Russ Columbo.

Russ Columbo (1908–34), immensely popular at the time, was a contemporary of Bing Crosby who might have achieved more lasting fame had he lived. Adored by his fans, privately he was a deeply disturbed individual. In September 1934 he had a tiff with his photographer lover, Lansing Brown, who had been showing him his collection of antique pistols. One of these went off accidentally: the bullet ricocheted off a table top and entered Columbo's eye, killing him almost instantly. Mario Lanza would later cover one of his songs, 'When You are in Love', from *Wake Up and Dream*. More ironically, the singer's biography would later be penned by a Joseph Lanza, no relation to Mario.

In September 1935, Freddie moved to the South Philadelphia High School for Boys. Academically, he was a non-achiever: though reasonably articulate, he played truant a lot and his only interests were boxing, weightlifting and mixing with the wrong crowd from the Italian quarter who gathered most evenings at the South Philadelphia Boys Club, on Moyamensing Avenue. Freddie and his gang of roughnecks were the scourge of the neighbourhood, scrapping with other gangs, robbing delivery trucks and generally causing mayhem. To earn money for beer, they would mug the smaller, weaker boys outside the school, steal their textbooks, then sell them back to them the next day. 'I must have been a little bastard,' Lanza later told *Time* magazine, 'but I was always the leader!' And in his parents' eyes he could do no wrong: if the Cocozzas received a visit from the police over some incident, to their way of thinking it was always someone else who had been involved, never Freddie. If he became upset – which happened often, when he wanted his own way – they would pander to his whims by feeding and pampering him.

The Lanzas appeared to live well for humble shopkeepers, especially given the size of their family. One minute they were complaining about the cramped conditions on Christian Street, the next Salvatore was buying a summer house at Wildwood, the resort centre in New Jersey, 35 miles from Atlantic City and 90 miles from Philadelphia. According to the legend, when Antonio overheard 16-year-old Freddie singing along to his favourite recording – Caruso's then definitive 'Vesti la giubba' once more – he was so overwhelmed that he summoned a family meeting, and it was decided that the boy should be given private lessons to mould him for the operatic career that had evaded his mother. Salvatore was firmly against the idea, but was overruled by the rest of the clan: begrudgingly, he agreed to pay. Freddie had already started to develop the ego which would frequently blight his later career, and immediately saw himself partnering the likes of Rosa Ponselle at the New York Met. It was at this stage that his music professor, the baritone Antonio Scarduzzo, whipped the rug from under him by warning him that, as his voice was not properly broken, he ran the risk of permanent damage to his vocal cords by even attempting to hit the same notes as his idol. Instead of singing, Scarduzzo suggested, he should first learn *solfeggio* (the 'sol-fa' system of sight-reading), and also take lessons in German, French and Italian so that if and when the time came he would be well prepared for the concert platform. Scarduzzo also suggested that he learn a musical instrument. Eager to please the fickle youth, Maria bought Freddie a violin – which in a fit of rage he one day flung out of his bedroom window. To make up for her mistake, Maria bought him a pianola which, thankfully for anyone who happened to be passing by, did not suffer the same fate!

Salvatore hired a language tutor for his grandson, and the results were surprisingly good, bearing in mind his lethargy towards other school work. Freddie would master French, Italian and Spanish with sufficient fluency to sing any aria of his choosing without slipping up, though he was the first to admit that he would never have been capable of holding a conversation in any language but English, other than the swear words. 'Mario Lanza could say *fuck* in twenty different languages,' offered Tallulah Bankhead, with whom he would later work on the radio. As for Antonio Scarduzzo, Mario completely ignored his advice to avoid singing too much, and for the next year or so he studied hard, practising his scales at home. The holidays he spent in Wildwood with the Lanzas, inviting all his friends along and helping to pay for his keep by driving a trolleybus. Years later, locals would recall how easy it had been to work out which bus he had been on – they had heard his singing half a mile away. The job did not last long, however: he was fired for letting his friends and every pretty girl in the neighbourhood ride for free. Unfazed, Mario and a friend, Joe Siciliano, took up busking in the streets. Siciliano would play his guitar, whilst Mario belted out Neapolitan love-songs. 'When a man in a blue uniform approached, we'd take off like gazelles for another concert in a safer sector,' he told *Modern Screen*, some years later. 'It may have been illegal, but it didn't hurt anybody and the few brushes with the law we had were a very steadying influence on Joe. He grew up and became one of the best, and best-liked, cops in Philadelphia.'

Privately, Salvatore was hoping that Freddie would grow out of his obsession and find himself 'regular' employment. All this changed during his senior year at South Philadelphia when he got into an argument with one of his teachers: when the teacher called him 'dirty wop', Freddie chinned him and was expelled. Many years later, in a *Time* magazine feature, one of these teachers would describe Mario Lanza as 'One of the biggest bums to ever come through the public school system.' This expulsion would also set a precedent: comfort eating, resulting in episodes of obesity followed by intense, harrowing periods of fasting. In this respect, Mario would not be unique: Lou Costello, Sidney Greenstreet, Orson Welles and Wallace Beery all had similar problems, but more attention would be focused on Mario because the ups and downs in his weight had much less to do with gluttony than his trying to strike a happy medium between the traditions of operatic requirements – the belief that excess weight pushed the voice forwards – and looking good on the screen in the days when overweight people were invariably portrayed as villains (Greenstreet) or generally behaving stupidly (Costello). Photographs taken at the time suggest Mario might have been tipping the scales at 240 pounds, and he had not stopped growing. And though his family would dismiss this alternately as 'puppy fat' and 'good living', the problem would recur time and time again throughout his life and eventually contribute towards his downfall. At 15, Mario could clear a plate with two pounds of steak and six eggs – and this was just for breakfast. Alternatively, he would wolf down an omelette containing 24 eggs!

With just six months left to finish studying for his high school diploma, the Cocozzas enrolled Freddie at the Lincoln Preparatory Academy, a private establishment which this time was paid for by Maria. More importantly, and much more crucial to him than finishing his education, he was introduced to Irene Williams, a 52-year-old retired soprano who had sung with the Mormon Tabernacle Choir, and the Chicago, New York, Los Angeles and San Francisco Symphony Orchestras. Additionally, she had duetted with Nelson Eddy. Now, Williams ran a voice academy in Philadelphia. Her services did not come cheap, and when Salvatore Lanza learned how serious his grandson was about pursuing his singing career, he refused to cough up, leaving Maria to pay for the thrice-weekly lessons. This meant her taking on extra work and being forced to get up most mornings at 5.30am.

When Mario complained that the noise of his mother 'pottering about' disturbed his sleep, Antonio starting taking him breakfast in bed so that he could catch up on his rest. His grandfather, on the other hand, ranted and raved that he too should have been out earning money and doing a real man's job, not lounging about the place. One lazy slob – Antonio – was more than enough in the family, Salvatore Lanza declared.

According to Irene Williams, Mario was not a model pupil. 'Sometimes he would be barely awake when he came for his lesson at two in the afternoon,' she told *Time* magazine in 1951. 'I used to chide him for being so lazy when his mother worked so hard.' Mario refused to practise his scales and breathing lessons, and still had not mastered the art of *solfeggio*, which has always been absolutely imperative for all opera singers. Indeed, he never would, preferring to stick a record on the turntable and sing along to this, picking up the singer's flaws and adding embellishments of his own, frequently way over the top but thrilling just the same. Then, as later, he would also have the annoying habit (for some) of hitting a top C without even working up to it. Friends recalled his 'party trick', when he would creep up behind them and suddenly let rip with a resounding note which all but burst their eardrums.

Sources who claim to have heard Freddie Cocozza singing in Irene Williams's workshop would later draw comparisons between his teenage voice and that of Fritz Wunderlich. This is true to a certain extent: he had the power, and the unmistakable and sincere sob in the voice, but primarily on account of his lethargy towards rehearsing he would never be possessed of Wunderlich's unmatched, almost superhuman breath control and on-stage stamina. Later, Pavarotti and Callas blasted their way through mighty careers with absolutely no one capable of surpassing them. It is therefore unfair to compare him with anyone from the legitimate operatic world because his career veered off in a more glitzy direction. Maybe, had he stuck with his studies and auditioned for one of the major opera houses, things would have turned out differently – maybe we would now be comparing him with Franco Corelli, Callas's favourite partner, also born in 1921. One only has to listen to Lanza's first known professional (as opposed to acetate) recording, 'Mamma mia, che vo' sape', made when he was 27, and Wunderlich's 'Einmal hat mir zur Frühlingszeit das Gluck gelacht', recorded when he was 23, to determine the uncanny similarity in their vocal techniques. It is also interesting to note the prejudice there has been from supposed 'experts' towards the Lanza voice, simply because they stubbornly refused to acknowledge that he was a great classical artist. In a recent poll conducted by the personnel of *BBC Music Magazine* to list the world's top twenty tenors, whilst Wunderlich came in at number 4 (Caruso came second, after Placido Domingo), Lanza does not show at all. Indeed, how many of the general public would have even heard of Peter Schreier, Wolfgang Windgassen and Sergey Lemeshev – and where were Andrea Bocelli and Roberto Alagna? As a result of the omission, many Lanza fans would claim that this was just another example of the classical world not accepting him as one of their own.

Freddie Cocozza studied with Irene Williams for almost two years, and it was probably she who suggested that he would never get anywhere with a name like Freddie Cocozza unless he made it on the opera stage – which also suggests that despite his enthusiasm, and in her opinion, with his lack of discipline he would never become the next Caruso. He had been toying with this idea himself, as a subsequently discovered schoolbook proves: on one page he has scribbled several names, including Al Cocozza and Fred Lanza. The one he favoured now was Mario Lanza, the masculine form of his mother's maiden name, which of course led cynics to home in on his Oedipus complex – the fact that, when his parents accompanied him anywhere, Antonio usually hung around in the background whilst Maria clung to her son's arm. Bearing in mind that they were so close in age, this indicated to some of those not in the know that Mario and Maria were a couple. Next, Williams introduced him to his first public – that of the society drawing room, soirées arranged mostly by middle-aged matrons, or young wives whose husbands were serving in the military, now that war had broken out in Europe.

Some of these early performances are said to have been embarrassing to watch. Though strikingly handsome and, in those days, not too overweight, he took up an ungainly stance in front of the piano and never knew what to do with his hands. He also suffered badly from stage fright, and made no secret of the fact that he was singing to people he mostly despised: though he would become very rich, Mario Lanza always looked down his nose at snobs. This said, there is little doubt that Mario fancied himself as something of a gigolo – to his way of thinking, if a woman could flaunt her wealth in his face, then she could also pay for his services in the bedroom. When asked by his closest friend, Terry Robinson (who was to anecdotes almost what Tallulah Bankhead would be to one-liners, and of whom more later) about the secret of his magnificent voice, he would reply, 'It's all sex, Terry. When I'm singing, I'm scoring. That's me. It comes right out of my balls!'

An early would-be conquest appears to have been another man, the first of several similarly disappointed suitors, cited by some sources as a wealthy member of the Astor family. Freddie – virulently heterosexual, but never homophobic – very abruptly knocked him back, according to Robinson, with the excuse that his pride would never permit him to accept money – which of course is exactly what he *was* doing at the time. Then in September 1940 he encountered a woman known only as The Countess, a visiting 'society dame' who was so impressed by the youth and his voice that she invited him to visit her in New York at the end of the year. The deal was that she would put him up in one of Manhattan's finest hotels, in exchange for being able to show him off to her society friends. Some sources maintain that Mario travelled alone, others that he took former busking buddy Joe Siciliano along for company. He actually stayed at her suite in the Hotel St Regis between 8 and 18 December, and would have stayed longer, had it not been for his family wanting him to return to Philadelphia for Christmas.

Again, we only have the Lanza 'tall tale' as to what happened in New York. One of the Countess's treats was an evening at the Met, where he met one of his idols, the great Swedish tenor, Jussi Björling (1911–60). Joe Siciliano told one biographer, Derek Mannering, of how they had met the soprano Rosa Ponselle. He also said that Björling had spectacularly cracked a top C whilst singing 'Di quella pira' during a performance of *Il Trovatore* – furthermore that he had stopped the orchestra, mid-opera, and started the aria again. This is not true. Ponselle was touring at that time, and Björling did not perform *Il Trovatore* until the following year. On 12 December 1940, the evening in question, records state that he was singing the part of Riccardo in Verdi's *Un Ballo In Maschera*, and performed flawlessly, according to contemporary reviews.

In New York, on 16 December, courtesy of the mysterious Countess, Mario paid his first visit to a recording studio. Here, accompanied simply by a piano, he put down three acetates which occasionally crop up on bootleg albums. The first was the Neapolitan favourite, 'Torna a Surriento', followed by a very brave attempt at 'Che'lla mi creda', from Puccini's *La Fanciulla del West*. And finally, what was by now his unofficial theme, 'Vesti la giubba', though when he later claimed that he had recorded the latter as a gift for his parents' 20th wedding anniversary, Mario would be shooting himself in the foot. Maria and Antonio are generally believed to have married in January 1920, but if they had married in December of that year, as their son now claimed, then he was effectively declaring himself illegitimate. Back in Philadelphia, Antonio Cocozza had these acetates copied, in the event of anything happening to the fragile originals. The tapes were distributed amongst friends, and word of Mario's magnificent voice quickly spread around the city. On Christmas Day, local bandleader Earl Denny – a regular feature at the Cathay Tea Garden and Palumbo's Café – invited him to guest at a morning mass he was hosting at St Mary Magdalene. Mario sang just one piece: the Bach–Gounod 'Ave Maria', but the response was unprecedented. 'People literally went down on their knees afterwards,' Denny recalled. 'They kissed Mario's hands and some, perhaps the most touched of all, were speechless.'

Such adoration would be bound to go to any young man's head, particularly before the high altar in a church, though Irene Williams – who frequently suffered the brunt of the temper tantrums which were already starting to take over – convinced Mario that he was not yet ready for the concert platform. He resumed his social soirées, until on 1 April Williams added him to the roster in a so-called 'Pops' concert at Sam Wanamaker's department store. This was a prestigious event conducted by Emanuel Balaban, currently working with Paul Robeson on his *Songs For Free Men* cycle. Amongst the first to take to the stage in a very full bill, Mario performed 'Cielo e mar' from Ponchielli's *La Gioconda*, and returned later in the programme to partner soprano Carolyn Long in three duets including 'O soave fanciulla' from *La Bohème*.

Amongst the local entrepreneurs sitting in the audience was William K. Huff, the director of Philadelphia Forum Concerts, and a man with considerable clout. It was he who suggested to Irene Williams that her pupil apply for an audition with Sergei Koussevitzky, who was in town for a series of concerts at the Philadelphia Academy on Locust Street. Since 1924, Koussevitzky (1874–1951) had been principal conductor with the

Boston Symphony Orchestra, a tenure he would hold until two years before his death. A tetchy, discerning character, he ran summer concerts and workshops at the orchestra's headquarters, Tanglewood, near Lenox in the Berkshire Mountains, Massachusetts. Each year, Koussevitzky would personally interview and invite 300 students of every classical denomination. Amongst his famous alumni was Leonard Bernstein, who worked as his assistant that year.

Once again, Mario exaggerated when recounting his induction into the Tanglewood workshop. According to him (in a story subsequently embellished by MGM), he was visiting the Philadelphia Academy the morning after the Pops concert and helping workmen to shift a grand piano when he suddenly burst into – yes, 'Vesti la giubba'. Koussevitzky, he claimed, was in the next room having a massage, and rushed out to felicitate him, with a scholarship application form he just happened to have in his hand ready for Mario to sign. 'He put both arms around me, kissed me in true Russian style, and said "You will come and sing for me in the Berkshires",' Mario said in a 1958 interview with a German radio station. None of this was true, of course. Irene Williams had submitted her pupil's application along with several others – he was registered as Alfredo Cocozza – and Mario attended an audition a few days later which he nevertheless passed with flying colours. He was then informed that in due course he would receive his scholarship papers in the post.

In the meantime, on the strength of his acceptance to study under Koussevitzky, Mario was asked to audition for William Judd, the director of Columbia Concerts, in New York – later Columbia Artists Management. Again, he chose 'Vesti la giubba', but this time his 'lucky' aria failed him. Judd liked what he heard, but declared that Mario was not yet ready to join his 'firm'. He was told to practise more, acquire discipline, learn *solfeggio*, then reapply in twelve months' time. Judd also criticised Mario's attitude: his comment, 'He's untamable. He'll end up the greatest tenor in the world, or just another singing waiter,' made Mario see red. Mario would never take kindly to criticism or rejection, and he cursed the air blue. Compensation came on 5 April, Easter Sunday, when as a result of a cancellation he was a last-minute addition to the programme at Haddon Hall, in Atlantic City, New Jersey. It was a tremendous rush to get to the venue on time but he made it, and received a standing ovation for a powerhouse rendition of 'Ombra mai fu', from Handel's *Xerxes*. He also sang arias from *Andrea Chénier* and Cileas's little-performed *L'Arlesiana*, but the real highlight of the evening was his sequence from *Cavalleria Rusticana* with soprano Josepha Chekova.

On 5 June, Mario received his papers to enter Tanglewood. His sponsor was listed as 'Miss Alice Clapp', who may well have been his mysterious Countess, or alternatively some other wealthy matron he had charmed. His tenure with the Berkley Music Center (now the Tanglewood Music Center) ran from 5 July through to 15 August, and such were his delusions of grandeur that, before he left Philadelphia, Irene Williams got him to sign a contract which would guarantee her the usual 10 per cent of his earnings, should these exceed $7,000 in a year. When he arrived at Tanglewood he very nearly headed back to the railway station upon learning that most of the workshops and the Berkshire Music Festival itself had been cancelled because of the involvement of the United States in the war. Some buildings had been commissioned by the Red Cross, and the main auditorium had been transformed into an entertainments canteen for servicemen on leave. He was persuaded to stay by Romeo Cascarino, a fellow South Philadelphian who would also go on to better things, but at a much more leisurely pace. Cascarino (1922–2002) would take 25 years to compose his opera, *William Penn*, about the founder of Philadelphia – and this would receive just two performances during his lifetime, though Cascarino was to achieve more lasting fame after his death. It was he who signed the petition urging Koussevitzky to reinstate the Music Festival. This happened on 7 August when, under the baton of Boris Goldovsky, another of the maestro's protégés, Mario sang the role of Fenton in an English-language version of Nicolai's comic opera, *The Merry Wives of Windsor*.

The whole purpose of Tanglewood was to learn one's craft, under privileged conditions, with neither ego nor outside financial influence, and without taking liberties. That Mario was a difficult, headstrong student was evident in the number of complaints Koussevitzky received from Goldovsky and stage director Herbert Graf regarding his attitude, his mood swings, and especially his drinking and womanising. Irene Williams was summoned from Philadelphia to give her investment a lecture and hopefully pull him back into line. Graf (1903–73), a producer with the New York Met who later worked with the fiendishly fiery but supremely professional Maria Callas, once confessed that she had been a 'doddle' compared with Lanza. His peers – Williams, Koussevitzky and Goldovsky – subsequently confessed that they tolerated his bad behaviour at Tanglewood because, as an artiste, he left nothing to be desired; but said that, even so, they would not relish working with him again. A few years later, with movie fame beckoning, Mario would return to Tanglewood as a special guest and find himself snubbed by Goldovsky and others, who mostly remembered him only for being 'a pain in the ass'.

Sergei Koussevitzky may have muttered 'Caruso redivivus!' (Caruso reborn!) after hearing Mario singing the third act duet from *La Bohème* with fellow student Irma Gonzalez – but at this stage he still had some way to go before anyone would recognise him as the tenor par excellence he thought he was. The critic with the *New York Post*, whilst noting that he was astounding, added of Mario's interpretation of Fenton, 'If Lanza's natural abilities are developed in the proper direction, he will own a splendid voice. At present he needs more fundamental training and rudiments of style.' Similarly, the *New York Times*'s Noel Straus observed, 'Mario Lanza, a twenty-year-old tenor, is an extremely talented if as yet not completely routined student whose superbly natural voice has few equals among the tenors of the day in quality, warmth and power.' Even Herbert Graf, who disliked him, could not resist the quip in *Opera News*, 'A real find of the season was Mario Lanza.'

One man who recognised Mario's raw but unquestionable talent at this time was concert promoter Michael de Pace, whose agency was based at the RKO Building in New York. De Pace was used to temper tantrums – his clients included Giovanni Martinelli, now coming towards the end of his career but still thinking himself the world's greatest tenor, and the baritone Robert Weede, who took a shine to the young singer and opted to give him lessons in his spare time. California-born Weede (Robert Wiedefeld, 1903–92) had trained in Milan, and made his debut with the New York Met in 1937 – singing in *I Pagliacci* – so the two already had a common bond. Later, Weede would partner Callas in *Tosca* and *Aida*. Though he could not get Mario to stay calm whenever things were not going his way, which was most of the time, Weede did teach him invaluable breath control and, almost as impor-tant, how to stand on a stage without looking like a lump of wood. He and Weede recorded excerpts from *La Bohème* on acetate at around this time, accompanied at the piano by Weede's girlfriend, Dora Reinhardt. Again, these pieces frequently turn up on bootleg albums.

Mario was a big fan of the Italian bass, Ezio Pinza (1892–1957), who appeared in over 750 performances with the New York Met. A few years hence, Pinza would embark on a second career as a Broadway star, and triumph in the stage and film versions of *South Pacific*. Robert Weede arranged for them to meet, a rendezvous which would later lead to arguably the most hilarious private recording session of Mario's career. In 1949, Pinza would cut an acetate of 'The Shit Song' with the Budapest String Quartet. This begins with the bass singing quite earnestly and without once cracking up, 'I shit more in the summertime than I do at any time of year'. In 1952, Mario got a technician to play and re-record this at a Los Angeles studio, where he added a few interjections of his own – pronouncing 'Oh, shit!' thirty times before rounding the whole thing off with a roisterous 'Go fuck yourself!' This recording subsequently turned up on the 'Lanza Blue Tape', of which more later; and this rendezvous led to better things for Mario, courtesy of Pinza's personal assistant, the wealthy and mysterious Maria Margelli.

Though she was twenty years Mario's senior, from her point of view it was love at first sight – and he did not baulk at offering his charms and hunky frame in the interest of career advancement. As had happened with the Countess, Margelli appointed herself his patron, financing private voice lessons, fixing him up with a classy wardrobe, even paying him a weekly retainer in the hope of preventing him from straying. Maria Cocozza detested her from the start and tried to discourage her son from seeing her – livid that he had found another figure who might replace her in his affections. Some years later, long after both protagonists were in their graves, a young tenor named Victor Lanza would come forward, claiming to be Margelli's son and Mario's love-child.

Between them, Robert Weede and Maria Margelli – using his influences and her money – began assembling a concert tour for their protégé which was scheduled to kick off in January 1943 and take in much of the East Coast. A letter forwarded by his mother, two weeks before Christmas – addressed to Alfredo Arnoldo Cocozza – put paid to this. Mario had received his call-up papers.

Chapter Two

The Singing Private

*If the voice was blessed by God, the temperament and
discipline and attitude weren't…his blustering temperament
masked his perennial state of panic.*

Constantine Callinicos, accompanist and friend

Mario's peers, claiming to be friends, did their utmost to get
him excused from military service. To their way of thinking,
his duty lay not in serving his country, but in satisfying his
ego and their pockets by propelling him towards the concert platform for
which, not so long before, they had considered him unprepared. His
former benefactress, the Countess, dispatched a letter to the parole
board in Philadelphia, claiming that she had connections in high places –
no less than President Roosevelt himself – who she would personally ask
to intervene, if they refused her request to have her friend's call-up
cancelled. And in any case, she added, Mario had a 'lazy' eye, the result
of a childhood convulsion, and therefore should be declared unfit for
combat training. Michael de Pace, writing in the capacity of the singer's
manager (Mario had signed a contract with him, well aware that he was
already legally committed to Irene Williams), chose an even more
implausible approach. Arrangements had been made for his client to
audition for the New York Met, and no less a figure than the great
Giovanni Martinelli would be sponsoring him. Therefore it would be
inappropriate for Mario to be drafted now. Nobody at the parole board
had even heard of Martinelli, by now a minor figure in entertainment
circles. The letters were binned, and Mario was given an ultimatum: he

would complete his military service, or face the consequences for draft-dodging.

On 31 December Mario left New York, and on 5 January 1943 he was sworn in as Private Alfredo Cocozza, Service Number 33477918, at the army base in Miami Beach, Florida. This brought about his first complaint, for he had wanted to be known only as Mario Lanza. Here, he completed his basic training with the same lack of dedication that he had applied to his studies. Mario's attitude to 'warmongering' was, 'Let somebody else do it. Some of these volunteered – I didn't!' Today, of course, he would be permitted to have his point of view, but in 1943, like every other able-bodied man under the age of 40, he had his duty to perform.

Because of his lethargy towards training, Mario was transferred to the AB Squadron in Marfa, Texas. Twelve years later, the location would be used for James Dean's last film, *Giant*. Ever the loyal camp-follower, Maria Margelli rented an apartment in the town so that she could be near him. She found him in a lamentable state, in tears because after just a few days his throat was inflamed, he said on account of the desert dust. Margelli had complained on his behalf before, and was reluctant to do so again, so Mario contacted Michael de Pace and asked him to use his influence – de Pace had none – to get him transferred to another base where the conditions would not harm his voice. The request was ignored and he was assigned to military police duties, patrolling the Mexican–American border on a jeep. When even this proved a strain, Mario was appointed a chaplain's assistant, which at least offered him the opportunity to sing at morning and evening service. Even so, he became depressed and coped with this by gorging on food – and the more he ate, the more depressed and bad-tempered he became, piling on the pounds at an alarming rate. The army medics warned him that he was putting a strain on his heart. His buddies joked that he was a candidate for *Sad Sack*, the comic strip immensely popular at the time with its motley collection of military odd-bods, including the archetypal 'fatso soldier' who never got the girl – though in Mario's case, the latter trait never applied. What was far from amusing was the fact that Mario would binge for three days, then purge himself for the next three. How he managed to find all this food, on army rations, is not known.

Salvation of sorts came when Mario was granted a pass to attend a recital by visiting tenor Jan Peerce – popularly known in pre-political correctness days as 'The Jewish Tenor'. He later boasted of how the two had embraced like old friends, just as he had spun the yarn about kissing Rosa Ponselle in Jussi Björling's dressing room at the New York Met – she had actually been performing overseas at the time. At the Peerce concert, Mario met the Hungarian-American radio star Johnny Silver (John Silverman, 1918–2003), a recruit at Marfa who had been put in charge of arranging a concert party. What Silver was describing to *Time* magazine, eight years later, was the archetypal obese slob: 'His shirt was open, he didn't have a hat, no laces in his shoes. He hadn't taken a bath in six months. He hadn't even taken his socks off in six months, and the guy weighed 287 pounds. He just didn't give a damn.'

When one sees pictures of them together, one almost imagines a Lanza and Silver comedy double act – Silver was almost as round as he was tall, standing just over five feet. Mario, however, was aiming for a bigger goal. When he learned that the impresario-showman Peter Lind Hayes was due to arrive in Marfa to audition acts for his revue, *On The Beam*, scheduled to tour army bases around the country, he put both his name and Silver's forward, and promptly applied for leave. It is said that his superiors could not wait to sign the papers to be rid of him. Neither, it would appear, could Maria Margelli, who returned to Los Angeles without saying goodbye.

On The Beam had been hastily composed by Hayes and Frank Loesser, who later triumphed on Broadway with *Guys and Dolls* – with Johnny Silver playing one of the leads. Mario later claimed that a sore throat caused by breathing in desert dust had prevented him from auditioning in the conventional way, therefore he had given Hayes a 'test-recording' he had made before being called up – actually a recording by another tenor, Frederick Jagel, whose name he covered up with a sticker. A few days later, he got around to singing properly for Hayes who, still unaware that he had been tricked, congratulated him on having a better voice 'in the flesh' than on his recording! Needless to say he got the part – retrospectively, to the detriment of his hoped-for operatic career. Had he completed his national service and *then* auditioned for one of the major opera houses, he might have followed in the direction of contemporaries Franco Corelli and Giuseppe di Stefano. Because of his impatience, however, by accepting a part in a modest musical revue, he had effectively kissed goodbye to any of his operatic peers ever taking him seriously. Though his show-stopper was a serious operatic aria, 'E lucevan le stelle' from *Tosca* – this brought the house down at every performance and often had to be sung twice – never in a million years would one imagine Caruso portraying a character named Sylvia Storecheese in a comedy routine! Another sketch, entitled *Carmen*, had more to do with Spike Jones than anything Bizet had ever conceived. Two soldiers, one of which was Jerry Adler (harmonica player Larry's brother) were mopping the floor when Don José (Mario) entered, clowned around, and launched into the famous bullfighter aria. On the positive side, of course, he had sown the seed for an enterprise which would turn him into a living legend and see him reaching a far bigger worldwide audience than he could have imagined at the time.

On The Beam hit the road and Mario's lucky break, the event that widened almost beyond redemption the gap between his classical and show-tunes career, occurred in July 1943 when the show played Visalia, in the San Joaquin Valley. Here, he was billed as 'The Caruso of the Air Force'. The playwright-showman Moss Hart was in town, holding auditions for his latest production, *Winged Victory*, which had already been allocated a slot on Broadway. This was the brainchild of talent scout Irving Lazar, who in the distant future would represent artistes as diverse as Lauren Bacall, Diana Ross and Madonna. Lazar had approached the top brass in the US Army, Air Force and Navy, and between them they had decided upon a plan to raise funds for the Emergency Relief Fund. Hart had been commissioned to write a semi-romantic but nevertheless gung-ho drama which would portray the patriotism and devotion of American airmen as they went about their duty, along with the support they received from their loved ones. Like the *Hollywood* and *Stagedoor Canteen* films, which used unknown actors in the major roles whilst big movie stars appeared in cameos as themselves, *Winged Victory* would prove invaluable as a morale booster to encourage enlistment.

Hart had just one condition when it came to casting: he would recruit only servicemen – 300 men and 42 women, who of course would work for free, but nevertheless were actors – along with their real-life wives and girlfriends. His final roster was impressive: Leo J. Cobb, Karl Malden, George Reeves (who became the first television Superman), Red Buttons, opera star Gary Merrill, *Prince And The Pauper* twins Billy and Bobby March, future *Dynasty* actor John Forsythe, Brad Dexter, Kevin

McCarthy, Edmund O'Brien, and Barry Nelson – who in 1954 would be the first actor (and the only American so far) to play James Bond.

With his customary delusions of grandeur, Mario was hoping for one of the leads in *Winged Victory*, but had to be satisfied with being offered a part in the 50-strong chorus which performs the stunning, anthemic title song under the baton of Lieutenant Leonard De Paur. He joined the company for rehearsal in August, and the try-outs ahead of the Broadway run took place in Boston, Massachussets, early in September. The play opened at New York's 44th Street Theater on 20 November, following a gala dress rehearsal held the previous evening at the Shubert Theater. It played to packed houses here until 20 May 1944 – a total of 226 performances to almost 400,000 people. The production also had two spin-offs: the touring version, which visited local military camps, and *Yellow Jack*, a musical revue written by Sidney Kingsley. This played simultaneously on Broadway, using those cast members from *Winged Victory* who fancied a change of scenery. Mario appeared in all three, but though his voice soared high above every other in the chorus, few noticed him – because of his girth, the producer positioned him behind the other servicemen.

In New York, there was a reunion of sorts with Maria Margelli, who for reasons known only unto herself was still supporting him financially, but apparently no longer interested in having a lover who by now tipped the scales at 350 pounds – and who also made no secret of the fact that he was sleeping with a different woman every night of the week. There is a photograph, snapped in front of the stage of an empty Hollywood Bowl, where he is belting out a favourite aria and looking positively enormous, with a massive beer-gut hanging over trousers two sizes too small around the waist. This did not surface until after the war, when Lanza had become a household name. He tried his best to have it suppressed, buying up all the copies he could find, and of course the more he complained, the more this picture cropped up in features about his career. What is amazing is that this was the man witnessed by his army colleagues as being irresistible to women: females of every size, shape and age flung themselves at him, even when he was just plain Private Alfredo Cocozza.

It was Maria Margelli who paid for Mario to enter the Melotone Studios on 22 May 1944, an occasion which may be clearly defined as a turning point in his career. Though flawed in parts, these recordings have to be heard to be believed. Lanza's take on 'Addio alla madre', from *Cavalleria Rusticana*, simply blows the listener away. His diction and control are nothing less than remarkable. Similarly, 'Come un bel di di maggio' from *Andrea Chénier* and his reading of 'E lucevan le stelle' are near-definitive, though 'Vesti la giubba' would be improved upon. It is, however, his interpretation of that other aria from *Andrea Chénier*, 'Un di all'azzurro', which makes the hairs on the nape of one's neck stand on end. Absolutely no one can perform this as well as Mario Lanza. Therefore it comes as no surprise when one hears Margelli's voice in the background, muttering what we know already – how wonderful he sounds!

After the Broadway run, *Winged Victory* embarked on a national tour: 445 performances in San Francisco, Denver, Chicago, Detroit, Baltimore, Kansas City, Washington, Richmond – and Hollywood, where Twentieth Century-Fox shot the film version with George Cukor at the helm. It was a strange choice, for Cukor (1899–1983) had always been regarded as 'the woman's director', bringing to heel such temperamental sirens as Joan Crawford, Jean Harlow and Ingrid Bergman. The difference between the stage and film version was that the latter starred Judy Holliday, and also Lon McCallister, the young unknown who had played one of the central roles in *Stagedoor Canteen*. By now, however, Mario had had enough of standing behind 50 men and barely getting noticed. Word of his sensational singing had spread across Hollywood, and suddenly he was in great demand at celebrity parties. When darling of the bobby-soxers Frank Sinatra famously quipped, 'That kid's singing knocked a hole through me – for once in my life, *I* swooned!' his future was more or less assured. Mario sang at the homes of Joan Crawford, Irene Manning, Barbara Stanwyck – and Nelson Eddy, who should have been jealous to discover that he had a rival, but instead introduced him to his agent, Art Rush.

Rush was the West Coast agent for RCA Victor's Red Label, which also happens to have been Caruso's label. Not a man to sit on his haunches, he recognised the undisputed genius within this cocky, almost abrasive young tenor, whose voice, he believed, was even better than that of Nelson Eddy, whose fine tone still veered towards the tinny in its upper range. Mario did not tell Rush that he was contracted to the *Winged Victory* movie, or that he was on projected leave from the army.

When the executive promised him a modest record contract, providing he could get through the obligatory audition for RCA's board of directors, Mario was on the next plane to New York, and the deal was clinched. He came clean about the army, and the head of RCA informed him that the contract would be his once he had been discharged from active service.

Not content with 'sneaking off' to New York, Mario committed the cardinal sin by failing to turn up on the *Winged Victory* set two mornings on the trot – the first because he had a hangover, the second because he had a 'prior appointment' with Warner Brothers. His reputation preceded him, and so too did his legend. Here was a young man, already hailed as one of the finest singers in town, and as yet with neither contract nor engagements diary. One manager, Irene Williams, had given up on him. Another, Michael de Pace, had begun to tire of his partying and womanising, and of being constantly undermined by Maria Margelli: whilst de Pace was making excuses for him with George Cukor (who had decided to elevate him from choir member to bit-part), Margelli arranged for Mario to be auditioned by studio chief Jack Warner. As usual, he sang 'Vesti la giubba', only to be appalled by Warner's no-nonsense reply, 'Great voice, but the guy's way too fat for movies!' Later, Mario would spin a yarn to Dwight Whitney of *Collier's* magazine that Warner had offered him a $750-a-week contract, which he had turned down.

Mario returned to the set feeling dejected. He had already filmed several scenes where he can be seen – just – singing and mucking in with the other soldiers. Cukor had pencilled him in for the 'Whippenpoof Song' scene – Mario would sing the opening lines of the famous college song, and lead the other men into the chorus. Now, the director unceremoniously fired him. And if this was not enough, tired of his carousing, Maria Margelli announced that she wanted nothing more to do with him. *Winged Victory* would prove no great shakes as a movie. Although it was popular with the box office – Abel Green of *Variety* wrote, 'It's not a play, but a symbol' – earning $650,000 for the Emergency Relief Fund, unlike the Hollywood canteen films which retain a certain curiosity value because of the musical numbers performed by the likes of Gracie Fields and Tallulah Bankhead, it dated very quickly and has now been assigned to obscurity.

Mario returned to his unit in Marfa, where he stayed until the end of the year. One may only sympathise with his frustration – the fact that he had so much to offer the concert platform, when all he was doing was 'rotting away' in an army base, whilst rumours were rife that the war was almost over. Freedom came in December, when he was hospitalised with severe tinnitus in his right ear. The condition was genuine, the cause fabricated. Mario's perforated eardrum had come about through excessively loud singing, and not on account of noise experienced during active service. In the new year he was transferred to the army base at Walla Walla, Washington, and on 29 January 1945 he received his discharge papers and was granted a 60 per cent disability pension. Like most of his colleagues, through no fault of his own he had not spent a single day engaged in military action, and though he left the army as he had enlisted – Private Cocozza – the discharge was an honourable one.

Mario's parents wanted him to return to Philadelphia, but there was nothing there for him any more, he declared. Neither did he want to live in New York, as he was still angry with RCA for 'duping' him. Therefore he headed for Hollywood, where he rented a small apartment at 1871 North Kingsley Drive. During the Los Angeles run of *Winged Victory* an army sergeant friend, Bert Hicks, had introduced him to his 21-year-old sister, Betty, and it had apparently been love at first sight. Betty Hicks was as quiet and unassuming as he was brash, vulgar and outspoken. Even so, they seem to have been perfectly matched and in time she would tame him as much as was possible with a man who was very obviously as addicted to sex as he was to food. Within days they had discussed marriage, but with one proviso: to marry they needed money, and as they had very little of this right now – whatever Mario earned one day usually went the next on partying and entertaining friends – they had decided to wait until Mario had launched his recording career, or when the war ended, which-ever came soonest. In the meantime, on 29 August 1944 they had secretly become engaged. Mario had decided not to tell his parents: his father had always wanted him to marry a woman of Italian extraction, whereas Betty was part-Irish – a few years later, he would record 'My Wild Irish Rose' in her honour. Maria Cocozza, on the other hand, wanted her son to remain single and concentrate on his career. Once he hit the big time, she had drilled into him time and time again, then he could take a wife. She was of course intensely jealous of Mario being involved with anyone because she was terrified that the day would come when another woman would deflect his attention away from herself.

In March 1945, Mario was summoned to New York. RCA were offering him a five-year contract, with a starting salary of $250 a month, the first year's salary in advance of record sales. This was a pittance compared with what the likes of Bing Crosby and Frank Sinatra were raking in, but by assigning him to the Red Seal label, RCA were grouping him with some of the leading lights of the classical world. The deal was also sufficient to make him change his mind about waiting to marry Betty, particularly when he received his first cheque at the end of the month. Mario went out and bought a special licence – along with a $6 ring which she wore until the day she died – and the ceremony took place on an 'unlucky' Friday 13 April 1945 at Beverly Hills City Hall. Here, Elizabeth Janette Lyhan Hicks became Mrs Alfredo Cocozza. Mario's parents were not informed.

There was to be no honeymoon. At the beginning of May, Mario travelled alone to New York to discuss his future with the RCA executives – or rather, to warn them that unless they recorded him soon, he would break his contract and ask his agent to find him another deal. He also needed to find an apartment in the city: Hollywood no longer interested him because it was too glitzy. Knowing how much he was missing Betty, his old friend Johnny Silver – newly discharged from the army and about to embark on a tour – loaned the couple the use of his apartment until they could find a place of their own. Betty would have been on the next train, but Mario forestalled her when he received an unexpected visit from his parents, who swallowed the story that he was in New York looking for a bachelor pad. No sooner had they returned to Philadelphia than Betty joined him. Two weeks later, unable to keep up the charade any longer, Mario invited the Cocozzas back to New York, and came clean. Their feelings were hurt, naturally, but not because their son had married without telling them, rather because it had been a civil ceremony. Mario promised to rectify the position as soon as he could.

In the middle of June, Mario made six test recordings for RCA: 'Mattinata', 'Vesti la giubba', 'I'm Falling in Love with Someone', 'La fleur que tu m'avais jetée' from Bizet's *Carmen*, 'Che gelida manina', and 'E lucevan le stelle'. The session went well: all six tracks were put down in single takes and the head of the company, J.W. Murray, promised that he would get back to him after his 'second' wedding. This took place in New York on 15 July at St Colombo's Church, though if Mario was hoping that he had made amends with his mother, he was mistaken. Although she would always be civil towards her, Maria Cocozza would never like her daughter-in-law, or forgive her for taking her son away from her.

J.W. Murray was true to his word, though his response was not what Mario had anticipated. The test recordings were good, he said, but not quite up to the standard he was certain Mario would achieve with a little more discipline and training. Murray had found no problems whatsoever with his lower range and those sizzling top Cs, but Mario needed to return to the rehearsal room to polish his middle register. Then, and only then, would RCA permit him to return to the studio. Mario accused Murray of duping him, which was partly true. What the record company could be accused of was snapping Lanza up at a very affordable price, knowing only too well that he was improving almost on a daily basis and as such upping his market value. Had RCA waited the time they estimated was needed for his voice to be in perfect form – a minimum of 12 months – they would not have acquired him for a measly $250 a month.

Money was always a problem with Mario – the more he had, the more he wanted, and his fun-loving nature and generosity towards others dictated that it always burned a hole in his pocket until it was all gone. Once again, Robert Weede came to his aid. The baritone lived on a farm at Nyak, on the outskirts of New York, but also had an apartment not far from the Rockefeller Center. The Lanzas were informed that they could stay there as long as they wanted, for a nominal rent. Weede then set about organising a voice coach, whilst agent Michael de Pace found him work on the recital circuit. His first performance under this new regime took place on 5 September when he topped the bill at the Atlantic City Convention Hall, New Jersey. There is no record of what he actually sang: one assumes there would have been the trusted arias from *Tosca* and *Pagliacci*, although Mario had added German lieder to his repertoire – 'Ich liebe dich' – and a few show tunes. What made the evening of great significance is that he appeared with the NBC Symphony Orchestra under the baton of Peter Herman Adler, a feisty individual who would not have offered him the time of day unless he was guaranteed an exemplary performance. Many years later, Adler would applaud Mario's 'peasant aggressiveness and vitality', and his 'complete disregard for money'. Even in these early days he was displaying the latter trait: Adler paid him $500 plus substantial expenses, which he frittered away within a week, entertaining friends, with little care where the next dollar was coming from.

The engagement led to Mario being offered a lightning tour of Canada with the soprano Agnes Davis. His pianist was Joseph Blatt, who would regularly accompany him over the next two years. Again, details are sketchy: we know that on 10 October, the two appeared at the Montcalm Palace, Quebec. Gilles Mercier of the *Quebec News Review* observed, 'He is able to interest even those who do not *like* classical music' – a compliment which was misinterpreted by Mario, who now assumed that the audience had only turned up to hear him perform popular songs. To his way of thinking, if this was all that the public wanted, who would take his operatic aspirations seriously now?

Popular song was also the order of the day when, after the Quebec recital and courtesy of Robert Weede, Mario was auditioned for an appearance on Celanese Hour, radio's weekly extravaganza, *Great Moments In Music*. The concept for this, unusual in those days, was to broadcast a full opera bill one week, and show tunes the next. Ironically, perhaps, Weede put Mario's name forward after Jan Peerce cancelled due to illness. The producers were so astonished by his voice that they booked him for ten programmes, with a combined fee of $3,500. The first of these was broadcast, live of course, on 24 October and for the first time ever, Mario panicked before facing an audience. It was, he said, not the prospect of facing the thousand or so people in the audience which terrified him and made it impossible to keep anything down before the show, but the millions of unseen faces across America who would be hearing him for the first time – not that this stopped him from gorging himself almost into a stupor afterwards. On the plus side – if this really was one – he did not have to worry too much over his physical appearance on the radio, for he was still making the scales groan at over 250 pounds.

What those closest to Mario – friends and mentors – failed to comprehend was the way in which he gave more of himself when singing items such as Victor Herbert's 'I'm Falling in Love with Someone' and Irving Berlin's 'Blue Skies' than he did when performing operatic arias which he was ordered to sing, when these might have been left off the evening's list. In one programme, he soared woefully and it would appear purposely off-key during 'Vesti la giubba'. Neither did he care much for his soprano co-stars, with the exception of Frances Yeend, with whom he would soon record some of the most stunning duets in the operatic repetoire. Indeed, their recording of the love duet from *Madama Butterfly* easily compares with what many believe is the definitive reading by Maria Callas and Nicolai Gedda. Jean Tennyson he particularly disliked, arguing with the producer after their first coupling that she 'could not sing for shit', and adding that he would rather throw in the towel than work with her again. The producer told him that he would have no choice – dire or not, Tennyson was the wife of Camille Dreyfus, the Celanese Hour's chief executive and founder! Importantly, during the broadcast of 26 February 1946, he sang a selection from Sigmund Romberg's *The Student Prince*, a role he would reprise – as will be seen, in some kind of pyrrhic victory – eight years later. Also, in this sixth *Great Moments In Music*, he introduced what would become a Lanza standard, Romberg's stunning 'Golden Days', which he sang as a duet with Robert Weede. The studio audience went wild. Earlier, he had tackled arias from Verdi's *Otello*, and at 24 had strained at a part sung mostly by much older, more experienced tenors, and now he informed the producer that from now on he would perform only material of his own choosing. When the response came that he would sing what he was told to sing – clearly from a man who did not know what he was talking about – Mario stormed out of the studio. His last four appearances on the show were cancelled, and his pay docked by $1,200.

Through Robert Weede, Mario was introduced to Polly Robinson, a New York-based teacher of English songs: it was she who put him through his paces for the Victor Herbert song, and standards such as 'If', and Noel Coward's 'I'll See You Again', which cropped up regularly in his repertoire. Robinson worked from the Carnegie Hall Building, in Manhattan, and naturally filled her pupil's head with dreams of topping the bill at America's most prestigious music hall. Another of her pupils was 32-year-old Sam Weiler, a tenor-baritone and an unscrupulous individual who would later be sued by the Lanza family for bootlegging Mario's recordings. Weiler claimed to be a multi-millionaire real-estate baron who owned hotels and other properties up and down the country, and that he had only latched on to Mario because he liked him, not to make money out of him. He was no such thing. Though reasonably well off, he actually worked as a real-estate agent for his brother, Jack D. Weiler, the president of New York's Jewish Philanthropy Society. Even so, he genuinely believed that cash, and not talent, would see Mario Lanza carving his niche in the opera world. It becomes obvious reading and watching interviews with Weiler that, like Terry Robinson (of whom more later), he seems to have developed an unreciprocated crush on the young singer.

As such, Sam Weiler seduced Mario with the one thing he enjoyed almost as much as sex – food, and lots of it. For over a month he wined and dined him in some of the city's most exclusive eateries. Mario spoke of his dreams and ambitions: Weiler reassured him that these would all be achieved. Once he had secured the singer's confidence he began working on Betty, filling her head with all kinds of nonsense about opulent apartments with all mod cons, and boasting of how, under his tutelage, Mario would be able to afford the best schools for their children, if and when these came along. On account of Mario spending money faster than it was coming in, the couple were in debt to the tune of $3,000. Weiler settled with their creditors – later he claimed to have invested $100,000 in Mario, which was utter fabrication – and put him on a weekly retainer of $70, along with any reasonable expenses he incurred. In return, in February 1946 Mario was coerced into signing a contract with Weiler which would guarantee his new agent just 5 per cent of his earnings. The contracts with Irene Williams and Michael de Pace still held good, but for the time being Mario had pushed these people to the back of his mind. When asked why he was taking such a small percentage, Weiler remarked that he did not need the money, but that the law decreed that he had to take something. The following year, his cut would be increased to 10 per cent, and by 1951 he would be taking 20 per cent and Mario would have revised his opinion of this 'kindly benefactor' considerably.

Retrospectively, one of the few commendable things Weiler did for Mario was to cancel all of his engagements for the foreseeable future, and find him a decent voice coach – one who would elevate him to the status of grand opera star. He came up with the best – 72-year-old Enrico Rosati, who some thirty years earlier had tutored Beniamino Gigli. Rosati, as famed for his colourful vocabulary and put-downs as for his coaching skills, initially wanted nothing to do with a singer already renowned for his sloppy attitude towards training and discipline. Mario too was dubious of anyone thinking that he wanted to follow in Gigli's footsteps. A compromise was reached wherein Rosati agreed to listen to him for just five minutes. Weiler dragged his charge to the maestro's cluttered, dusty studio on West 57th Street, where Rosati personally accompanied him on his set piece, 'Vesti la giubba'. Sources who quote him as telling Mario, 'I have waited thirty-four years for you. You have a voice blessed by God!' are not quite accurate. What he actually said was, 'I have waited thirty-four years for you to come along. Now get to work, you lazy no-good bum!' And only a man like Rosati would have persistently got away with calling a hitherto devout Italian-American Catholic boy 'motherfucker'. Amusing too was Rosati's response to Mario's shock over being expected to pay his fees – $1,300 for 13 one-hour lessons – upfront. When the singer asked how he could be expected to come up with such a sum, Rosati quipped, proving that Mario's reputation really did precede him, 'Go fuck some rich old woman who's got plenty of dough!' Sam Weiler later shot himself in the foot – confirming that he was carrying a torch for Mario – when repeating to Constantine Callinicos how he had told Rosati, '*I'll* be the old woman. I'm ready to invest my money in this boy!'

In December 1949, Mario would tell *Etude* magazine, 'Under Rosati, I had to practise every day to achieve what the Italians call bel canto. Eventually, Rosati and Edward Johnson of the Metropolitan Opera in New York invited me to join the company, but without the necessary time for me to prepare for it in peace, I did not think it would be an advisable step for me to take.'

In fact, the decision for Lanza not to augment the New York Met's roster was twofold. Both Rosati and Johnson, the company's general manager, agreed that he was ready to take this ultimate step, despite his still clumsy stance and a voice which, albeit magnificent, tended to go off the rails when he over-embellished above what was printed on the sheet music. What the Met were prepared to do was to offer him secondary tenor roles within his range – whereas he was demanding to start at the top or not at all, with heavy roles such as Otello and Macbeth – roles which he had fought against singing for Celanese Hour, declaring that he was not yet ready for them! A couple of arias on a radio programme,

Rosati and Johnson argued, were a far cry from a three-hour production, under scorching lights and in full costume. Therefore the decision was made that, until further notice, he would stick with the concert platform. For the rest of his life, Mario would regret never doing grand opera; yet setting his sights too high at the time, added to his recurring lethargy brought about mostly by his eating habits, meant he would prove his own worst enemy. Maria Callas, a supreme disciplinarian who went to the extreme length of swallowing a tapeworm so that she could lose weight, and who never spared herself where her career was concerned, said of him, 'Mario Lanza could have become one of the greatest operatic tenors in the world. The only reason that never happened was because he was too lazy and undisciplined. That is *not* the sensible approach to bel canto!'

One example of this lethargy occurred three weeks into Rosati's tutelage, when the maestro arranged for Mario to be auditioned by the legendary conductor, Arturo Toscanini, almost 80 and still going strong. The piece they had in mind was Verdi's *Requiem*. Rehearsals went well at Rosati's studio: it was a difficult piece which Mario mastered with comparative ease. Yet when the time came to sing for Toscanini, Mario failed to turn up, offering the excuse that worrying over not being good enough for the great man had made him ill.

A few days after Toscanini had all but blacklisted him, Mario was contacted once more by William Judd of Columbia Concerts. Since rejecting him, Judd had seen him in concert and, unaware that he was now with Sam Weiler, had called Michael de Pace – who until then had known nothing of the contract with Weiler. Mario auditioned for Judd, and this time was taken on – resulting in a furious row between Mario and de Pace, who more than willingly signed his contract with Mario over to Columbia Concerts. His first big engagement through Judd was a recital in front of 25,000 people at Chicago's Grant Park Shell on 6 July. Here he shared the bill again with Frances Yeend, a stablemate from RCA. Yeend (Frances Lynch, 1913–2008) had debuted three years earlier in *The Merry Widow*, which had taken Broadway by storm. Later in 1946, she would sing at Tanglewood in the US premiere of Benjamin Britten's *Peter Grimes*. Her recorded work with Mario Lanza is nothing short of sensational. She may have ended up disliking the man, but as an artiste she considered him second to none. 'The best in the business,' she said. 'With him it was always all or nothing. He never spared the horses.'

It was after this performance that Mario was championed for the first time by Claudia Cassidy, the acerbic critic with the *Chicago Tribune*. Cassidy (1899–1996) was one of those people who, though possessed of no great musical knowledge, for some reason commanded so much respect from her peers – and fear from those she dug her claws into – that a production could close on the strength of one of her put-downs. She was a particular thorn in the side for Maria Callas, who gave her the well-deserved nickname, 'Acidy Cassidy'. The fact that she liked Frances Yeend and Mario was an enormous point in their favour: 'What few of us really anticipated was the impact of those two voices. Mr Lanza came first, a handsome, dark-haired boy with wide shoulders and a disarmingly modest presence. With the two *Tosca* arias he left no doubt that he is a true Italian tenor, beautiful, ardent and exciting!'

There were other recitals with Yeend, but the one that got him really noticed was a solo recital in Ottowa, with the city's Philharmonic Orchestra, on 13 November. Mario was on stage for 90 minutes, sang virtually nothing but opera, and after being made to sing Leoncavallo's 'Mattinata' twice, he received a 10-minute standing ovation. Drawing especial attention to the large number of top Cs he had totted up during the evening, Lauretta Thistle enthused in *Arts Review*, 'Mario Lanza has that golden quality to his voice which is given to few tenors.'

The great Lanza years were about to begin.

Chapter Three

The Bel Canto Trio

I sing each word as though it were my last on earth.

Mario Lanza

Much has been written about the meeting between Mario Lanza and Constantine Callinicos, the man who eventually became his accompanist, trusted friend, and more than occasional whipping boy, taking the brunt of his sometimes ferocious temper. On 14 April 1947, Mario was engaged to appear at the 5,000-seat State Teachers College Auditorium, in Shippensburg, Pennsylvania. He breezed into the town his usual loud, ebullient self, only to be told that his regular accompanist, Joseph Blatt, was indisposed. Mario's initial reaction was to call Sam Weiler and cancel the concert, but Weiler would not hear of this and promised to find him a suitable pianist in time for curtain-up. This man was Constantine Callinicos, an eminent New York-born musician of Greek extraction who had studied at Juilliard; he could be just as tetchy as Mario. Neither wanted to work with the other – Mario because he did not want a stranger to 'fuck up' his programme, Costa (to give him his more familiar name) because he had never heard of Shippensburg or Mario Lanza. Matters were only worsened when Costa called Mario and asked for a late-afternoon rehearsal. This particular tenor did not do rehearsals, he was told: he had better things to do before a performance – such as eating – and therefore Costa would have to follow his lead, as Blatt had always done.

Costa's recollections of life with Mario (*The Mario Lanza Story*, with Ray Robinson) are so contrived in parts, gushing with what are almost certainly 'tall tales', and so exaggerated, that they almost defy belief. He was of course writing immediately after the singer's death, when emotions were running high and he himself was still in deep shock – and writing about an event which, in 1947 when Mario had been virtually unknown, had been considered just another routine engagement. One feels that had the two men's paths never crossed again, had Mario not achieved world acclaim, Costa would have obliterated the evening from his memory instead of treating it as the most singular event of his career. Having agreed to eschew the essential rehearsal, Costa writes that he agreed to meet him in Shippensburg two hours before the concert – hardly the professional stance one would expect from a man said to be proud of his reputation, one who had accompanied such luminaries as Lauritz Melchior, Lily Pons and Jussi Björling. And all for the princely fee of $25? The truth is that Costa only set out for the venue once Sam Weiler had agreed to a very substantial increase in his fee, and even then there was another hitch when Mario revealed that he did not have the requisite tuxedo, and that he would be singing in an ordinary business suit, which no self-respecting opera singer would have even considered doing in those days.

Costa's account of hearing the Lanza voice for the first time is extremely highly charged:

> For as the rich tones flowed effortlessly from Mario's throat, I knew I was listening to one of the greatest tenor voices since Caruso. Through Mario's vocal cords and through those bony cavities in his throat, nose and mouth which are called the resonators, emerged phrases of such opulence, warmth and velvety quality that I sat there feeling some incredible joke had been played on me. The notes were round and rich, satisfying and meaningful, and his breath control, on the long phrases, was truly amazing... 'Mario, Mario, what a voice!' I exclaimed. 'You haven't heard anything yet,' Mario laughed.

What he was describing, of course, and with great accuracy, was the Lanza voice of the early 1950s, when he truly was one of the most remarkable singers on the planet. The reviews for the concert back up Costa 100 per cent, though any admiration he may have had for Mario did not make him in any particular hurry to accompany him again. Indeed, he had been horrified when Mario had first walked on to the stage and turned his back on the audience – regarded by many as the supreme insult – whilst Costa had been playing the introduction to his first aria, Stradella's 'Pieta Signore'. 'Leaning casually over the grand piano, he winked, then smiled at me,' Costa recalled.

For Mario, the Shippensburg concert was little more than a rehearsal for Columbia Concerts' next major enterprise: the Bel Canto Trio, which toured America, Canada and Mexico between July 1947 and May 1948, performing at 86 venues which included not just theatres, but Indian reservations, high schools, and the occasional college campus, mostly packed to the rafters. The Bel Canto Trio was the brainchild of Arthur Judson, the head of Columbia Artists, and the set-up was devised for Frances Yeend. The budget for each concert was $1,500: $500 for Yeend, around $300 each for the tenor and bass-baritone of her choosing, and the rest to be divided among the accompanists. She chose Mario, and between them they plumped for Montreal-based George London, whom Mario had befriended during the run of *Winged Victory*. Yeend would later regret her decision, for when it came to irresponsible behaviour London (1920–85) was little better than Mario. 'We overate, overdrank, overslept, overdid things generally,' London told Costa, adding that Betty had travelled with them some of the time but always stayed back at the hotel when the pair hit the town after the performance. London was however critical of his friend's sloppy attitude to his work, telling Costa, 'If he only could have crawled out of his own skin and listened to his own voice, he might have lived his whole life differently.' After this tour, London would be snapped up by the Vienna State Opera. He would also become a favourite of Maria Callas: the crowning glory of their partnership was a performance of the whole second act of *Tosca* on the *Ed Sullivan Show* in 1956.

The Bel Canto Trio made their debut on 8 July 1947 at the Emil Blatz Temple of Music, in Milwaukee. Then the tour took in towns in Iowa, North Dakota, Indiana, Michigan, New York State, Alabama, Connecticut, Minnesota, Texas, Wisconsin, West Virginia, Nova Scotia, Newfoundland and Mexico. The varied itinerary caused untold problems for Frances Yeend, for whilst she commuted by plane, Mario refused to fly – claiming that this affected his perforated eardrum. Out of sympathy, George London accompanied him, both men drinking heavily and sometimes arriving at the venue the worse for wear and with only minutes to spare. Again, there were few legitimate rehearsals: Mario and London frequently rehearsed on the train or bus, giving the other passengers the thrill of their lives. The three singers were also given every say in their programme, which only makes one rue the fact that hardly any of their work was recorded. The reason was Mario's 'Johnny Opposite' tendency to please himself when he was erring on the side of caution and to completely disregard the advice of his peers. It was only because RCA wanted him to record some of his most critically acclaimed work that he refused to entertain the idea, otherwise his fans would be able to listen to these pieces today. Had Arthur Judson *not* wanted him to record them, he would have insisted on doing so.

In all 86 concerts, the order and content rarely varied. The trio opened with 'Qual volutta trascorere' from Verdi's *I Lombardi*, and closed with a selection in English from *The Barber of Seville*, or the heavy-going 'Prison Scene' from *Faust*. In between there was the usual fare from *Tosca*, *Carmen* and *La Traviata*, along with stirring extracts from Puccini's *Manon Lescaut* and Donizetti's *L'Elisir d'Amore*. The Lanza–Yeend showstoppers included 'Nobody Could Love You More' from Franz Lehár's *Paganini*, which does crop up on the odd bootleg album, and Mario's 'M'appari', from Flotow's *Martha*, which he recorded several times.

Leading the plaudits for the first of two concerts at Chicago's Grant Park, which took place on 19 July, was Claudia Cassidy, though even she was critical in pointing out that Mario still had some way to go:

> A coltish youngster with the wide shoulders and the general just-out-of-uniform air of *Call Me Mister*, Mr Lanza sings for the indisputable reason that he was *born* to sing. He has a superbly natural tenor which he uses by instinct, and though a multitude of fine points evade him, he possesses the things almost impossible to learn. He knows the accent that makes the lyric lines reach the audience, and he knows why opera is music drama... The crowd roared while Mr Lanzo happily mopped his brow, and he seemed more surprised and just as delighted as anyone else.

The first Chicago concert had been attended by a crowd of 45,000. On the strength of Cassidy's review in that morning's *Tribune*, 75,000 people flocked to Grant Park that evening. Such was Cassidy's power, of course, that had she decided *not* to like Mario, the Bel Canto Trio could easily have played to a near-empty venue.

What Mario did not know was that his peers, current and future, were plotting behind his back to send his career zooming in a direction he had never dreamed of. In the middle of July, a copy of 'Mattinata' – one of the test recordings he had made for RCA two years earlier – ended up in the hands of Ida Koverman, MGM chief Louis B. Mayer's assistant and adviser. Koverman, a woman of considerable influence, had previously worked as executive secretary for both Calvin Coolidge's and J. Edgar Hoover's presidential campaigns. Additionally she served as a director for the Opera Guild and the Municipal Arts Commission, and she was actively involved with the Hollywood Bowl. The photograph of Lanza, in Mayer's words 'looking a beached whale in uniform', accompanied the recording. Koverman was Mayer's most loyal, trusted servant, and her recommendations were always taken seriously by the man whom everyone called – though never to his face – 'the Messiah'.

An English adaptation of 'Mattinata' – 'You're Breaking my Heart' – had just been composed by Pat Gennaro and Sunny Skylar. It would be published the following year, and would subsequently prove a massive hit for Al Martino and a minor one for Britain's Gracie Fields. Ida Koverman envisaged Mario singing this in a movie: she showed Mayer photographs of the slimmer Mario, and Mayer agreed, after listening to the test recording and without even meeting Mario, that the idea would work. MGM's star couple, Jeanette MacDonald and Nelson Eddy (who had parted company with the studio in 1942), were now old hat; the public needed someone new, and who better than this hunky, dark-haired, handsome Italian with a voice so magnificent, Mayer said, that next to him Eddy sounded like a cat howling? Koverman got in touch with her contacts at the Hollywood Bowl, and they agreed to stage a concert to showcase Mario's formidable talent.

There was just one snag. Mayer had asked for 28 August, and on that evening a concert had been scheduled featuring the Italian tenor, Ferruccio Tagliavini (1913–95), hailed by many as the successor to Gigli. Tagliavini was asked to step down – he still got his fee – so that Mario and Frances Yeend could take his place. Mario objected to this. Much as he liked Yeend, this was supposed to be his night – and she would be getting paid twice as much as him. His pleas fell on deaf ears.

Even Mayer had to agree with the organisers that the chances of an unknown singer filling such a prestigious venue were virtually nil, and Yeend needed to be there to guarantee at least a decent turnover of tickets. Yeend would also be topping the bill, with Mario billed as her special guest star. George London would not enter the equation. This brought complaints from Arthur Judson, who protested that the Bel Canto Trio should appear as such, or not at all. A compromise was reached: London would be welcome at the concert, but he would have to sit in the audience with Mayer and 25-year-old Kathryn Grayson, the soprano who was to partner Mario in his debut movie. Grayson (Zelma Hedrick) was being promoted as MGM's answer to Deanna Durbin: she had recently starred in *Anchors Aweigh* and *Till The Clouds Roll By*, but would not reach her peak until after working with Mario, when she appeared in big-budget musicals like *The Vagabond King* and *Showboat*.

Contrary to what has been written by some biographers, the Hollywood Bowl concert was not a sell-out. Far from it: less than 4,000 tickets were sold for a venue which seated around 18,000, whereas back in 1936, even the aisles had been packed when Lily Pons had sung to an over-capacity crowd of 26,000. To make up the loss of revenue, the director of the Hollywood Bowl had sold broadcasting rights to CBS radio. To listen to the recording of the event today is a treat indeed: there are not enough superlatives in the dictionary to even begin to describe how good Mario and Yeend sounded. The programme was pretty much the one they had performed dozens of times before; but minus those items which Mario, Yeend or both had sung with George London, this left the organisers with just 33 minutes of operatic arias, so musical interludes were incorporated at the last minute. Before either singer appeared, the orchestra, conducted by the legendary Eugene Ormandy, played Bach's *Passacaglia und Fugue* – this droned on for fifteen minutes and made the performers and the audience restless. Mario was so nervous that he tripped over a speaker wire. Even so he managed to crack a joke: 'I guess if I fail here tonight, folks, they'll say Lanza fell flat on his face!' Unsure of how Mario would be received, Mayer had paid for 'shriekers' and 'claquers' to be strategically placed in the crowd to ensure that each aria would receive a good ovation. These proved unnecessary, for despite a few boos from disgruntled Tagliavini fans, Mario acquitted himself well. He opened with 'Una furtiva lagrima', which received only sparse applause, then went straight into 'Un di all'azzurro spazio', from *Andrea Chénier*, which fared little better. The real applause came after 'E lucevan le stelle' – and after his first duet with Yeend, 'Parigi, o cara,' from *Tosca*, the audience finally realised that they had a major star on their hands. Nothing, however, compared to their performance of the love duet from *Madama Butterfly*, which earned them a 12-minute standing ovation. Only Maria Callas and Nicolai Gedda would sing it as well – though some critics maintain Mario and Yeend's to have been the superior version – and such was the emotion that both singers almost missed their cue for their final piece, 'O soave fanciulla' from *La Bohème*.

The critics, most of them in Mayer's pocket, had been asked to write 'favourable' reviews of the concert but to concentrate only on Mario. All of them did, not just because they did not want to be excluded from the MGM lot for displeasing Mayer, but because they truly liked what they had heard. His champion, Claudia Cassidy, had been barred from the Hollywood Bowl just in case she – a law unto herself – changed her mind and wrote something bad about him. The *Los Angeles Times* called his voice, 'The sort of tenor voice that every operatic stage had been yearning for, lo these many lean years.' The *Los Angeles Daily News* praised his 'native artistry which, rightly developed, should prove to be one of the most exceptional voices of his generation'. The *Los Angeles Examiner* claimed that there were too few superlatives in the dictionary to describe his brilliance.

After the concert, Mario was approached by several producers and agents, each of whom was hoping to poach him from Mayer. Had this been an ordinary operatic concert, Mario would almost certainly have been signed up by a legitimate opera company. It was not, and he was compelled to decline every offer and therefore throw away the one career he had truly wanted for himself. Two days later, Mario was summoned to MGM's Sound Stage One, in front of which every executive from the studio – along with those of its rivals – gathered in anticipation of witnessing Mayer's latest foible. The mogul had given them no clue as to who or what they were about to witness, save that it was 'somebody sent by God'. Mario was still a very corpulent 230 pounds, and Mayer did not wish him to be prejudged on his appearance before they had heard his voice. Contrary to what has been said, including by herself, Kathryn Grayson was not involved in this or the previous Hollywood Bowl performance other than as a spectator; Mario was totally alone. From behind a curtain, he sang 'Che gelida manina', then Victor Herbert's 'Thine Alone', from *Eileen*. When Mayer dabbed his eyes, most of the others followed suit, genuinely moved. Then the mogul stood up and announced, 'Gentlemen, you've heard the voice. Now I want you to meet the singer.'

Having gained the approval of his executives – and the enmity of Jack Warner, who would always regret rejecting Lanza when he had the chance to sign him up – Mayer took his discovery to lunch, and after watching him eat a meal which would have more than satisfied four men, realised why he had such a problem with his weight. A few years later, *Collier's* magazine would observe, 'Mayer regards Mario as his own discovery, nominated for stardom because he has the Mayer trademark of a pleasant face to go with his other talents. L.B. treats him as a father treats a son. "Mario, my boy," Mayer tells him, "you are going to be a singing Clark Gable some day."' Mayer always spoke this way of his favourite stars – the ones he mostly tolerated only because they were bringing in the most revenue – but at times he could be the most ruthless 'father'. As wily as he was tightfisted, he quickly latched on to Mario's inarticulacy – not to mention Sam Weiler's infatuation with his charge – and set out to ensnare Mario for next to nothing, as had happened with Gable, Crawford, and most of his other stalwarts who had been plucked from the 'lower reaches' of society. This was the tyrant who in 1936 had promised the cancer-ridden star Marie Dressler a $100,000 bonus providing she promised to 'hang on' until she had finished the trio of films he had lined up for her. In tremendous pain, Marie had made it – and Mayer had paid her just $10,000, declaring that there was little sense in paying her any more because she would not live to spend it. Mayer's attitude towards Mario would be little different.

Usually, new recruits to MGM were offered the standard seven-year contract, and put on a weekly salary. When Mayer saw how big Mario was, how much food he could put away at one sitting, he suspected that this recruit might not live the requisite seven years. He offered him a non-negotiable three-picture deal: $15,000 for the first, $25,000 for the second, $30,000 for the final film. On top of this, just to ensure that he did not dawdle and allow himself to be poached by Warner Brothers,

Mayer promised Mario a $10,000 bonus just for signing the contract. Mario did so, rubbed his hands with glee, and told Mayer that he could not wait to start shooting.

At this stage, Mayer dropped his bombshell. Mario's first picture was to be *This Summer Is Yours*, directed by Joe Pasternak – the man who had discovered singing sensation Deanna Durbin, and had taken Marlene Dietrich off the 'box-office poison' list by putting her into the phenomenally successful *Destry Rides Again*. The film, however, would not go into production until Pasternak could be assured of his new star facing the camera without looking ridiculous. In his memoirs, *The Easy Way*, he recalled his first impression of Lanza's screen test: 'The voice was rich, warm, sensuous, virile, capable of incredible highs and able to go down in register as deep as a baritone. My spine tingled.' Maybe he would have been better off saying this to Mario's face instead of telling Mayer, in front of him, 'He's way too fat and his hair looks like a horsehair mattress that's bust at the seams!' In those days Mario's hair was jet black, and he always wore it unparted and ruffled. Pasternak also criticised Mario's then dreadful dress sense – his oversized suit, and the tent-like shirt he wore outside his trousers which made him look even fatter than he was. Given Mario's volatile temperament and complete lack of restraint when criticised, it was a miracle that he kept his counsel. 'He could be almost saintly when he wanted to be,' Costa recalled, 'and that day his graciousness towards Pasternak was sincere and heartfelt. [But] it was to make Mario's future behaviour upsetting and equally puzzling to Pasternak.'

Jack Warner had also called Mario fat to his face, but Mayer was more subtle than this. He also valued Pasternak's opinion, so much so that Mario was told that he would have to wait a few days for the result of the screen-test: at this stage, MGM were still deciding whether to go ahead with him or not. In the end, it was the voice which convinced Mayer and his executives, though there would be certain conditions. Work on *That Midnight Kiss* would not begin until June 1948, enabling the singer to undergo a 10-month 'grooming' schedule – rigorous diet, vocal training, lessons in deportment, a new hairstyle and, more importantly, a more controlled lifestyle. This was Hollywood, the town of double standards. Mario would have to be seen with his wife, and when away from her would 'keep his pecker inside his pants'. There is no evidence yet that he was cheating on Betty – he would do so openly and with unbridled gusto, later on – but Mayer had heard the rumours and in keeping with MGM's strict family-values policy, Mario would have to behave himself.

In his biography of Louis B. Mayer, *The Lion Of Hollywood*, Scott Eyman publicly states what he claims most of the MGM executives thought about Mario Lanza:

> The tenor quickly proved himself to be amongst the most obnoxious people ever to walk onto the Culver City lot. He was crude and vulgar – he referred to Ethel Barrymore as 'that old bitch' – and he was an egomaniac who squabbled with old MGM hands about how they did their jobs. But Mayer loved him – 'Mr Mayer would cry every time Mario sang,' said Joe Pasternak – and MGM had another star on its hands.

Joe Pasternak put it more succinctly. 'Lanza never made a pretence of being a good boy, or easy to get along with,' he observed. 'He had Dietrich's ability to think outside of himself. "Mario, you sing like a sonofabeech," he would say after hearing a playback of himself that delighted him.'

Yet his movie career almost ended before it began when Mayer ordered him to 'clear his diary' for the foreseeable future. No one told Lanza what to do, and Mayer was informed in no uncertain terms that before he could devote himself entirely to MGM, he would have to finish off the Bel Canto tour, and that this would keep him almost fully occupied until the following May. Until now, only Greta Garbo had been able to get away with disobeying a direct command from the Messiah, but an uneasy compromise was reached. Mario could resume the tour, but he would have to return to MGM on 8 September to make two test recordings: 'Vesti la giubba' and 'Che gelida manina'. This session went well; he was accompanied at the piano by 18-year-old André Previn, then starting to make a name for himself in Hollywood.

On 20 November, the Bel Canto Trio arrived in Mexico, where they inadvertently found themselves in trouble with the police. Such was their popularity that Columbia Concerts had organised two extra dates: Chihuahua on the 27th, Torreon the next evening. Unfortunately, what the agency had not reckoned with was the country's peculiar tax laws, which stated that foreign working visitors pay income tax, in cash, before leaving. Columbia Concerts had paid this in advance for the rest of the tour, but not for these extra shows. Mario, Frances Yeend and George London were asked to cough up $500 after the Torreon concert – money which they did not have. As the banks and telegraph offices were closed for the night, they were arrested and forced to spend the night in a cell at the local constabulary.

Mario returned to Hollywood, vowing never to visit Mexico again as long as he lived. Louis B. Mayer, incredibly, had not found out about the fiasco, otherwise he might not have been in the mood for renegotiating Mario's contract to bring it into line with those of his other stars. This last-minute change of heart had come about as the result of an angry exchange with Sam Weiler, who enlightened Mayer about his client's reluctance to be in the movies in the first place – all Mario really wanted, Weiler explained, was to tread the boards at the New York Met. Mayer, who saw only the invisible dollar signs over Mario's head, knew that he would make much more money for all concerned by sticking with the big screen, and he was willing to shell out a little more to keep Weiler on side. Mario could keep the $10,000 Mayer had paid him for signing the contract, but now he was put on a 20-week retainer at $750 a week. He would still get the $15,000 upon the completion of his first picture, and his fee would be increased by $15,000 for each one he made, save that now there would be seven films. Additionally, he would only be contracted to work 26 weeks out of every year – the other 26 would be for concert, operatic and recording work, and for vacations. There was, however, a very significant snag. As with every star on its roster, MGM now owned Mario Lanza, and as such he would have to adhere to the studio's previously mentioned family values policy: no sex outside marriage, no heavy drinking, no other activities which might bring the studio into disrepute. The unwritten laws enforced a decade earlier by the National League of Decency still held strong. Mario was warned that should he waver even slightly from these iron rules, MGM would be permitted to suspend him without notice – and if suspended, he would not be permitted to do any other work until the suspension was lifted. Mario signed the new contract and promised Mayer that, from now on, he would be the very model of respectability.

Few would deny that the MGM contract, and the sudden wealth this brought, went to Mario's head. Over the next few months his behaviour became increasingly tetchy and unpredictable. Though he had cut down on his food intake, for the time being, his drinking was still out of control much of the time – it was not impossible for him to sink 20 pints of beer in one evening session. He was more than a little tipsy when he appeared on *The Edgar Bergen Show* on 14 February, though no one seemed to mind because it did not affect his performance as straight man to Bergen's puppet, Charlie McCarthy, who after a great deal of clowning around got him to sing a thrilling 'Vesti la giubba'.

Mario had always been a prankster. As a youth he had lifted sweets from local candy stores just for the sheer hell of it – returning them later, dumping them on the counter and accusing the owner of not being vigilant. However, stealing sweets and chocolate as a grown man, and whilst on the tour circuit, was another matter, even if he did empty his pockets and pay for them at the checkout. Years later, he would make a habit of stealing clothes from the studio wardrobe department, and boast to all and sundry where they had come from. He had also developed a complex about Ferruccio Tagliavini, since being booed by the tenor's fans at the Hollywood Bowl. Each time the Bel Canto Trio hit a new town, Mario would head for the nearest music store and, if they had any Tagliavini recordings, take the shellac disc out of its cardboard cover, bite a chunk out of it, and put it back!

Infantile or hilarious, depending upon how one wishes to interpret it, was the way he would hide behind the curtain, out of sight of the orchestra, and urinate loudly into a bucket or flash at Frances Yeend whilst she was performing a solo – not for sexual gratification, but in an attempt to make her crack up. Clearly, she did not see the funny side, as others might have done. In *Tenor In Exile*, Lanza biographer Roland L. Bessette quotes from a letter he received from Yeend in 1995, in which she writes, 'His personal life was characterised by a lack of regard for others, both socially and professionally... He provided a great treat for the ear, but there was nothing for the mind.'

Mario's signing with MGM made the trade papers, and the news that he would still be devoting half his time to the classical stage was greeted with approval by conductor William Herbert, the director of the New Orleans Opera, who had had his eye on the young tenor for a while. Herbert had attended the Bel Canto Trio's concert in Chicago the previous year, and now offered him the part of Pinkerton in two performances of *Madama Butterfly*. Cynics have suggested that Herbert was in Louis B. Mayer's pocket, and that Pinkerton was the easiest role he could come up with – he appears in the first act, where he sings the stunning love duet with Cio-Cio San, but does not return to the stage until the final scene. If this was a ruse perpetrated by Mayer and Herbert, were they suggesting already, as would be said so many times over the next ten years, that Mario lacked the stamina for a heavier role? Or was he being offered Pinkerton simply to allow him to fulfil his ambition to sing opera in a major hall, in the hope that once he had got it out of his system, he would apply himself more seriously to his movie career?

Mario caused Walter Herbert a mighty headache from the word go. In his opinion, there had only been one Pinkerton – Gigli. Therefore, when he turned up for rehearsal at the New York studio of the San Francisco Opera's veteran Armando Agnini, he refused to work from the score – insisting on using as his yardstick Gigli's 1939 Rome recordings with soprano Toti Dal Monte. Even the most serious Gigli devotee would have agreed that this performance was flawed in parts, and by learning the entire opera solely from singing along with Gigli, Mario picked up these same flaws. When Agnini's pianist, Rudolph Scharr, politely pointed this out, Mario flew into one of those tantrums usually reserved for only the most bad-tempered prima donnas, stormed out of the room, and declared that he would not return until Scharr had been fired. Agnini refused to do this, and the next day Mario arrived with Robert Merrill's coach, Leila Edwards, who had formerly worked for Agnini as a rehearsal pianist. An uneasy equilibrium was established – with both Agnini and Walter Herbert vowing never to work with Lanza again. Edwards, who seems to have had a way with difficult artistes, immediately put Mario in his place; he agreed to sing Pinkerton as written in the score, and henceforth the rehearsals ran smoothly.

Madama Butterfly was staged at New Orleans Municipal Auditorium on 8 and 10 April 1948. Singing the role of Cio-Cio San – indeed, she would hardly ever sing anything else in her career – was Japanese soprano Tomiko Kanazawa. For two months, Mario had been on a crash diet, and he had lost so much weight – he was down to 160 pounds, less than half of what he had been during his Marfa days – that he looked gaunt, almost skeletal in some photographs when posing next to a robust-looking Mme Kanazawa. By all accounts, it was a splendid performance, one which was carried by Kanazawa and baritone Jess Walters as Sharpless, but for which Mario received all the allegedly paid-for plaudits. Laurence Odel of *St Louis News* criticised William Herbert's orchestra for being 'too brassy', and said of Kanazawa, 'She is to be congratulated for bringing an otherwise ridiculous tragedienne to life for a change.' Of Mario, Odel enthused:

> Mario Lanza performed his duties as Lieut. Pinkerton with considerable verve and dash. Rarely have we seen a more superbly romantic leading tenor. His exceptionally beautiful voice helps immeasurably. The general run of the mill succeed only in disillusioning an audience. The combination of good looks and vocal ability should prove most helpful to Mr Lanza in any of his more earnest undertakings.

After each peformance, Walter Herbert walked on to the stage to warmly embrace the two leads – an act where Mario was concerned, for neither could stomach the other. The press reported that Herbert was so pleased with his new star that he had signed him up for two performances of *La Traviata*, as part of the New Orleans Opera's 1949 season. He would sing the more demanding role of Alfredo, opposite Herva Nelli's Violetta. Mario would later claim that he had had to turn the part down in favour of his movie career, but the truth is, he had never been offered the contract in the first place. The company had decided early on in the proceedings, when he had ousted the much respected Rudolph Scharr from the rehearsal room, that he would never cross their threshold again. As a budding opera star, Mario had shown enormous potential, but that singular tantrum had put paid to any operatic career he might have had coming his way.

Chapter Four

Vinceró! Vinceró!

When this roaring rampaging tenor was offended, windows were
shuttered, doors bolted: friends and other victims fled to the hills.
Pavarotti's occasional and probably exaggerated outbursts were
tranquility itself compared with the verbal, and sometimes
physical carnage that raged around the life and times
of Mario Lanza.

Donald Zec, critic and occasional friend

In May 1948, Mario was informed that production on his debut
movie had been postponed until the end of the year. Kathryn
Grayson had fallen pregnant, and her doctor had advised her to rest
as much as possible, and to cancel all her engagements until further
notice. In *Tenor In Exile*, Roland L. Bessette quotes an alleged conversation between Mario and Albert Robinson, a Columbia Artists
employee, wherein Robinson had said to Mario, referring to his urgency
to get the film out of the way so that he could get on with his concert
work, 'Well, there is just nothing to be done until her baby arrives,' to
which Mario is said to have responded, 'Ah, but you'd think there would
be!' Such a comment would not have been entirely out of character for
him, of course. But would he, a devout Catholic who worshipped
children, truly have advocated abortion? One thinks not. Grayson's only
daughter would be born on 7 October, the day Mario and Betty Cocozza
legally changed their name to Lanza, and a date no Lanza fan would
come to forget.

Also in May, Mario played his final dates with the Bel Canto Trio, in

Nova Scotia and Newfoundland. During the press conference after their concert in Halifax, when a journalist remarked that he had sung especially well that evening, Mario levelled, 'I should say so. Tonight I sang five high Cs. Caruso only ever managed two in the same evening!' Two days later, offering no explanation, he dropped out of the tour and returned to Los Angeles – for the last three concerts audiences would have to make do with the Bel Canto Duo, until Arthur Judson found Frances Yeend and George London an emergency replacement. More than half of those who had bought tickets for these concerts demanded their money back. Although he was troublesome and temperamental, there was no questioning the fact that Mario was the star of the show. He joined them for one last time on 18 June for a recital in New York, part of which was recorded. The fourth act of *La Bohème*, sung in English, remains the only surviving record of the Bel Canto Trio.

Louis B. Mayer coerced Kathryn Grayson out of temporary retirement on 24 July, when she and Mario topped the bill in an MGM concert at the Hollywood Bowl, partly organised by Lionel Barrymore to showcase his *Hallowe'en Suite: A Musical Fantasy*, a piece the actor had composed for orchestra and voice. Mario and Grayson sang several of the items he had formerly performed with Frances Yeend, and at Mayer's behest he included 'Nessun dorma', from *Turandot*. Famed movie score composer Miklós Rózsa conducted the Hollywood Bowl Symphony Orchestra, and the event was recorded and broadcast live by CBS. Another last-minute addition to the programme was Bizet's 'Agnus Dei'. In the future, Mario would often be requested to sing it again, and for some reason he always refused. His duets with Grayson, though, were not a patch on those with Yeend. Like Jeanette MacDonald, Grayson tended to overdo the vibrato on her high notes and sound tinny and shrill.

A few days after this concert, Mario announced glad tidings of his own: Betty was pregnant with their first child. It was, however, his own rapidly swelling stomach that provided MGM with a dilemma, now that their new star was footloose and fancy free whilst his wife was compelled to take things easy. Since the first Hollywood Bowl concert, Mario's weight had soared back up to 200 pounds, and producer Joe Pasternak declared that he would have to shed at least 30 pounds before they began work on their film, whose title had now been changed to *That Midnight Kiss*. The man hired to get him back into shape was Terry Robinson, a musclebound and loquacious former Mr New York City five years Mario's senior who, like Sam Weiler, gives every impression of having developed an unreciprocated crush on the singer. Robinson's introduction to Hollywood had come about when Louis B. Mayer had hired him to treat him for a back ailment. One of his first duties as Lanza's friend and more than occasional dogsbody had been driving the removal truck when he and Betty, who was eight months pregnant, had moved house. As a personal trainer, he was certainly efficient: by the time the film went into production on 3 November, he had brought Mario's weight down to 180 pounds. Pasternak told a press conference, 'This is the first time I'll be able to let an operatic tenor sing and know the audience isn't closing its eyes and visualising Van Johnson.' What he did not add was that he had insisted upon weighing scales being installed in Mario's dressing room so that he could weigh himself, like a boxer before a big fight, each morning before stepping in front of the camera.

Over the years, Terry Robinson has attracted more than his share of criticism from some Lanza fans, notably on account of his colourful reminiscences in interviews and in the book he co-wrote, *Lanza: His Tragic Life*. The fact that he was Mario's closest friend cannot be denied, and as such he would have been party to his most intimate confidences. Whether Mario would have wanted some of these antics and outbursts broadcast to the world is another matter – this may explain why only 75 per cent of the script submitted to the publishers actually ended up in the book, the remainder being deemed 'by way of common decency, unsuitable for publication'. And yet, who is to know what really happened, or what was said during those lengthy bonding sessions when these two were alone together, far from the restraints and oppression of Hollywood? Angel or demon, Robinson was always central to Mario's existence, and should accordingly be afforded the respect he deserves. He cannot be ignored simply because his recollections do not always fit well with the so-called *honorable société* of the Lanza fanbase who have set their hero on a pedestal of saintliness which no mortal could possibly have lived up to.

On 9 December, Betty gave birth to a baby girl, who Mario insisted on naming Colleen – in honour of the 'Irish colleen' (sic) he had married. He shocked his family and his Catholic friends by asking Sam Weiler and his wife, Selma, to be godparents – the couple were Jewish, as indeed were the majority of the people he had been involved with since arriving in Hollywood. Only weeks before, the Lanzas had moved into their first proper home, a duplex at 236 1/2 South Spaulding Drive, off Wilshire Boulevard. The father was conspicuous by his absence: he and Kathryn Grayson were at the MGM studio, recording the sound-track for the film.

Mario had been put through his paces by the studio orchestra's Charles Previn (uncle of André) and sexagenarian Giacomi Spadoni, who had briefly coached Caruso and had been a close friend of another Lanza idol, the great Russian bass Fyodor Chaliapin. Mario and Spadoni had met at a fundraiser at Pickfair, the fairytale home of Mary Pickford and Douglas Fairbanks Jr. This had been organised by Louis B. Mayer's sister, Ida Mayer Cummings, to raise money for the Jewish Home For The Aged. It was a project which amused Mario: Mayer never stopped drilling into his stars how important families were, yet here was his sister working for an organisation which helped fund the retirement homes the Jewish community disapproved of! The bash was attended by 300 wealthy Jewish women who chattered noisily during his first two arias, and only quietened down when he made strangulatory gestures with his hands. He also learned a valuable lesson, that most of these people were much less interested in Lanza the man than they were in the curiosity of his voice. Mario fulfilled several more such engage-ments, but the crunch came when he was 'summoned' to Mayer's mansion to perform for the mogul's friends. He was fine with this until Mayer ordered him to stand on an upstairs balcony, like a prize exhibit, and sing to the diners below. Halfway through his first piece, angered by the clattering of the cutlery, he uttered a few very loud profanities, stopped the pianist, and left in a huff.

Mario's decidedly short fuse caused just as many problems on the film set as elsewhere, though this time he was concerned about staying in shape until the picture had been completed. Then, he declared, he would 'live life to the full' until the next studio call, six months from now. He loathed having to start work at six in the morning, which sometimes meant missing his usual colossal breakfast. On at least two occasions he stopped the camera during a key scene when, having glanced at himself in a mirror, he decided that an immediate workout with Terry Robinson would rid him of some wedge of fat he had missed before. This meant a two-hour break afterwards to shower, have his make-up fixed and his hair re-coiffed, and for the technicians to reset the lighting equipment. Recurring heavy benders the night before led to his missing at least five studio calls for scenes to which he was crucial, resulting in the set having to be closed down for the day. Then there were the pranks, such as sending toilet rolls to people he did not like – in his words, 'An asswipe for an asswipe,' – perpetrated to annoy Kathryn Grayson and 69-year-old Ethel Barrymore, who had branded him an 'upstart' before meeting him. The first time she turned her nose up at him on the set, he called her 'a fucking old bitch' to her face and accused her of stealing every scene they appeared in together. This was true: some might argue that all the Barrymores had forgotten more about acting than Mario and the other MGM musical stars would ever learn, but nothing will alter the fact that she had been rude to him in the first place. In his memoirs, Costa recalls Edmund O'Brien, one of the stars of *Winged Victory*, visiting the set and bumping into an extremely irate, much changed Lanza:

> And as he raved on about Ethel Barrymore, Mario's eyes, ordinarily so bright, narrowed into searing pinpoints of hate. O'Brien was powerless to stop the tirade. 'Maybe I should have recognised it at once,' O'Brien says, 'but who looks for paranoia in a friend? Mario suddenly believed that he was being persecuted, that almost everyone was insidiously working against him. To most of us at the time, Mario was only a youngster with a wonderful, thrilling voice. We thought we could kid him and make jokes about him without having him hate us. Lord, that hatred must have been burning inside him all along!'

Costa then offers his personal, very similar take on the Lanza hostility and psychosis:

> Later I became intimately acquainted with him on our concert trips around the country. The generous, affectionate side of Mario, his boundless warmth for ordinary people, his love and loyalty for his friends, made it impossible to regard him as a sick man. The ugly side of Mario was overlooked until darker days, when it was too late to give him the help he needed so badly.

Costa was being too critical. Mario was not a sick man, other than by way of an inability to control his monstrous appetite. No, his great problem – one he shared with contemporaries such as Piaf, Callas and even Sinatra – was his awareness of his own genius, which cannot have been easy to live with, and an inability to cope with those peers who wanted only to take advantage of this, rather than wanting to get to know the individual lining their coffers. For Louis B. Mayer and his cronies at MGM, Lanza was a magnificent voice which earned the studio millions of dollars. The stress and physical exertion they put him through mattered little to them, so long as they gained their pound of flesh.

This sense of persecution would stay with Mario for the rest of his life, to be dealt with by tantrums and unruly, sometimes childish behaviour. As had happened with Frances Yeend, he would expose himself in front of Ethel Barrymore and Kathryn Grayson, then urinate in whatever receptacle was available – be this a potted plant, or a hat someone had left lying around. 'And sometimes he wasn't just satisfied with urinating,' Marlene Dietrich said. News of his antics were relayed to Louis B. Mayer, who summoned Mario to his office and informed him that from now on he would be supplied with an on-set 'babysitter', such as the ones the studio provided for some stars' wayward children who could not be left alone without causing mayhem. Mario caused more problems for Mayer towards the end of shooting by barging into his office – one thing absolutely no one got away with doing – and demanding that his name should appear above those of Grayson, Iturbi, Barrymore and Keenan Wynn in the credits. His argument was a valid one. The critics who had seen the rushes were already hailing him as the star of the picture, whereas the other stars barely warranted a mention. Neither had his ego been helped by one journalist telling him that one day he would be as great as Caruso. Never more serious, Mario had responded, 'I already am!' Mayer begrudgingly offered a compromise: instead of being fourth billing, as planned, the banner 'Introducing Mario Lanza' would appear at the end of the credits, in letters the same size as in Grayson's name.

That Midnight Kiss was directed by Norman Taurog (1899–1981), who in 1931 had won an Oscar for his weepy, *Skippy*, featuring his nephew, the child star Jackie Cooper. Later, he would direct nine films for Elvis Presley, ranging from the staggeringly successful *Blue Hawaii* to the not-so-hot *Speedway* and *Live A Little, Love A Little. That*

Midnight Kiss is a better than average film made great solely by way of Lanza's singing, though the tagline – 'The Biggest Kiss in Movie History' – had some critics howling. The screenplay, by Bruce Manning and Tamara Hovey, was loosely woven around the Mario Lanza biography – or at least the one part-fabricated by MGM – with some aspects of this applying to the Kathryn Grayson character. Therefore it is millionairess Abigail Budell (Barrymore) and not Maria Cocozza who wants to put her soprano granddaughter, Prudence (Grayson), on the opera stage so that she might have the career which evaded her. To make this easier, Abigail has founded her own opera company and engages legendary conductor-pianist-producer José Iturbi (playing himself, whilst later in the film his pianist sister, Amparo, also plays herself) to put her through her paces. Prudence has just returned after five years studying at the finest academies in Europe, but this cuts no ice with the tenor Iturbi provides her with. Guido Betelli (Thomas Gomez) fits the bill as the then archetypal tenor – fat, bad-tempered and full of himself; he starts off by assuring Prudence that she should consider herself fortunate to be breathing the same air as him.

To an extent, the tenor is right. As a popular singer in vehicles such as *Showboat*, Grayson was fine, but she is deplorable when attempting to tackle grand opera, sounding (and looking, here) like a caricature of Disney's Snow White – warbling shrilly and way too fast, like a 45rpm record playing at the wrong speed. To hear her screeching her way through Alabiev's 'Russian Nightingale' is quite painful, assuring one that no legitimate opera company would have gone within a mile of such a horrendous noise. Cut to Mario, aka truck driver Johnny Donetti, sitting in Prudence's living room at the piano he has just delivered – as is supposed to have happened chez Koussevitzky – and belting out an impromptu 'Mama mia, che vo' sape?' The scriptwriters have also slipped in another Lanza *truc* – the bellowing of that lengthy top C down the ear of some unsuspecting victim. He looks good in the wake of his training regime, though the studio should have either come clean about his real height of 5 feet 8 inches (1.73m), or not cast him alongside actors who dwarf him. Even Grayson is almost as tall as he is. In his leather jacket and denims, he looks like a street kid, though what makes this street kid special is the way he launches into a pretty spectacular 'Una furtiva lagrima', minus the extraneous hand gestures which would come a little later in Lanza's career. One becomes so mesmerised by the beauty of his voice that one forgets to ask why there just happens to be a piano in the garage in the first place.

Even so, Iturbi has his doubts about hiring Johnny. The voice is fine, he says, but on stage the young tenor would look awkward and stiff – exactly what they had said about Mario, of traits which never really left him. Unsure what to do with his large, shovel-like hands, he would frequently wave them around indiscriminately, punching the air like a prizefighter. Also like the real Lanza, Johnny has worked in army concert parties and trained with a maestro, only to give it all up and find more realistic employment as a truck driver. Prudence begs Iturbi to rethink his decision, and workmate Artie (Keenan Wynn) appoints himself his manager when Iturbi tests him out on the concert platform – no ordinary performance, but one accompanied by a 40-piece orchestra. The aria is 'Celeste Aida', which earns him a standing ovation, along with $250 to buy new wheels for his truck. And the audience have barely recovered from this spinetingling experience when the mood changes to high camp. Johnny turns up at Prudence's house in the middle of the night, the orchestra on the back of his truck, to re-enact the most famous scene from *Romeo and Juliet* as he serenades her, on her balcony, with 'They'll Never Believe Me' – dropping his voice when she joins in, so as not to drown her.

Iturbi still is not convinced that Johnny will make the grade as an opera singer, arguing that there is a vast difference between a six-minute aria and a full two-hour production. Betelli is therefore reinstated, and hits the roof when a newspaper article announces that Philadelphia now has *two* great tenors – a line which brought another outburst from Mario against Ethel Barrymore, who in a recent article discussing *That Midnight Kiss* had been hailed as another great Philadelphian, whilst the writer of the piece had failed to mention him. Betelli tears up his contract, leaving Iturbi in the lurch, though we instinctively know that he will now choose Johnny as his replacement. This coincides with a misunderstanding between the tenor and Prudence when Mary (Marjorie Reynolds), the secretary at the truck depot, gives her the impression that it is she who Johnny will marry. The next time he turns up at her house to serenade her – with 'I Know, I Know, I Know' – he is sent packing. Now, with the two no longer on speaking terms, Iturbi persuades Betelli to return to the production. All ends well, of course, when the couple's friends sabotage the opening night by switching Betelli's costume for the one bought for the much slimmer Johnny. Betelli trashes his dressing room, and Johnny takes his place on stage for what must be the briefest and most tuneless opera ever. The curtain opens on the main aria, 'Love Is Music', and the performance ends immediately after it – but not before allowing the lovers to kiss as the credits prepare to roll.

The six-month period between completing the film and its release were arguably the busiest of Mario's career. By the terms of his contract, he had fulfilled his obligation to MGM and should have been allowed to pursue his operatic interests. Columbia Concerts – and a hefty pay packet – persuaded him to change his mind by throwing together a promotional tour of America which, in retrospect, was a huge mistake. Though just about everyone in the country knew what he looked like by now, Mario had released no commercial recordings, and only a small percentage of the American public had listened to him on the radio. Even Louis B. Mayer's behind-the-scenes machinations had only permitted him to partly fill the Hollywood Bowl, and in fact most of the audience had been there to see Frances Yeend. As Mayer's power did not extend beyond the Hollywood confines, none of the major concert halls wanted to risk booking him, which resulted in him being hired by similar venues to those he had played with the Bel Canto Trio.

This only brought out the very worst in Mario's temperament. He had boasted of being greater than Caruso so many times that he had come to expect the same treatment afforded an operatic megastar, along with the same salary, which of course was not forthcoming – indeed, the pittance paid to him by Columbia Concerts definitely meant they were taking advantage of him, and it barely covered his expenses. Mario's first bust-up with the company occurred when they tried to block his decision to engage Costa as his accompanist. He offered them an ultimatum: no Costa, no Lanza. There were many other problems along the way: for example, if he turned up at a particular town he took a dislike to, he simply cancelled the concert.

Citing invented illnesses, Mario opted out of the first concert on 7 March at Bluefield, West Virginia, and the last one on 25 May at Lincoln, Nebraska; in between, there were thirteen others he cancelled at the last minute. One cancellation which caused long-lasting enmity towards him and almost saw him blacklisted by tour organisers across the country was a benefit scheduled for 19 May (for which he had been paid $1,200 in advance, which he subsequently kept) in Centralia, Illinois, for the families of the 111 men who had died in the town's mining accident of March 1947. The organisers were told that Mario could not make it because he had been hospitalised with pneumonia. Concerned reporters called all the major hospitals in Chicago, drew blanks, and eventually located him at the city's Bismark Hotel, where he had thrown a party for the other guests. Columbia Concerts contacted Sam Weiler and instructed him to bring his charge to heel. Weiler, who had earned nothing from this tour because of all the cancellations, tried his best to control him. As usual, Mario pleased only himself.

The tour took in such 'off-the-beaten-track' venues as Fort Wayne, Indiana; Duluth, Minnesota; Chicago and Minneapolis; Tulsa, Oklahoma; Wilmington, Delaware; New Orleans; Troy, New York; Portland, Maine; Charleston, Illinois; Clinton, Iowa; Zanesville and Athens, Ohio; and Sylcauga, Alabama, which Mario wanted to cancel because he had never heard of it, but decided to give it a go. Though he had got over being physically ill before a performance, he had by now developed another paranoia: worrying over his repertoire, which was not extensive then, outside the recording studio, and which would become even more limited later on. There was absolutely nothing wrong with his memory; he just became increasingly terrified of fluffing his lines in front of an audience where there could be no retakes, and believed that the only way to combat this problem would be to learn as little new material as possible. For this tour he included the material he had been singing for the last five years, along with a handful of works by Monteverdi, Pergolesi, Scarlatti – and Sigmund Romberg, whose music provided Mario with an early showstopper, 'Softly as the Morning Sunlight', with its rather ominous warning, 'The light that gave you glory will take it all away.'

Mario had also rehearsed several songs by Hugo Wolf, but ditched these at the last minute. Costa worshipped the ground Mario walked upon, yet never held back when criticising him, sometimes severely, for his lethargy. 'He was lazy, irresponsible, and lacking a proper sense of the importance of the tour to his development as an artiste,' he recalled. 'But he was also in a state of continuous fright, just as he had been at the prospect of singing for Toscanini.' Yet some of these concerts turned out to be memorable. When told that he would be performing in Oklahoma, he asked to be accompanied by the State Symphony Orchestra, and the request was granted. He was on stage for over two hours, and at the end even received a 20-minute standing ovation. The critic with the *Daily Oklahoman* called him 'possibly the greatest of our young tenors who might fill the long-vacant shoes of Caruso'.

Now that he had completed his requisite six-month stint for MGM, whilst waiting for his next studio call Mario devoted much of his spare time to eating and drinking, and of course the pounds he had struggled to lose now piled back on. Costa had introduced him to *taramosalata*, a fattening traditional Greek dish of cod's roe, olive oil and onions. The pianist recalled how Mario would eat five double servings of this in one sitting, then order a four-inch-thick steak. If he wanted something simple, he would call room service and order 'twenty fried eggs, sunny side up, with three orders of bacon and three orders of toast and three orders of sausages'. He was not drinking as much beer as before, but it was not unusual for him to wash this lot down with two or three bottles of strong red wine, Italian of course.

In the midst of this melee, Mario managed to spend some time in New York, where he cut his first proper recordings for RCA Victor (as opposed to tests, and the soundtrack for *That Midnight Kiss*, recorded the previous December). Backing him would be 45 musicians, mostly from the New York Philharmonic. Again, he made special demands that the first session would take place at the massive Manhattan Center, on West 34th Street, and that he should be given three top conductors to choose from. How Mario was able to get away with this, bearing in mind that he was building his own legend on what the critics had said of a film which the public was yet to see is both baffling and a testimony to his extraordinary nerve. On the one hand RCA had Lanza the shrinking violet, sometimes afraid of his own shadow – on the other the tyrant who did not care whose toes he trod upon so long as he got his own way, which with his impeccable judgement almost always turned out for the best for all concerned. He chose the New York City Opera's Jean-Paul Morel (1903–73), regarded as one of the key conductors of the French repertoire. At just 18, Morel had begun teaching at Fontainebleau before moving on to work with Reynaldo Hahn. In 1949, he had augmented the staff at Juilliard. Such plaudits, however, cut no ice with Mario once someone else began throwing their weight around for a change. Morel, no less feisty than Enrico Rosati, loudly pointed out one afternoon in front of the whole orchestra where Mario was going wrong with 'Celeste Aida', declaring that Mario had made the same mistakes whilst performing this in *That Midnight Kiss*. Mario retaliated with more expletives than the conductor had heard in his life, then promptly stormed off the platform. The next morning he called Manny Sachs, RCA's vice-president and another tetchy individual feared by all who had the misfortune to work with him. Sachs was given an ultimatum: Costa would conduct the orchestra from now on, mindless of the fact that he had only done so once before, albeit at Carnegie Hall, an unnerving experience which he said he never wanted to repeat! To his credit, Mario also offered to pay the $5,000 for the session out of his own pocket, should Costa fail to come up to scratch. Such was his confidence in his friend.

The first session took place on 5 May, and could not have passed more smoothly, though the experience was a nightmare for Costa. Because he rarely sang the same piece twice in the same way, Mario instructed Costa to watch his eyes for direction – only to close them when effecting an unexpected key change or embellishment not in the sheet music. Despite this, the end result was sheer perfection. Like other tetchy perfectionists – Piaf, Callas, Dietrich, Wunderlich – his first take would always prove the best, and Mario would be applauded as a technician's dream. Indeed, he made it clear that if he was going to put his heart and soul into a performance, as happened on the stage, then unless it was someone else's fault there would be no second take. The first aria laid down during the afternoon was 'Che gelida manina'. Mario would record this several times over the next few years, and numerous takes have turned up on live recordings, but he never sang it nearly so well as he did on that day. It contains just one tiny, excusable flaw – when he rushes the ending as if afraid that he might crack the final note. Even so, this may still be the definitive version of the aria, which explains why it was voted operatic recording of the year by the National Record Critics Association, and why it remains in RCA's Hall of Fame catalogue to this day. This was followed by 'Mama mia, che vo' sape' and the complete version, transposed up a tone, of 'Celeste Aida'. In the film, Mario had scored a first by singing the entire piece, but without the lengthy recitative which he added now (until then, only fragments of operatic arias had been permitted on the screen so as not to bore audiences). Finally, he recorded a Neapolitan favourite, 'Catari, Catari', listed in the catalogue under its official title, 'Core 'ngrato'. This he would improve upon in subsequent concert performances, though even this 'flawed' (in his opinion) reading is better than anyone else's.

Three more popular songs were recorded in the session of 23 August, which took place at the more easily accessible Republic Studios, in Hollywood: a solo version of 'They Didn't Believe Me', 'Mattinata', and a second take of 'I Know, I Know, I Know' because Mario had disliked the version he had cut for the film soundtrack. By now, Ray Sinatra had replaced Costa as conductor. Sinatra also conducted for the final session, on 28 October, when Mario cut 'Lolita', 'O sole mio', and two versions of 'Granada', the second of which would only be superseded by Fritz Wunderlich's definitive recording of 1965, which he would sing an astonishing two keys above the written score. This session had originally been scheduled for the end of September, but the date changed when Mario was summoned back to Philadelphia, where Maria Cocozza had been hospitalised with suspected kidney stones. In fact, it was much more serious than this and she underwent surgery to remove a tumerous kidney. For Mario, who never hid the fact that he loved his mother more than he could possibly love anyone else, including his wife, this was the last straw. He stayed at the hospital until she had recovered from her operation, and promised that he would find his parents a house in Hollywood as soon as possible so that he would never have to be separated from them again.

The previews for *That Midnight Kiss* took place in July and coincided with Mario's first press interview, a feast of well-deserved praise and tall tales which was compiled during the last the week of the month and published in the 3 September issue of *Collier's* magazine. Though the public were yet to see this new sensation, all hope of Mario embarking on the operatic venture he had dreamed of was fading: he had a wife and daughter, and courtesy of MGM a blossoming movie career and extravagant lifestyle which he would never have afforded had he been working as second tenor for the New York Met. Though he had privately forced himself to accept this, when interviewed by Dwight Whitney he continued to boast of the non-existent offers coming his way. According to Mario, he had received an offer from La Scala, Milan, to open the 1950 season in a special production of *Andrea Chénier*, under the baton of Victor de Sabata. There was even talk of him partnering Maria Callas, though an examination by this author of La Scala's records in February 2007 revealed that no actual offer was ever made. Other offers had supposedly come in from the New York Met, which he had also rejected. 'I may be the first *sensible* young American singer,' he told Whitney, 'but I'm not yet experienced enough for the Met. Caruso didn't come into his own until he was thirty-three. At twenty-seven I'd be rushing into it. I want to leave my mark in music. As long as I have a good voice, they need it!' Rudolf Bing, who had recently taken over as the Met's general manager and would rule the establishment with a rod of iron until 1972, did not think so. MGM, he declared, had made a mockery of opera by making films about it, and as such, Mario Lanza would never appear in any Met production whilst *he* was running things.

MGM had furnished *Collier's* with an 'official' Lanza biography, which he too was ordered to adhere to: they had knocked one year off his age, and added four inches to his height. 'He is six feet tall but gives the impression of being a still bigger man,' Whitney observed. 'He has a chest like a wrestler and the manners of a old-world diplomat.' For some reason he had now been born in New York, but relocated to Philadelphia as a child. Those close to Mario who had suffered the brunt of his foul moods must also have been amused to read, 'Lanza is neither ineffably modest nor a swelling egotist...his sense of humour extends to himself, and he will burlesque his own situation mercilessly.' The studio had also come up with a new take in how Alfredo Cocozza had come by his more famous monicker – courtesy of Sergei Koussevitzky, who had argued in a letter to Mario's father that the word *cocozza*, mispronounced, 'sounded like a personal reference of the grossest and most unprintable sort'. Nonsense, of course. Similarly, MGM had changed the already almost certainly fabricated story of how Mario had cheated during his audition for *On The Beam* by sticking a label with his name over that of another tenor. No one had heard of Frederick Jagel, Louis B. Mayer maintained, so the tenor's name was changed to – Caruso.

Other notes included in Whitney's briefing claimed that Mario had had a quiet, religious upbringing and that as a child he had been timid. This he scoffed at and, incurring Mayer's wrath, he came clean about his youth. Now, the bobby-soxers in the cinema who would leap on to their seats whilst he was singing 'Celeste Aida' – screaming as if they were at a Sinatra concert – would learn that as a youth their idol had led a gang which had terrorised the streets of Philadelphia, raiding bakery trucks, smashing windows, brawling. Betty Lanza, already the long-suffering spouse, was also brought into the equation, telling Whitney of her husband's constant demands. 'Our life is a merry-go-round. There are certain requirements in the life of an artiste, you know. When I'm sick, who gets the coffee in bed? *He* does!'

For the benefit of *Collier's* readers, Mario described his typical day:

I get up early – at ten o'clock. My wife serves me black coffee in bed. A half hour later, Terry arrives. I look at him blearily, I hate him. He drags me up to the roof [to the gymnasium] and I still hate him. Towards the end of our workout an hour and a half later I begin to like him. He rubs me down for half an hour. Then I warm up my voice in the shower. Sometimes I get dizzy from the wall vibrations. Luckily the neighbours like music. At one o'clock I have a breakfast of three poached eggs, skimmed milk and fruit. Then I have a one-hour session with my coach, Giacomo Spadoni, then a dramatic lesson, next a half-hour chat with my producer Joe Pasternak. Sometimes I visit the movie sets and watch Deborah Kerr work, or I sing a duet with Walter Pidgeon. I get home at six and want to eat. It is my one important meal of the day – steak or liver and a monstrous vegetable salad.

Only the first part of this statement was true: the enforced workouts with Terry Robinson. Mario was still wolfing down enough food to sustain four men – three days of bingeing, followed by three days of near-starvation – and when hungry he was impossible to handle. On 16 August, to publicise the film, a tubbier Mario and Kathryn Grayson were among the artistes who appeared at the Hollywood Bowl in the extravaganza, *Salute To MGM*. A mixed bag pat-on-the-back if ever there was one, this event saw Mario walking on to the stage after Eleanor Powell and Carmen Miranda, to change the mood completely and shake the foundations with a roisterous 'Celeste Aida'. He also hit a stunning D flat during 'Addio, addio', the duet from *Rigoletto* for which he insisted he be partnered by soprano Mary Jane Smith, technically far superior to Grayson, as the surviving recording proves.

On 28 August the stars of the film, their families and most of the MGM executives headed for Philadelphia, where *That Midnight Kiss* was to have its world premiere. Over 3,000 hysterical fans were waiting for Mario outside Salvatore Lanza's store on Mercy Street. As he climbed out of the car, his shirt and jacket were almost ripped off his back and a dozen policemen manhandled him inside the building where, ten minutes later, still wearing his torn clothes, he flung open his old bedroom window and, *a cappella*, belted out an impromptu 'Vesti la giubba'.

The next evening, an open-topped limousine, flanked by six motor-cycle cops and with Mario perched atop his seat, headed the motorcade which drove through the packed streets of the city to the Boyd Theater. In the extremely unlikely event of someone not knowing who he was, a banner with his name in foot-high letters was tied to the car. The studio had arranged for Kathryn Grayson to travel with him, but she – and Betty – were relegated to the car behind, with Antonio Cocozza and the Mayor of Philadelphia, and Mario insisted that his mother share with him his moment of glory. The motorcade was halfway along the main street when, without warning, a coal truck swerved to a halt in front of it, causing Mario's driver to jam on the brakes and all but catapult him over the windscreen. The truck contained two of his old schoolfriends, and the parade was held up for ten minutes whilst Mario hugged and kissed them – then insisted that they latch on to the back of the motorcade and attend the premiere, grimy overalls and all! Other old friends were waiting outside the theatre, and Mario took the time to embrace every one, completely ignoring the local dignitaries who he 'didn't know from Adam'.

President Truman was also in town, staying at the Bellevue-Stratford Hotel. Mario and Grayson had been engaged for a short recital of songs from the film here, but because of the delays caused by meeting his friends, and staying behind to chat with them after the screening, Mario arrived late, by which time Truman had been assigned to a midnight nationwide radio address. Walking on to the podium, it was *he* who grabbed the microphone and announced, 'Ladies and gentlemen, I want to apologize to Mr Lanza for asking him here and then not allowing him enough time to sing for us!'

The next day, Mario and Grayson appeared on the WCAU Radio, an event which turned into a very noisy affair when the two coal merchants turned up again – barging past the reception and into the actual studio, along with eight members of the former 'Lanza gang' that had wreaked havoc on the city streets a decade earlier. Like Mario himself, all were reformed characters who had done well for themselves. 'There were the Capones. Dick, now an eye specialist and rather formal in manner, his brother Eddie, very proper and handsome,' he later wrote in *Modern Screen*, 'the Graziano boys, now owners of the King Laundry. Vince Bartolomeo, Dr Eddie Lucente, the kindly baby doctor. Tony De Simone. We grinned in memory of the pranks we played and the mischief we shared.' That evening, Mario and Betty should have attended a social function with the cast of the film and the MGM executives. He opted out of this to paint the town red with his buddies.

That Midnight Kiss was immensely popular with the box office, but only on account of him. The *New York Times*'s Bosley Crowther, a frequently hateful but extremely influential man who could close a revue or end a movie's run with just one acid comment, observed, 'Lanza's voice has quality and warmth. And he has a nice personality.' Harold Barnes of the *Herald Tribune* was not so impressed, saying, 'He may have a resounding tenor voice, but he has a lot to learn about acting.' The critic from *Variety* disagreed with this:

> His standout singing and capable thesping should provide an extra word-of-mouth fillip for exhibitors... In addition, far from resembling the caricatured opera tenor, he's a nice looking youngster of the average American boy school who will have the femme customers on his side from the start.

This was true. As a beginner, Mario's acting abilities were way above average and easily compare with those of 'singing actors' such as Gordon MacRae and Howard Keel. But the one review which went to Mario's head and enhanced his claim that his name really should have topped the credits appeared in *Newsweek*:

> Aside from José Iturbi's music, virtually the only excuse for this one is Mario Lanza, a singer whose talents would be conspicuous

even outside a film devoted to opera. He can act as well as sing. But his efforts in both directions are hampered by an inconsequential story which enmeshes him with Kathryn Grayson – a girl who neither sings nor acts in his league. Its tenuousness is mitigated neither by the music of Tchaikovsky nor the presence of Ethel Barrymore.

A few days after the premiere, against both stars' wishes, Mario and Grayson embarked on a brief tour promoting the film. This took in venues in Philadelphia, New Haven, New York, Kansas City – and concluded in Hollywood on 29 September with a concert for the Screen Guild Theater Program which was broadcast on NBC Radio. On stage for just 30 minutes, Mario sang 'I Know, I Know, I Know' and 'Mamma mia, che vo' sape', before Grayson partnered him on 'They Didn't Believe Me' and a somewhat tinny 'Verrano a te sull'aure' from Donizetti's *Lucia di Lammermoor* – an aria which Mario had asked to be dropped from the film because he believed that his co-star could not sing it properly.

Everyone involved with *That Midnight Kiss* had by this stage had enough of Mario's fickle (but professional) ways, and asked not to work with him again – though Norman Taurog, Grayson and J. Carrol Naish (who had played his father in the film) had already been contracted to his next picture. Joe Pasternak, who had called him 'exasperating', would be saddled with him for another five years. Yet there is no disputing the fact that, exasperating or not, Mario would carry every production he was involved in.

Chapter Five

The Man with the Million-Dollar Voice

*I sing from the heart, from the top of my head to the tip of
my toes. I sing as though my life depends on it, and if I
ever stop doing that then I'll stop living.*

Mario Lanza

M ario's next film should have been an operatic version of
Deburau, based on the play by Sacha Guitry which tells the
story of the real-life French mime artiste and original
Pierrot, Jean-Gaspard Deburau (1796–1846), so memorably portrayed
on the screen by Jean-Louis Barrault in Marcel Carné's masterpiece,
Les enfants du paradis (1945). This concentrates on the relationship
between Deburau and Marie Duplessis, the courtesan-model used by
Dumas for *La dame aux camélias*, immortalised by Greta Garbo in
Camille. Neither Deburau nor his son Charles, the part pencilled in for
Mario, had appeared in the Garbo film – her love interest had been
Armand Duval (Robert Taylor), the man who had replaced both of them
in her affections. The part of Marie was to have been played by Kathryn
Grayson, and in the role of Deburau, Louis B. Mayer had decided upon
Ezio Pinza. Little wonder, then, that Mayer faced fierce opposition from
his board of directors. Pinza was coming to the end of his career – he
died in 1957. Also, one shudders to even think of Grayson following in
the footsteps of Garbo and, albeit inadvertently, lampooning legitimate
opera alongside two undisputed masters of the genre.

Instead, Mario and Grayson were put into *Kiss Of Fire*, subsequently changed to *The Toast of New Orleans*. This would again see him portraying the non-professional singer with the glorious voice, pursuing the world-famous soprano whose attempts at singing opera are unintentionally dire. And as before, the scriptwriter incorporated large chunks of the Lanza biography and transferred some of the singer's less endearing traits to his on-screen character.

As before, Mario embarked on a quickfire training programme with Terry Robinson – begrudgingly because, having read the reviews for his first film, he still considered himself first and foremost an opera singer, and as such considered looks secondary to vocal talent. In those days, even some experts believed that being fat was obligatory for classical singers – that it was necessary to have this excess weight to push the voice forwards. 'When Lanza was of a mind to eat,' Joe Pasternak observed, 'the secret service itself couldn't keep this trenchman in bounds.' The Casa d'Amor, one of Hollywood's most exclusive Italian restaurants where he was a regular customer, added 'The Lanza Special' to their menu – a whopping 20-inch wide, three-inch thick pizza with 12 toppings. So far as is known, Mario was the only customer they ever had who could eat a whole one and still ask for more! He would pat his paunch, laugh and boast that he owed his girth to 'good living'. By now, the three-day purges following his eating binges were being helped by vitamin shots, amphetamines and prescription drugs – there was never any shortage of suppliers on the MGM lot – and the more he became addicted to these, the more bad-tempered he grew, flying off the handle over the slightest triviality and sending everyone scurrying for cover.

Shooting began on 20 October 1949. Both Mario and Sam Weiler had petitioned Louis B. Mayer to give him top billing, and Mayer had compromised by billing him over his other co-star, suave and sophisticated British actor David Niven, but refused to remove Kathryn Grayson from the top of the credits, declaring that she was by far the greater star – true, at the time. What therefore looked like being a grumpy experience for Mario perked up when he was introduced to Niven. The first time these unlikely allies – against MGM, Grayson and the others – met was in Mario's dressing room during rehearsals, when Niven strode in with his best friend, Errol Flynn, another rebel against the Hollywood system. Niven and Flynn had founded the hellraiser group, 'FFF' – Flynn's Flying Fuckers – who painted the town red most nights they were together, in their quest for 'Quentin quail' (teenage girls and boys) and a good brawl, if this could be had. And if Mario did not take too kindly, at first, to being addressed as 'Nellie Melba', he soon warmed to the Tasmanian actor when Flynn dropped a bottle of vodka into his lap and barked, 'Get that down your neck, sport!'

Flynn's heroics and publicly conducted extra-marital affairs fascinated Mario, as did his exhibitionism – the latter was one trait the two stars had in common, along with the sad fact that they would die within a week of each other. Mario was fascinated by the story, related by Niven, of how Flynn's mother had once walked into his dressing room to find a young extra on his knees, administering a blow-job. 'Be with you in a tick, Ma – almost done!' he had panted, reaching out one long leg and kicking the door shut after her. Over the coming years, Mario would extract more than a few leaves out of the Errol Flynn encyclopedia of dissipation, and like Flynn, would execute them with accustomed humour, never malice. Though he would never develop the older actor's fondness for Class A drugs and lovers of both sexes, like him he was fond of whipping out his penis at the most unexpected moments. With Frances Yeend it had been discreetly, from behind the curtain, and meant only as fun. With Kathryn Grayson and Ethel Barrymore, it had been to shock and annoy. Now he began sneaking extras into his dressing room and purposely leaving the door ajar, so that anyone passing by could catch an eyeful. If there were no extras to tickle his fancy, he would 'buy in' – from the ready supply of hookers who were always available to be smuggled on to the lot, for a price. Neither did Mario keep his libido under control whilst at home. The faithful Terry Robinson would be asked to stand on the upstairs landing, keeping watch and doubtless getting a thrill out of listening to the noisy goings-on behind the bedroom door.

Neither was Mario averse to having sex with female fans who sent him nude photographs of themselves, or underwear for him to sign and send back. 'My mail is so hot that I need asbestos gloves to open it,' he told one journalist. Sometimes, at the exact moment of ejaculation, he would let out one of those piercing top Cs, which must have been very disconcerting for the woman involved.

Mario and Niven's drinking caused havoc on the set. Dismissing vodka as 'tasting like mule piss', Niven turned up each morning with a bottle of Chivas Regal whisky, which they had usually polished off by lunchtime. Since finishing *That Midnight Kiss*, Mario was also back on the beer – going through a dozen bottles or more before Norman Taurog called a halt to the day's shooting. He had also inherited one of Niven's traits – one he would share with Flynn, Gable and Joan Crawford – of befriending 'the little people', as he called them: clapper boys, canteen staff, hairdressers and make-up artists, technicians and extras. Appalled by their low rates of pay, he would sometimes deliberately fluff his lines or mess up scenes so that these had to be shot again, and earn these friends valuable overtime. On one occasion when a studio labourer's wife had just had a baby and he needed some extra cash, Mario complained that the artificial lagoon used for the boating scenes 'stank of piss and God know what else'. He had been using it as a toilet all week just so that the young man would be asked to drain it, and earn the money he needed. Each evening he handed out little gifts before heading off home: cigarettes, crates of beer, wrist watches, maybe a tie he did not wear any more. These people repaid him by ordering meals from the studio commissary and handing them over – to complement the two plates of food he ordered each lunchtime. But where anyone of authority was concerned, such as directors, producers and studio bigwigs, like Flynn he went out of his way to antagonise them.

The film's score was by Sammy Cahn and Nicholas Brodsky, an uneasy partnership initially. Cahn (1913–93) had written for just about every major star in America, and was used to working with composers who could mould their music around his amazingly articulate lyrics. Odessa-born Brodsky (1905–58) was, on the other hand, totally inflexible. Once he had completed a piece of music, he would have this printed and sent to the lyricist, who would be forbidden to alter a single note.

Though some of the numbers from *The Toast of New Orleans* may be deemed forgettable, one of them became Lanza's theme song, and when Brodsky forwarded the sheet music to Cahn, he cannot have imagined how popular this would become; 'Be My Love' will be for ever identified with him. Virtually every tenor has sung it at some stage of his career, and these renditions range from the sublime (Domingo, Carreras, and Pavarotti separately) to the downright awful (the same three as an ensemble towards the end of their huge run as the Three Tenors). Critics have frequently argued that the version by Fritz Wunderlich –

the only item he ever recorded in English – released in August 1966, only weeks before his death, is the better version. But the opera critic with *High Fidelity* observed:

> Comparisons with an original are always disadvantageous. Lanza's 'Be My Love' is, to come off it and tell the truth, one of the most exciting pieces of singing heard in the last twenty or thirty years, considered simply in terms of vocal quality and line. Wunderlich rings something of a change by singing it in a higher key, but this forces him to take a low ending where Lanza went up to the C, and the final effect is anticlimactic.

So there we have it.

Mario first recorded the song with Kathryn Grayson on 15 December 1949, and alone two weeks later. The definitive version with Ray Sinatra's orchestra and 'I'll Never Love You' on the flipside – the one which sold millions of copies worldwide – was cut on 27 June 1950 when Mario rounded off the song with the resounding, elongated top C praised by the *High Fidelity* critic. Sammy Cahn, who witnessed the event, wrote in his memoirs, 'No mechanical reproduction could capture the startling brilliance of that voice. It scared the hell out of you.' By this time, the song had been covered by Billy Eckstine and, in Britain, proved a hit for Dorothy Squires who insisted on using exactly the same arrangement. 'Soon afterwards, I met Lanza in Hollywood,' Dorothy told me, some years later. 'I asked him what he thought of my version of the song and he said, "You and every dumb motherfucker who tried to sing it sounded like shit. The song was written for a great singer, and I am that person!" Never in my whole life have I so wanted to slap somebody's face. That man really did have an opinion of himself. He was one of the best singers in the world, but as a person I found him utterly loathsome.' This song, as well as Brodsky and Cahn's 'I'll Never Stop Loving You' (written for Doris Day to sing in the Ruth Etting biopic, *Love Me Or Leave Me*) would both be Oscar-nominated, though the Lanza song would lose out to Jay Livingston and Ray Evans's 'Mona Lisa', written for Nat King Cole.

The film (aptly described by Roland L. Bessette as 'a Lanza–Grayson screamfest') opens at the turn of the century with a 'blessing of shops' ceremony in the swamp fishing village of Bayou Minou, on the outskirts of New Orleans, a backwater where time stands still. When opera star Suzette Micheline arrives to sing for them – a four-minute aria which Grayson zips through, again like a record being played at the wrong speed, in just two – no one has seen a motor car before. Cut to Pepe Duvalle (Mario), the brash and bold fisherman we first see winning an anchor-lifting contest, and wearing a skintight sweater which suggests that he gulped down one pizza too many. Pepe is more interested in ogling the pretty singer than he is in getting his uncle's boat to the ceremony – henceforth the old man (J. Carrol Naish) believes that it will be cursed. When Suzette launches into 'Be My Love', she is not bad at all – and when Pepe-Mario joins in, the result is breathtaking.

Suzette may not be pleased about this crude interruption, but her manager and would-be suitor, Jacques Riboudeaux (Niven) is mightily impressed; next thing he is tempting Pepe with the French Opera in New Orleans. The know-it-all young man turns him down upon being told that, despite his fabulous voice, he will have to train hard for several months before being put into a production. By way of contrast to what we have just heard comes the silly, instantly forgettable stuff, such as when Pepe sings 'The Tina-Lina', an upbeat item which would not have been out of place in an Yma Sumac concert. A clumsy dancer, he is joined on the stage by Tina (18-year-old future *West Side Story* actress Rita Moreno, in her second film role), who of course is jealous of the attention he has shown Suzette. Pepe changes his mind about not being an opera star when his uncle's boat sinks during a storm: now they need the money to buy a new one. Therefore he heads for New Orleans, and arrives at the theatre whilst Suzette-Grayson is murdering the classics once more – 'Je suis Titania', from *Mignon*. Jacques gives him money for new clothes and a haircut and instructs Suzette to spend time with him and relieve him of his rough edges.

Pepe is in love, and entertains the street-hawkers outside his house with the raucously stupid 'Boom-Biddy-Boom-Boom', a dire piece which one might expect to find in one of Norman Taurog's later pairings with Elvis Presley, once The King's 'travelogue' movies had run their course. Jacques takes him to see the famous maestro, Tellini, who puts him through his scales – his top notes rattling the chandelier above his head. Tellini tells him what others had told Mario: 'This voice – it's crude, it's untrained, it's unpolished. It's magnificent!' Pepe is taken on as a student, but still not considered ready for the opera platform. Tellini was played by real-life Dutch-born American pianist, composer and conductor Richard Hageman (1881–1966). A child prodigy at six, he had come to America in 1906 with the French chanteuse Yvette Guilbert (Mario would sing but never record her most famous song, 'Le fiacre'), and opted to stay here. In 1914 he had begun an 18-year tenure as principal conductor with the New York Met, and had subsequently worked with some of the biggest orchestras in the country – besides winning an Oscar for his score for *Stagecoach* in 1939. Mario got along with him famously, once he had got over Hageman asking him to crack his notes during this rehearsal scene. When the film was released, some less knowledgeable critics, who went too far linking the note-perfect singer to the trainee singer character, picked up on this, claiming that Lanza could not really hit those high notes, and that in his first film and in his recordings this had been effected by studio trickery. Some years later they would similarly attack Maria Callas for cracking her notes in the final scene of *La Traviata* – until she shot back with, 'Of course I cracked them. I was supposed to be *dying*, for God's sakes!'

Pepe, like Lanza, also proves annoyingly lethargic; additionally he is rude to everyone, and misses vital rehearsals to go off and have fun with his friends, including one occasion when he risks ruining his voice by hammering out a reprisal of 'The Tina-Lina' with a local jazz band. There is also the question of his lack of table manners and inability to act like the perfect gentleman – more actor-character links, along with Pepe's 'lazy' eye. At the city's top eatery he turns up wearing an ill-fitting, bright blue suit, bumps into everything, and sends the food back because it is not to his liking. He only exonerates himself when the band strikes up 'Be My Love' – he drags Suzette on to the stage to reprise the theme song exceedingly well, a whole octave above Brodsky's score. This is a far cry from their later 'Libiamo, libiamo ne' lieti calici', which has him rushing through his lines to keep up with her high-speed wailing.

Jacques decides that his new protégé must learn the essential society graces, and he complies – only drawing the line when his gay assistant, Oscar (Clinton Sunberg), tries putting him through his paces on the dance floor. From now on, Suzette will be his Svengali. This goes well: he takes her boating in his old stomping ground, and serenades her with the lovely 'Bayou Lullaby'. He will sing opera for six months of the year, he tells her, echoing the real Mario, and spend the rest of the time here, fishing. Then he spoils it all by kissing her – and she slaps him. She loves him, of course, but is afraid that any amorous involvement with a man not fully dedicated to his career will never work. On the rebound, she asks Jacques to marry her, though he knows that all she really wants is this former rough diamond who, because of their machinations, has become too much of a gentleman. Pepe's reaction to rejection is to almost throw in the towel, but Jacques persuades him to stay and we cut to the premiere – another slice of the Lanza story – when he makes his opera debut as Pinkerton in *Madama Butterfly*. The film ends with them helterskeltering through a truncated rendition of the beautiful love duet, in a scenario which would have had Puccini spinning in his grave. Mario is his usual majestic self, whereas Grayson is lamentable. This is not grand opera, but a burlesque of the very worst kind which ends with the lovers taking their curtain call (with two acts still to go). Pinkerton kisses her and she flutters her eyelids like some pre-Talkies vamp – and then promptly socks him on the jaw so that he can chase her around the wings and corner her in her dressing room, where this time she finally succumbs to his charms.

Mario had just filmed the dining scene when he was taken to lunch by Jim Henaghan of *Modern Screen* who, having dreaded meeting him in the first place, left the Hungarian restaurant assigned for their interview with the impression that the singer was more than slightly mad. Whereas Henaghan ordered a modest sandwich and side salad, Mario wolfed down two whole chickens and, displaying the most atrocious table manners and speaking with his mouth full, for no reason whatsoever launched a blistering attack on one aspect of the classical world:

> I hate opera singers, those fancy Italian opera singers. Every time I see one on the street I want to go up to him and punch him in the nose. Who the hell do they think they are? They sneer at good Americans because they don't think they love music or can sing. I'm a good one hundred per cent American Philadelphian wop, and I can sing better than any of them!

With this, Henaghan wrote in his piece – aptly titled 'Wonderful Madman' – Mario let out one of those shattering top Cs which had everyone in the restaurant covering their ears. The studio publicist had instructed Mario to keep a leash on his racy tongue – no tall stories. The biggest howler this time was that Sam Weiler had been an 'arts patron' who had first heard him singing at Carnegie Hall! Otherwise, he more or less stuck to the facts and was sometimes too truthful for his own good. When the reporter admired his jacket, he confessed that this had belonged to Van Johnson and that he had stolen it from MGM's wardrobe department. 'Only in America can an opera singer steal such a beautiful coat and tell people about it,' he added. 'In Europe, where every third guy is an opera singer, they claim they bought it or found it or something. They stink!'

Mario – though never homophobic – also inadvertently upset his then closeted gay fans, of which there were many, and also some of the more fervent opera buffs, with the suggestion that opera and homosexuality went hand in glove. 'To the tough kids I palled around with, anything artistic was sissy,' he said of his youth. 'It was as much as a kid's life was worth to express even a mild interest in anything sissy. But I am no sissy. I can still lick any kid on my street – and any of those fancy Italian singers with the high noses. The next one I see, I'll punch right on the nose!' To which Henaghan concluded, 'This man is indeed a lunatic, but a wonderful lunatic. The most exciting personality in years, and without a doubt the greatest voice since, well, anybody.'

The piece in *Modern Screen* brought hundreds of complaints from the people of South Philadelphia, who accused Mario of being unnecessarily nasty when speaking of his home town. In fact, other than making up the story that he had been born in New York and therefore hinting that he was ashamed of his origins, the real attack on the city and its inhabitants had come from Henaghan himself. 'The people of South Philadelphia are pitifully poor, which was the only reason they lived there,' he had written. 'Any education in any direction beyond grammar school was rare, and beyond high school completely unknown. A boy grew up and became a thief, a thug or a labourer according to his instincts. And the respect of his neighbours and contemporaries depended on his hewing strictly to this degenerate tradition.' Because of this, Mario received hundreds of abusive letters, including one – quite possibly from the Philadelphian underworld – which referred to the Lindbergh baby, and threatened to kidnap Colleen. The toddler son of the famous aviator had been abducted in 1932, and subsequently found murdered. Naturally, Mario was terrified and personally hired an armed guard to patrol his house. Back in Philadelphia, thugs attacked Salvatore Lanza's store, smashing the window and scrawling graffiti on the walls.

Nevertheless, it was Mario who was ordered, by Louis B. Mayer personally, to apologise to the magazine's readers for 'his' blunder. He did one better than this. He called the editor of *Modern Screen* and insisted upon 'putting the record straight' by telling his own story as it had really happened, as opposed to the fabricated version fed to the movie magazines by MGM. The first Mayer learned of this was when the publication hit the newsstands in the September. Fortunately, Mario was true to his word and for once told the truth about his upbringing. Regarding South Philadelphia, he could not praise the place enough, and there was no doubting his sincerity:

> Hometown. It has a great sound, doesn't it? You can lose a good friend, get fired from a good job, have your favourite girl chase you off her porch swing for keeps, but you can't lose your home town. It's like a birthmark, or a cowlick, or six toes on each foot if you've got them – your home town stays with you as long as you're alive, and when you're dead they mention it in your obituary. That's why you can't take any chances with alienating it from you. You belong to it, and if it ever abandons you, you're doomed to be a very lonely man for the rest of your life.

Mario brazenly concluded his piece by juxtaposing his own importance with that of his town of origin. Recalling the reception after the premiere of *That Midnight Kiss* when he had turned up late for President Truman, he observed, 'Maybe, as they say, South Philadelphia *is* on the wrong side of the tracks. But the President apologised to a kid from over there, so there can't be too much wrong with it.'

Like its predecessor, *The Toast of New Orleans* did well at the box office: it became MGM's biggest grosser of the year, but it had its critics, notably the *New York Times*'s Bosley Crowther. Having denounced the scenario as 'devoid of novelty or sparkle', Crowther concluded by way of a backhanded compliment, 'But since the music is richly rendered and the scenery is lovely to look upon, *The Toast of New Orleans* comes off better than it has a right to when the story is so hackneyed.'

Mario had been paid $25,000 for making the film, and a $25,000 bonus on its completion. Between these payments, he had received his first royalties cheque – a whopping $510,000. RCA Victor's Red Seal, like many classical labels, paid its artistes a 10 per cent (as opposed to 5 per cent) royalty on record sales, simply because they never sold as many copies as their pop contemporaries. By crossing the classical-pop divide, unheard of in those days, Mario had taken them by suprise. And money, he declared, was for spending and not sticking in some bank to rot. Even so, he invested half his new fortune in the corporation he formed with Sam Weiler, Marsam Enterprises – an amalgamation of their first names – which was run from a rented office in the Allen-Paris Building, in Beverly Hills. On the very day he received his first royalties cheque, he bought his first Cadillac.

Shooting on *The Toast of New Orleans* had been in full swing when the Lanzas moved out of Spalding Drive and into a much larger Spanish-style house at 810 North Whittier Drive, just off Sunset Boulevard. They left the old place in such a mess – Mario had smashed up some of the furniture during one of his rages, and urinated on the bedroom carpets whilst drunk – that the owners threatened him with legal action. He settled out of court, paying them $1,000 in cash. Two days later, the Cocozzas arrived in Hollywood. They had sold the property on Mercy Street, and without even discussing it with Betty, Mario changed his mind about buying them a house of their own and insisted that they move in with them.

Over the next two weeks, Mario missed seven studio calls, citing ill-health. On one occasion he had hurt his back helping the workmen clear the extensive grounds so that a swimming pool and gymnasium could be installed; this would contain a full-sized boxing ring, and the first bout would be between Mario and Rocky Graziano, who would of course lose. Another time, he told Norman Taurog that he had been up all night listening to records. When the director commented that at least he had been learning something, Mario responded that the records had been his own! The rest of the time, he stayed away from the set because he was suffering the after-effects of one of the many housewarming parties. One of his first guests was Jussi Björling, so naturally there was an impromptu concert which went on until dawn. Another was Judy Garland, whom he seduced in his bedroom while Betty was entertaining the other guests downstairs. A trick of his was to ask female guests who had caught his eye, 'Wanna come upstairs and see the family album?' This contained 'stag' photographs which he would collect over the years – Joan Crawford administering a blow-job in one of the porno films she had made before becoming famous, shots of Olivia de Havilland in scanty underwear, and photographs of Carmen Miranda and Jean Harlow minus theirs – which later ended up in Kenneth Anger's *Hollywood Babylon* books. A notable failure was Lana Turner. Mario had met her one afternoon during one of his delayed absences from the set, when he had wandered on to an adjacent lot to share a bottle of Chivas Regal with Ezio Pinza, currently filming *Mr Imperium* with one of the most slept-with women in town. Turner later ungallantly confessed that she had rejected him because she 'did not do wops'.

An unlikely alliance at this time was with Nick Adams, an 18-year-old stage-door Johnny, hustler and budding actor who made a small fortune on the side supplying drugs and prostitutes of both sexes to other actors and studio employees. Mario and Adams struck up a friendship at the Mocambo, where Adams was working as a waiter-doorman, when the star of the show, Pearl Bailey, cancelled her show due to illness. Adams, a capable mimic, had the audience in stitches with an impromptu act which saw him impersonating James Cagney, then playing a scene from Tennessee Williams's *The Glass Menagerie*, acting out all the voices. Afterwards, he persuaded Mario to get up and give a brief recital. What made Adams especially dangerous, though not so to Mario, was his position, long before becoming a household name, among Hollywood's so-called 'open secret' closeted gay community. He knew everything about this community's murky past, and was not averse to broadcasting this to anyone wishing to pay for the privilege. Later he would have affairs with James Dean and Elvis Presley. Almost certainly it was Adams who acted as go-between for the dozens of hookers who had been smuggled into Mario's dressing room at MGM. That he had his eye on Mario also goes without saying: predatory and promiscuous, he rarely showed the slightest interest in any good-looking man unless he expected sex to be on the cards, though with Mario he was barking up the wrong tree. Although he had been advised to stay well clear of him, Mario frequently invited him to his home and they also socialised with each other. Adams would subsequently appear in several successful films, including *Pillow Talk* with Doris Day and Rock Hudson, and the cult sixties television series, *Saints And Sinners*. In February 1968, aged just 36, he was found dead of a drugs overdose.

Whether Nick Adams later introduced Mario to Elvis Presley, as he once boasted, is a matter for conjecture. There is certainly nothing on record to suggest they ever met, though there is much evidence that Lanza, along with Jane Froman, greatly influenced Elvis's later repertoire, and his approach to powerhouse hits such as Joy Byers's tearjerker 'So Close Yet So Far' (where the Lanza influence is at its most potent), Domenico Modugno's 'Ask Me' and the religious songs. In 1972, whilst shooting *Elvis On Tour*, Elvis would tell directors Pierre Adige and Robert Abel, 'I had records by Mario Lanza when I was seventeen, eighteen years old. I would listen to the Metropolitan Opera. I just loved music. Music period.' When Elvis returned home from Germany after serving with the US Army, his first film in civvy street was *G.I. Blues*. It was directed by Norman Taurog, and shooting began in 1960, a few months after Mario's death. Elvis had owned a private copy of *The Student Prince* for some time, besides having the single of 'Serenade' on his juke-box at Graceland, and would insist on paying homage to Lanza in the new film – not by covering Lanza songs, but by insisting that Taurog incorporate two of Mario's favourite pieces into the soundtrack. These were Offenbach's 'Barcarolle' from his *Tales of Hoffmann*, and Strauss's *Tales From The Vienna Woods*, which in English became both 'Tonight Is So Right For Love' and 'Tonight's All Right for Love', although only the former would be used in the film. Four years later, also in honour of Mario, Elvis would record Cottrau's beautiful 'Santa Lucia'.

Maria Cocozza's arrival in Hollywood put a tremendous strain on her daughter-in-law: henceforth, whatever decisions Betty made about the running of her household were overruled. Mario, who much of the time had only taken his wife to social functions because MGM expected this, now started leaving her at home. His new 'companion', who he some-times introduced as his mistress just to get a reaction from those journalists who did not know her, was his mother! Maria was the first to be presented with the obligatory Hollywood mink, diamonds and Cartier watch. As had happened in Philadelphia, this brought a few ribald comments – a problem that Mario sorted out with his fists, as he did back then. When he was not in public with Maria, his 'factotum companion' was Terry Robinson. When Louis B. Mayer threw a party at his mansion to celebrate the completion of *The Toast of New Orleans* and the new contract Mario had signed, offering him a substantial increase in salary, Betty stayed home whilst Robinson was his 'date of sorts'. A decade later, *Confidential* magazine would investigate whether, on account of all the extraneous hugging, their relationship had ever progressed beyond the platonic. It never did, though one gets the impression that this was not without a great deal of wishful thinking on Robinson's part. Listening to him in interviews, there is little doubt that he carried a very big torch for Mario Lanza.

In March 1950, Robinson stayed home to babysit Colleen while the Lanzas travelled on the SS *Lorelei* to Hawaii where, accompanied just by Costa on the piano, Mario gave three concerts at Honolulu's McKinley Auditorium. Whilst there, Mario received the keys to the city and the couple socialised with Tyrone Power and his wife, Linda Christian. Errol Flynn had nicknamed Mario 'Tiger' on account of his aggressive personality, and visitors to his dressing room were met with the handwritten sign on the door, 'Don't Fuck with the Tiger'. It was while they were here that they announced they were expecting their second baby. Mario was over the moon, and told the press that the news coincided with his being offered another contract with La Scala, again for *Andrea Chénier*. This, he said, he had rejected because his wife's health was so delicate that overseas travel would be impossible. Betty was in fact very robust, and there had been no contract. He does however appear to have been approached by the San Francisco Opera to appear in a production of either *Tosca* or *La Traviata* with the Italian soprano Licia Albanese, scheduled for the October. This was cancelled because of his movie work, though there would be some compensation with the duets he subsequently recorded with Albanese, his finest since the ones with Frances Yeend.

On 22 April, Mario appeared in a very mixed bill at Los Angeles's Shine Auditorium, in a gala performance which included such diverse talents (though Mario did not think so) as Harpo Marx, Dean Martin and Jerry Lewis, Donald O'Connor, Robert Mitchum, violinist Isaac Stern, Phil Silvers, Jack Benny and, in one of his last appearances (he died at the end of the year), Al Jolson. Mario had never liked Jolson's over-hamming of the standards, or his claims that he was 'the world's greatest entertainer'. Jolson may have attempted to upstage everyone he came in contact with, but it was Mario who stole the show on this evening – singing his old stalwarts 'O sole mio' and 'Vesti la giubba'.

Mario designated April and May his 'opera months'. He attempted to learn new pieces, recorded some of them, but opted not to perform them on the stage because he was terrified of forgetting the words. RCA had engaged Ray Sinatra for an astonishing seven sessions at Hollywood's Republic Studios, but Mario baulked at this. Sinatra could not be bettered for show songs, he declared, but when it came to conducting the classical stuff, Costa reigned supreme. The arias put down at this time are as good as, if not better than, anything Pavarotti, Domingo and Carreras repeated a generation later. The first song taped during the 8 April session was 'La fleur que tu m'avais jetée', from *Carmen* – always introduced for simplicity as 'The Flower Song' – a version which would not be surpassed until Roberto Alagna came along during the 1990s. Yet, perfect as this was, Mario was dissatisfied and asked for a retake. He followed this with his second reading of 'M'appari tutt' amor', and 'O paradiso', from Meyerbeer's *L'Africana*. These had been pencilled in for the soundtrack of *That Midnight Kiss*, but dropped by Joe Pasternak.

Three days later, Mario recorded two takes of the love duet from *Madama Butterfly* which Kathryn Grayson had mangled in *The Toast of New Orleans*. They had recorded the studio version back in the December, with Johnny Green conducting. He liked Grayson very much as a person, he said, and 'would not have minded tumbling her', but as a singer he did not rate her at all. Unusually, though almost all of his solo work was put down in one take, he insisted on recording these duets twice – he got so carried away, he said, that it was only too easy to drown the soprano, therefore he would leave her to decide which take to have released. Singing with him now was the American soprano Elaine Malbin, who proves equally thrilling in their duet of the drinking song, 'Libiamo, libiamo ne' lieti calici', from *La Traviata*.

The briefest of these sessions took place on 11 May, when Mario and Costa dropped in at the studios to record the Bach–Gounod 'Ave Maria'. This took just fifteen minutes. Mario dedicated 15 May as 'Vesti la giubba' day, when he recorded the aria six times, 'just for the hell of it'. Listening to them today, all six versions are superb. He also re-recorded

'Una furtiva lagrima', along with 'La donna e mobile' and 'Questa o quella' from *Rigoletto*. On 18 May he recorded 'Un di all'azzurro spazio' and 'Come un bel di di maggio' from *Andrea Chénier*; and from *Tosca*, 'E lucevan le stelle' and 'Recondita armonia'. Two 'new' pieces which Mario had rehearsed half-heartedly were recorded on 29 May, with some difficulty. Mario warned the technicians before stepping into the booth that he would mess them up, and he did – several times stumbling over the lyrics. The finished result, however, was well worth the effort. The first aria was 'Parmi veder le lagrime' from *Rigoletto*, which he had not sung before; the second was 'Addio alla madre', from *Cavalleria Rusticana*, which he had test-recorded for Melotone back in 1944. For good measure he threw in 'Cielo e mar', from *La Gioconda*. A novelty religious item was Max Reger's 'The Virgin's Slumber Song', and Mario played an absolute blinder by recording 'O Holy Night', a song which had taken Paris by storm at the turn of the 20th century when, on the stroke of midnight, it had been sung in so many churches there that it had been impossible to walk down any street and not hear it.

Since returning from Hawaii, Betty had not been seen in public with Mario, and staying at home all day with her interfering in-laws quickly took its toll. Rather than show them the door, or make Mario aware of the hell his mother was putting her through – in front of him, Maria was all sweetness and light – Betty became merciless towards the household staff. Long lists of 'household orders' would be typed out and posted behind every door in the house, task sheets which her 'servants' had to tick off once a particular task had been completed, or else face the music. Few employees stayed until the end of the month. Mario's wife was also drinking heavily and popping pills to combat what appears to have been neurasthenic depression and, after each child, postnatal stress, which Mario (in keeping with the times) probably would not have recognised. Betty was reported as taking to her bed for three days at a time. It is not known if she actually threatened to leave Mario and take Colleen with her, or when and how the crunch came: the fact that the Cocozzas moved out of North Whittier Drive and into a rented property – paid for by Mario – on South Crescent Drive, a mere ten minutes' walk away, suggested some sort of ultimatum had been delivered. And to make sure that his mother was sticking to her fitness regime, Terry Robinson moved in with them – or so the press were told, though truthfully Betty had a zero tolerance of anyone coming between her husband and herself. Even so, little had changed: the Cocozzas ate all their meals at North Whittier Drive, Robinson still spent his every waking moment with Mario, and Betty kept on drinking.

Betty also had to contend with the dozens of stalkers and other cranks, whether potentially dangerous or not, which were then as now part of the package of being a major Hollywood star. Because he was so very accommodating with his fans – he was not averse to standing for two hours, in the pouring rain, to sign up to one thousand autographs at a time, rightfully declaring that it was the fans and not the studio bureacrats who made the stars – Mario assumed that all of these people genuinely loved him. Many, it is true, just wanted his signature, or a snapshot with their idol, but others would wait until he had left his home, then sneak into the grounds and rummage through the dustbins, hoping for some titbit about his private life – a discarded letter, maybe – which they would be able to sell on to the press. Others posed as repairmen, or claimed they were there to read the meter, or told Betty that her husband had commissioned some household work or other. She was sensible enough never to let any of these people into the house, and Terry Robinson was asked to organise an infallible security system. Whilst this was being installed, the lights were left on in every room of the house, 24 hours a day.

Mario had told 'his story' to *Modern Screen,* and in November 1950 it was Betty's turn to spill the beans on life with Lanza. She was in fact coerced into writing the piece by Louis B. Mayer, who was becoming more and more concerned that Mario's personal life was spiralling out of control with the food binges, drinking, prescription drugs, hookers and one-night stands. Such was the naivety of the cinema-going public in those days that, if Betty opened up to the fans about her 'blissfully happy marriage', the rumours surrounding her husband's 'lechery' would disappear. 'Being married to Mario Lanza is all any woman could wish for – it's my dream come true!' she announced in *Motion Picture,* before describing a typical day in the Lanza household:

> Every morning, the first thing I hear is Mario asking softly, 'Are you awake?' 'I'm lonesome,' he adds. By the time I'm really awake I'm starting one more fabulous day as his wife. Being married to a

man who is thrilled by all the possibilities in life is all any woman could wish. Until my door opened six years ago and Fate stood Mario there, I saw no signs of this story-book future happening for me. Then miraculously we both fell in love at first sight, and neither or us has experienced one dull moment since.

It was all hype, of course, with the accompanying photograph having been taken not at breakfast time, but in the mid-afternoon, when Betty was recovering from being bombed out the night before. What the photographer was unaware of was that the coffee she was sipping contained three shots of whisky. 'We have no secrets,' she went on, adding how lucky she considered herself. 'I constantly sense I am part of all he is doing or thinking.' None of this was true, and only lightly did she touch upon the subject of her husband's vicious temper – 'He gets so mad, so fast, he expodes!' – and of the way he manipulated her to make her more desirable to him, telling her exactly what she should be wearing, how to do her hair. 'He has definite ideas about women,' she wrote, 'so I pay attention to them. He likes to dress me in a very feminine manner, and wants me to have perfumes and jewels and furs.' Betty concluded that he had not bought her an expensive fur coat yet, and that the only diamonds he had given her were in her wedding ring. What she did not add was that Mario's mother had been given several minks, along with the diamond bracelets and necklaces Betty believed should have been hers. Clearly, she was a deeply disturbed, disillusioned, desperately unhappy woman.

Chapter Six

Caruso Reborn?

Who the hell do they think can play Caruso – Nelson Eddy?
Nobody but me can play that role! I am Caruso!

Mario Lanza

During the summer of 1950 MGM, like all the major studios, was starting to feel the pinch. One report revealed the enterprise to be over $6 million in the red. Theatre attendances too had dropped somewhat over the last six months. The culprit in all of this was the rapidly increasing popularity of television: for a fraction of what it cost to see a play or a movie, families could stay home and watch all their favourite stars. This necessitated making radical changes to how Hollywood's biggest studio was run. Hoping to help solve the dilemma, in 1948 MGM president Nicholas Schenck had brought in Dore Schary (1905–80), with whom Louis B. Mayer had always had a shaky relationship. Born in New Jersey, Schary had worked as a stock actor, then as a scriptwriter for Columbia, joining MGM in 1937 to work on Spencer Tracy's *Boy's Town* and *Edison The Man*. Six years later he had fallen foul of the Messiah's unpredictable temper, and left MGM to produce for RKO and Vanguard.

Politically opinionated, Schary made three immediate enemies on his return to MGM: Clark Gable, Mayer and Mario Lanza. Schary upset Gable by asking the ultra-macho actor to 'don a skirt' and play a Roman centurion in *Quo Vadis*. Gable told him to 'stick the script up his ass', and refused to do the picture. The new broom pushed Mayer's nose out of joint by triumphing with a number of film projects which Mayer had wanted to reject, deeming them uncommercial. Mayer further accused his rival of courting publicity by using these 'message movies' to exploit propaganda, which of course was true. The final solution to the Mayer-Schary problem was not decided until the following year, when Schenck took into consideration Mayer's failing health (he would succumb to leukaemia in 1957) and the fact that Schary was twenty years his junior. Then, Schenck was called upon to exercise the upper hand over which of these warring egotists would go. Each had his own agenda and band of sycophants, and should both have been permitted to stay, Schenck feared the studio would split into two factions and ultimately sink. The deciding factor would be money. Schary's recent films had taken more at the box office than Mayer's, and had attracted more Oscar nominations. According to Mayer's biographer, Scott Eyman, Schenck's task was made that much easier by Mayer having told director Bob Rubin over the telephone, 'You can tell Mr Nicholas Schenck and Dore Schary that they can take the studio and choke on it!' The next day, 31 May 1951, Mayer tendered his resignation and received as a golden handshake a cool $3 million.

Schary got on the wrong side of Mario by denouncing his first two films as 'million-dollar turkeys', and by dismissing him as 'a vulgar little wop' and 'like Gable, one of Mayer's shit-stirrers'. He and Gable would be summoned to Schary's office after Mayer's resignation and told in no uncertain terms that, if the mighty Mayer could be toppled, then absolutely no one in Hollywood was indispensable. In the meantime, opposing Schary – who considered the idea of making a 'full opera movie' preposterous – Mayer went ahead with his plans to make what he predicted would be regarded as *the* opera film of the century. Provisionally entitled *Life Of Caruso*, this would be changed during the production stage to *The Great Caruso*. Some Lanza biographers have got their facts woefully wrong in stating that Mayer left MGM before this went into production, and furthermore that Mario contacted Mayer after he had been 'fired' to offer his sympathy in such a way that Mayer burst into tears. This is nonsense. Mayer retained his vice-presidency of MGM until three months after the film's premiere.

Jesse Lasky (1880–1958), the founder of Famous Players-Lasky, had acquired the rights to Dorothy Caruso's not-so-revealing biography of her husband in 1949, with the hope of bringing his own obsession with the tenor to cinema audiences. In 1918–19, Lasky had produced two of

Caruso's (silent) films, *My Cousin* and *The Splendid Romance*, paying him a whopping $100,000 for each one, a salary only comparable to the one Mayer would pay Greta Garbo two decades later. The first film had been withdrawn from circulation after just three months, the second released only in Britain. An astute businesswoman, Mrs Caruso had demanded the same $100,000 fee for the rights, and added a clause to the contract that Lasky, one of the few people in Hollywood she trusted, should act as executive producer.

The tagline read, 'The Intimate Story of a Man with a Voice as Great as his Heart'. However, by the time scriptwriters Sonya Levien and William Ludwig had finished hacking away to remove just about every vestige of Caruso's private life, aside from the stupendous singing the storyline was on the verge of boring. As would happen with the later *Gone With The Wind*, commissioned from author Margaret Mitchell solely with Gable in mind for playing Rhett Butler, only one man was ever really envisaged to portray Caruso on the screen. The press ran endless anecdotes linking the two, some of them silly. Mario had been baptised by a priest named Caruso; Caruso's personal assistant at the time of his death had been called Mario; one great tenor had died the same year the other had been born and inherited his spirit; Caruso and Lanza had both been coached by Giacomo Spadoni, and so on.

Mario began recording the soundtrack for *The Great Caruso* before signing the contract. He was given carte blanche regarding the musical content, his operatic co-stars and conductor. Mayer hoped that he might select Johnny Green, or Costa if it came to the crunch. Mario wanted neither for such an important project and demanded Peter Herman Adler, which had everyone rushing for cover. Adler was virulently outspoken and hypercritical; having him working with Lanza was tantamount to waving a red rag in front of a bull. Mario promised to behave himself, no doubt with his fingers crossed behind his back, and as a gesture of goodwill insisted upon the fabled conductor staying with his parents for the duration of the recording and shooting schedule. Adler would push him to the limit and apparently enjoy doing so, just to see how far he could go before making him crack. Playing him at his own game, Mario took it on the chin – waiting until the film was in the can before letting rip. His opportunity came when a journalist asked Adler if, in his opinion, Mario really was as good as Caruso. Adler's response, 'Ask me that in ten years' time,' along with his yelling at him day in, day out in front of the cast, brought forth a string of invectives from Mario and the subsequent ending of their friendship. Mario's arrogance at this time almost cost him his friendship with George London, who had arrived in Hollywood for a series of recitals. When Mario called him at his hotel and invited him to his home for dinner, the baritone politely declined – he was actually performing that evening. Costa recalled Mario's outburst over the telephone when he snarled at London, 'I'm a greater star than you are. *You* can't brush *me* off!' Mario would forget what he had said, and London would not only forgive him, he would set him on a pedestal for the rest of his life.

The recording sessions – 14 for the actual soundtrack, along with several more for retakes – took place between 17 July and 18 December at the MGM Studios. All but two were with Adler, and these final two sessions were conducted by Johnny Green when Adler was assigned to another commission. At this stage, no one knew which pieces would be used for the picture, or how many, so Mario recorded almost indiscriminately just about every classical item that had been in his repertoire these past ten years, along with a clutch of popular songs Caruso had also performed. The latter were arranged by Irving Aaronson, who accompanied Mario at the piano. Two popular songs revived and re-adapted for the film would sell over a million copies. 'Quand tu viens à moi comme dans un rêve' (When you come to me as in a dream) had been written in 1902 by Guy d'Hardelot – actually Helene Rhodes (1858–1936), a Frenchwoman whose work had subsequently been recorded by Edith Piaf, Damia, Suzy Solidor and Gracie Fields. Caruso had recorded it in French in 1913. With English lyrics by Edward Teschemaker, it had been recorded by Nelson Eddy, amongst others, as 'Because', but more or less assigned to oblivion until now. Even older was 'Sobre las olas' (Over the waves), a waltz composed by the tragically shortlived Mexican bandleader-violinist Juventino Rosas (1868–94) when he had been just 19 years old. The English words, 'The Loveliest Night of the Year', were by Paul Francis Webster, who had written 'Black Coffee' for Peggy Lee. Two years later, Doris Day would perform his 'Deadwood Stage' and 'Secret Love' in *Calamity Jane*. Jesse Lasky and Louis B. Mayer fought against the director's decision to have Ann Blyth, the only non-operatic performer in the production, actually sing it herself – they wanted her to lip-synch to one of the sopranos. Mario was having none of this. Blyth, sounding like a young Jane Froman, does the piece beautifully.

For their first session, Adler erred on the side of caution by arranging for Mario to record 'Vesti la giubba', the aria which most linked him to Caruso and the one which had kick-started both their careers – an aria he knew so well, he once boasted, that he could sing it backwards and still remain pitch-perfect. For the opera sequences, Adler brought in the very cream of the Met's roster, again without being entirely certain that they would appear in the film. The baritone Guiseppe Valdengo and soprano Teresa Celli joined Mario for the torture scene from *Tosca*, whilst soprano Dorothy Kirsten (who had been assigned to the cast) and mezzo-soprano Blanche Thebom accompanied him on 'O terra addio', from *Aida*. The soprano Lucine Amara joined him for the 'Miserere' from *Il Trovatore*, whilst Thebom, Valdengo and soprano Olive May Beach sang with him the quartet from *Rigoletto*. For the finale from *Martha*, arguably the most dramatic scene Mario ever played, Adler used Kirsten and Maria Callas's favourite bass, Nicola Moscona. These two, along with Thebom, Valdengo and tenor Gilbert Russell, sang the sextet from *Lucia di Lammermoor*. Jarmila Novotná, of whom more later, partnered Mario in 'E il sol dell'anima' from *Rigoletto* – an aria which did not appear in the finished film. This completed the Adler sessions. On 17 and 18 October, under the baton of Johnny Green, he reluctantly recorded 'No, Turrido, rimani' from *Cavalleria Rusticana* with the soprano Marina Koshetz, and the temple scene from *Aida* with Nicola Moscona and the tenor Bob Ebright.

There are many who share Mario's opinion that Caruso remains the greatest tenor of all time. This is not entirely true. His place in history was initially assured him because he was a pioneer, the first tenor to be recorded. Indeed, such were the primitive techniques of the day that it is frequently impossible to determine which faults are in his voice – as with Lanza, he was far from flawless – and which are the glitches in the recording itself. Caruso has always been vastly overrated by senti-mentalists, and today would be regarded as one exceptional tenor amongst many. Indeed, at their best, Pavarotti, Alagna, Domingo, Wunderlich, Carreras, Björling, Corelli and of course Gigli were all considerably better than he was. Mario was so obsessed with him that it sometimes affected his judgement; for a time he genuinely believed that he was Caruso reborn. He began speaking like Caruso, dressing eccentrically and acting like him, even walking like him with a cane. For 'his' film, he decreed, he wanted no Hollywood actors playing the major parts – just singers from the New York Met, because this was where he would be headed, once this one was in the can.

Mario was given less than three months to shed the 45 pounds he had piled back on since his last film. Joe Pasternak arranged for him to train for six weeks at Ginger Rogers's vacant ranch in Medford, Oregon. Terry Robinson drove him there – he still refused to get on a plane – and they were later joined by Betty, Colleen and MGM public relations officer Jack Keller, sent along to keep an eye on him. Mario later said that these had been the toughest weeks of his life: Robinson had fixed him up with a fitness regime – jogging, throwing weights, push-ups and more jogging – which began at 5am and with few breaks went on until 8pm. The press were given details of his daily diet: three tomatoes, three hard-boiled eggs, the occasional very rare steak, lots of fruit juice and absolutely no alcohol. For a man with Mario's appetite, this would have been tanta-mount to starvation and of course no one believed it.

Another side of Mario emerged during his sojourn in Medford, when he was reunited with an old army friend, Dale Goodman, who appears to have been in *Winged Victory*. In March 1945, Goodman had suffered horrendous injuries during the battle of Iwo Jima, which had resulted in his having a lung removed. When he confided in Mario that his dream was to own a chicken ranch, Mario told him to go ahead – so long as he could have shares in it and therefore get free eggs for those famous 16-egg omelettes! Mario never visited the property in Rogue River, Southern Oregon, but kept in touch with Goodman and his wife. In October 1951, he learnt that the couple's baby was dangerously ill with a brain haemorrhage and paid for a specialist to fly out from Chicago. Thanks to Mario's generosity, the child survived, although Mario's friendship with Goodman would not.

By the time *The Great Caruso* went into production Mario was as slim as he would ever be, but staying below 200 pounds would always be for him a herculean effort. All the same, Terry Robinson's 'killer' routine would have its amusing moments if Mario was ribbed about his size, such as in the incident reported by *Time* magazine:

Once, in a moment of high spirits, he dispelled all the misery in the immediate vicinity by bursting out of his studio dressing room, clad only in an athletic supporter, and raced hilariously around the set, while girls fled in all directions. Though Mario's literary preferences lean to body-building and movie-fan magazines, his uninhibited zest for startling pranks sometimes seems inspired by the gutsier tales of Chaucer.

Costa recalled, 'Even now, as he was realising a lifelong ambition, Mario seethed with resentment and hostility and the compulsion to drink, to overeat, and to defy authority... There were times when he showed up for work under the influence of alcohol. And there were times when he drank right on the set.' The drink, Mario would sneak in under his clothes. As for eating, he would call the commissary and pretend to be one of the actors who shared the dressing-room block – Robert Taylor, Clark Gable, even Ava Gardner – and wait for food to be delivered, relieving the busboy of his order and scoffing the lot on the stairs. 'When he got through, there'd be a graveyard of bones,' Joe Pasternak observed. Needless to say, by the end of shooting he had regained the 45 pounds he had lost, and as the film was not shot in sequence, this fluctuation in weight was seen on the screen.

Mario returned to Hollywood on 16 July to be given a pep talk by Dore Schary. The shooting schedule would be tight – eight weeks, from 30 July until 24 September, though this would be amended when Mario sprained his ankle. He was instructed to behave himself at all times, and warned that he would be fired if he showed the same tardiness as he had during his last picture and would be replaced by an actor who would lip-synch to Caruso's voice – a ridiculous notion, for Caruso's recordings were way too dated for this. Mario's response to Schary over this was, 'Go fuck yourself, buddy. I work for Mr Mayer, not you!'

Mario's leading lady, playing his on-screen wife, was 22-year-old Ann Blyth, then as now best known for her role as Joan Crawford's spiteful, scheming daughter in *Mildred Pierce*. Hiring her brought Jesse Lasky the threat of legal action from Dorothy Caruso, who wanted to be portrayed on screen by her favourite actress, Joan Fontaine. Lasky told her to go ahead and waste her money: having assigned the rights to him, she had no say in the production. Blyth had a reputation for being strait-laced and, according to Terry Robinson, the cast and crew – and Mario especially, who could outcurse anyone – were instructed not to swear in front of her. Mario was also ordered to keep his trousers buttoned, and to use the proper facilities and not the set if he needed to go to the toilet. 'Excuse us, especially me, if I yell once in a while,' he is quoted as telling her upon their first meeting. 'We have a big picture to make about a man who was known to yell and swear. He had balls.' Blyth saw the funny side, and the two became friends.

Of the opera stars used in the film, the best known was probably Czech-born Jarmila Novotná (1907–94), a major star since 1925 when she had made her debut, aged just 18, in Smetana's *The Bartered Bride*. Her debut with the Met had been as Mimi in *La Bohème*. Her most famous role, however, had been a non-singing one as the Auschwitz prisoner looking for her son in *The Search* (1948) opposite Montgomery Clift. The director was Richard Thorpe (1896–1991), the ex-vaudeville star revered by Louis B. Mayer for almost always completing his films on time and under budget – though not particularly liked by some actors for the pressure he put them under to achieve this. Thorpe never made any blockbusters, though he did triumph with two of the Johnny Weissmuller *Tarzan* films, and today he is probably best remembered for Elvis Presley's *Jailhouse Rock*. Thorpe later said that *The Great Caruso* was one of his most demanding projects, not just because of Mario's inordinate demands, but because of the hold-ups when no shooting could take place – 21 days in all, though 14 of these were on account of Mario's injured ankle. Even so, he and Mario got along well, with very few tantrums, and although the film was completed four weeks behind schedule, it did not exceed its budget.

The film opens with Caruso's birth in 1873 – with the voiceover stressing that this took place in Naples, *Italy*, in case American audiences did not know where Naples was – and with the usual Hollywood stereotyping, all the Italian characters speak to each other in English, with heavy accents. Similarly, there is a playbill announcing each opera. It zips through his childhood: the death of his mother when he was 10 (he was actually 15) whilst he is singing in a street parade, the young Caruso with his childhood sweetheart, Musetta (Yvette Duguay), and his busking for coppers in pavement cafés – Mario bursting on to the screen with 'Marechiare'. Truthfully, the real Caruso never sounded half as good. In order to win Musetta's hand in marriage, he agrees to give up 'begging' and takes a job with her father's flour company, only to be fired when he leaves the flour barrels out in the rain to be ruined. 'You were born a beggar, and you'll die a beggar,' the old man tells him. Of course, when we hear him singing 'La danza' for his drinking pals, we know otherwise.

Next, Caruso is mixing with the elite of the opera world, and singing in the chorus of *Aida*. His success from this point is rapid, again light years away from what really happened: bit-parts in *Tosca* and *Cavalleria Rusticana*, then the lead tenor role in *La Gioconda* before he wows Covent Garden with his *Rigoletto* and becomes embroiled in an onstage altercation with snooty soprano Maria Selka (Novotná), who denounces him as an Italian upstart. In the original scene, having been told this was how Novotná perceived *him*, Mario acted off the cuff; grabbing her by the wrist, he hauled her to his chest as if to kiss her, then flung her aside like a rag, causing her to hit the deck. According to Mario, Novotná approached him the next day in the street and, rather than slapping his face as he anticipated, congratulated him for devising such an unexpected, emotional scene! Richard Thorpe did not agree, and ordered the scene to be reshot, whilst the original footage ended up on the cutting-room floor. Unfazed, Mario delivers a boisterous 'La donna e mobile', proves a massive hit and heads for New York with his newly appointed manager – former tenor Alfredo Brazzi (Ludwig Donath), now reduced to working as a doorman. At the Met he is befriended by soprano Louise Heggar (Dorothy Kirsten), and sings a stunning 'Celeste Aida', which is performed, like most of the solo arias here, in its entirety. It is also interesting to note that it was at this stage in his career, through emulating Caruso after studying old film footage, that Lanza brought in those extraneous hand movements. But if Louise recognises the tenor's greatness, her friend and mentor, millionaire lawyer-physician Park Benjamin (Carl Benton Reid) thinks him common and hates him on sight.

Hollywood's depiction of Caruso's lovelife is pure bunkum. Having mistaken Benjamin for Louise's father, he goes to his home to apologise and meets his pretty daughter, Dorothy – Ann Blyth making her entrance 40 minutes into the film. In a near-repeat of the scene in *That Midnight Kiss* she falls for him after he serenades her at the piano with 'Torna a Surriento', and naturally Papa disapproves. And because

Benjamin dislikes him and spreads the word, the public treat him with disdain, rewarding him with a glacial silence after arguably the most stunning 'Che gelida manina' ever recorded – until Dorothy starts the applause, whence he receives a standing ovation. It is she who advises him to sing to the 'diamond horseshoe' – the section of the stalls containing the critics and the elite. He ignores this, declaring that as a common man he belongs only to the galleries – though each time we see him taking a bow the camera homes in on the bejewelled, tuxedoed social set, compounding Hollywood's stereotyped theory that opera was only for the rich.

Caruso asks Dorothy to marry him, a union which her father forbids. Louise also believes that marrying this egotistical man will be a big mistake: 'You marry a voice and you'll be waiting around with the rest to see that voice. Don't give up your life for someone else's voice.' The couple elope, but not before Caruso has stood her up to reflect whilst singing 'Ave Maria' in the local cathedral – an inspiring scene where he 'duets' with a boy soprano. This was in fact a child actor lip-synching to the voice of soprano Jacqueline Allen. They are congratulated by heads of state from around the world, but still ostracised by Park Benjamin. During their honeymoon, Dorothy throws a surprise birthday party, sings 'The Loveliest Night of the Year', and announces that she is pregnant. Their daughter, Gloria, arrives while Caruso is on stage performing in the sextet from *Lucia di Lammermoor*. Sadly though, from now on it will be all downhill as he develops lung disease and his health fades. Even so he adopts Canio's creed of 'On with the Motley', refusing to rest or see a doctor, disguising his condition with an ether spray whilst the voice remains flawless as ever. For the last time, before a performance – Flotow's *Martha* – he prays to his mother, tells Dorothy how much loving her has enriched his life, and expires beautifully as the curtain swings to during 'The Last Rose of Summer'. The film ends with his friends laying a wreath at his memorial in Naples.

As a showcase for Lanza's talents, *The Great Caruso* is a masterpiece. As a historical document chronicling the life of the tenor, however, it is worthless and should therefore only be regarded as an exceptionally fine musical drama in the tradition of Mario's first two films. Dorothy Caruso, though forewarned of Hollywood's tendency to reinvent history, never stopped complaining throughout shooting, and at one stage became so troublesome that Jesse Lasky threatened to bar her from the studio. She grudgingly managed to shake hands with Ann Blyth, but loathed Mario without even meeting him. He was, she said, far too young, at 30, to be playing her husband and indeed should never have been offered the part in the first place because, whilst the real Caruso had graced every major opera house in the world, Lanza had only sung opera once, and then not in what she considered to be a major production. She also objected to the Lanza Caruso dropping dead on the stage, in full voice. In December 1920, Caruso had suffered a haemorrhage during a performance of Donizetti's *L'Elisir D'Amore*, since which time he had suffered failing health not helped by two daily packs of full-strength Egyptian cigarettes. Cause of death had been pleurisy and peritonitis brought about by a burst abscess.

However, if the tenor's widow complained about MGM's distortion of the facts surrounding her husband's health and career, there was one aspect of his personal life which she would truly have objected to, had Lasky's scriptwriters stuck to the facts: Caruso's foul temper, docker's language, and inordinately high sex-drive, which had caused her considerable embarrassment. Nothing was mentioned in the film about the so-called Monkey House incident, where at the Bronx Zoo he had been arrested and charged with indecency. Caruso had always had a problem with pinching women's bottoms, though in this instance it had subsequently been revealed that this particular incident had been stage-managed by a rival to discredit him. Also omitted from the storyline was the other major character in Caruso's life – the soprano Ada Giachetti, with whom he had performed *La Traviata* in 1897. She was a married woman with a child who became his common-law wife, suffering two miscarriages and bearing him two sons. Having achieved some recognition, though nowhere near as renowned at this stage as she was, Caruso had forced her to abandon her career to look after him. Ada had rewarded him by running off with his chauffeur and confidant, Cesare Romati – after which Caruso moved in with her sister, Rina, who he had been sleeping with for some time!

Caruso's sons, Rodolfo and Enrico Jr, also had their say, though they had nothing but praise for Mario, as will be seen. Their hackles had first risen a few months earlier with the release in Italy of *Enrico Caruso: leggenda di una voce*. Directed by Giacomo Gentilomo, this is a woeful telling of the Caruso story, even less accurate than the MGM version. It starred the appropriately named Ermanno Randi as the lusty tenor (the singing voice was provided by Mario del Monaco) and a 23-year-old sex-bomb named Gina Lollobrigida as his love-interest, Stella. She was no stranger to opera movies: after uncredited parts in *Lucia di Lammermoor* and *L'Elisir D'Amore* she had played twice opposite Tito Gobbi, performing Canio's wife in *Pagliacci*, and his lover in *Follie per l'opera*, both in 1948. Initially a flop in Italy, the film was released in Britain and America during the summer of 1951 as *The Young Caruso*, badly dubbed and with more shouting than singing – not to compete with the MGM film, but to launch La Lollo, as she became known to the English-speaking public. The Caruso brothers' beef with the Italian film was that it only lampooned their father. They successfully sued Tirenna Films, in Rome, and had the film withdrawn from circulation, though Tirenna fought back and had the ban lifted – resulting in it becoming much more successful the second time around. The reason for their lawsuit against MGM was quite different: they accused the studio of insensitivity for not including them in the film. In Europe, where morals were more relaxed in those days, this would have presented no problem. In America, however, this meant the brothers revealing that they were illegitimate as a result of their father having lived in sin with his mistress. Though this had nothing whatsoever to do with Mario, with the National League of Decency still prominent in the movie world, a knock-on effect would have been inevitable. The NLD never had enough power to actually ban films, but their sway over the distributors could have persuaded some cinemas not to show it. Stupid as this may seem today, with Lanza boasting to all and sundry that he *was* Caruso, the blinkered moral majority would have assumed that he had inherited some of Caruso's more unsavoury characteristics and would have insisted on him being penalised for this. The matter was therefore kept out of the newspapers as much as possible: MGM reached a compromise by paying the Caruso brothers undisclosed 'damages', and agreed to remove *The Great Caruso* from circulation in Italy.

The Great Caruso album was rush-released when shooting wrapped, and within a month had sold 250,000 copies to fans who genuinely believed that they were listening to the actual soundtrack. In fact, all the arias were retakes sung by Mario, and most of these were not even in the film. Even so, as a tribute to Caruso and a showcase for Lanza's superior talents, it is the ultimate concept, and by the end of 1951 it had shifted three million copies worldwide, the first operatic album to have surpassed the million mark. The film also revived interest in Caruso, as more and more of his recordings were released.

The film premiered at the Egyptian Theatre, on Hollywood Boulevard, on 16 April 1951. MGM had gaslights installed outside the theatre and the foyer decked out to represent 1905, the year Caruso had arrived in America. This time, Betty shared Mario's limousine, sandwiched between him and Jesse Lasky. The Cocozzas, Terry Robinson and the pianist Artur Rubinstein were there; the guest of honour was Deborah Kerr. In the foyer, Mario walked straight past Dore Schary, refusing to acknowledge him. Schary had opposed the film from the start, and was sufficiently hypocritical to have sent a hamper of fruit, flowers and champagne to Mario's home, the morning after the first press preview. Mario had sent them back. MGM's biggest money-earner of the year, the film went out on general release in May, and was a smash hit around the world. At New York's Radio City Music Hall, America's biggest cinema, it played to a full house several times each day for 10 weeks, grossing over $1.5 million in this theatre alone. It received an Oscar for Best Sound Recording – awarded to Douglas Shearer, the brother of actress Norma whose producer husband, Irving Thalberg, had done more than anyone to put the studio on the map. Peter Herman Adler and Johnny Green were joint-nominated for Best Score, whilst Gile Steele and Helen Rose were nominated for Best Design and Best Costume – all three categories were won by MGM's other big hit that year, *An American In Paris*.

The critics, whilst almost universally applauding Mario, not surprisingly came down on the hackneyed storyline. The *New York Times*'s Bosley Crowther called it, 'The most elaborate "pops" concert ever played on the screen.' Crowther denounced Richard Thorpe's 'mawkish, bathetic style', and the scriptwriters' 'silliest, sappiest clichés'. Of 'The Loveliest Night of the Year' he wrote, 'Miss Blyth's bland rendition typically indicates the bed-rock romantic level on which the story of this picture transpires.' *Variety* said of Lanza, the thespian, 'His acting conveys something of the simple peasant Caruso essentially was... Lanza's talent is obviously of high artistic calibre and quite stirring.' Louella Parsons proclaimed in her syndicated column, 'Be proud that motion pictures have made this possible with as great an artiste as Mario Lanza!'

Pre-promoting the film and the album during the run-up to the premiere, Columbia Concerts dispatched Mario on a 22-date tour of America. This time the venues were more select, and he would be compelled to wear the tenor's more traditional tuxedo and bow tie: New York, Richmond, Pittsburgh, Columbus, Miami Beach, Daytona, Orlando, Tampa, New Orleans, Chicago, St Louis, Milwaukee, Wichita, Cincinnati, Kansas City, Ogden, Omaha, and Fresno – 'Places I've actually heard of,' he joked, and every one a sell-out. He also proved more reliable than during the last tour, cancelling just one engagement due to genuine illness.

Orchestras around the country clamoured to accompany him, but Mario was not interested: with just one exception, he was accompanied at the piano by Costa. Success came at a price, however. Sam Weiler, in a deal which would see him pocketing 20 per cent of Mario's income, had recently negotiated a management deal with the Music Corporation of America – Lanza had become too big for him to handle alone – and the head of MCA, Lew Wasserman, declared that he would have to slim down considerably by the time the tour kicked off at Scranton, Pennsylvania, on 16 February. Moreover, he would have to lose a minimum of twenty pounds while on the tour circuit. The company rented a house near Palm Springs, complete with gymnasium and sauna; it was essential to get Mario away from Hollywood, they declared, where his favourite restaurants were a temptation. Initially, he refused to comply, claiming that he needed the excess weight to push his voice. He soon changed his mind, though, when Columbia Concerts informed him that the tour would be cancelled unless he cooperated, and that he would lose out to the tune of $5,000 a day, the average fee they had negotiated for each concert – a formidable amount in those days. 'He was inspired now,' Costa recalled. 'It was remarkable to see a man who had descended almost to the level of an animal suddenly reverse his course and act with maturity, responsibility, and self-abnegation.' Such extraneous exercise, forced upon a man already in poor shape, could have killed him. All that mattered from his peers' point of view was that audiences would be seeing Lanza as they would be seeing him on the screen. Since completing *The Great Caruso*, his weight had ballooned to 240 pounds, and once more he embarked on a gruelling fitness programme devised by Terry Robinson, who appears to have derived some sort of sardonic pleasure out of watching Mario toil and sweat: dragging him out of bed at 4am, Robinson had him jogging around the park wearing a heavy rubber sweatsuit, then it would be an hour in the gym throwing weights, followed by another five-mile jog, an hour sweating it out in a steam-room, a rub down – and then a two-hour rehearsal with Costa.

Yet behind the radiant smile and general air of bonhomie there lurked the archetypal melancholy of the clown Mario had so often emulated, in or out of costume, whilst performing 'Vesti la giubba'. According to Costa, the fans and even some of his friends never saw the real Mario Lanza:

> When a man earns over $100,000 for less than three months of singing, when he stays at the country's most luxurious hotels, when he eats the finest steaks daily, when the public applauds his every gesture and reacts to each of his groans and grimaces, there is hardly any reason to suspect he is suffering any excruciating agony. Yet, not withstanding the success and acclaim that inundated him, Mario was never truly happy... Sitting in his hotel room – which he practically never left, except to keep his concert dates – he had too much time to brood, to think about himself, to let the nagging doubts consume him, to rage at the torments of the heretical critics, to invent enemies and doubt his friends. During the Caruso tour, he considered himself the highest paid prisoner in the world.

There were a few surprising additions to Mario's repertoire, bearing in mind his fear of fluffing lyrics. 'Be My Love', 'Because' and 'The Loveliest Night of the Year' received standing ovations even if he made mistakes; no one seemed to notice. The problems came with the 'novelty' items: Ernest Charles's lovely 'The House on the Hill', and 'Bonjour mon coeur, bonjour ma mie', a 16th-century French madrigal by Pierre de Ronsard, set to music by Orlando Lassus. Mario sang this just twice, concluded that it was not taking with audiences, and never recorded it.

Each evening, after belting out one of the songs from the film, Mario would disappear into the wings and return with a copy of *The Great*

Caruso album, hold it aloft and announce that if copies were not available in the foyer after the show, then fans would be able to buy them at their local store. Such blatant publicising of an artiste's own work was unheard of in those days, and frowned upon by so-called 'opera traditionalists'. Another thing the stuffier members of the press could not get their heads around was his habit of applauding himself during a standing ovation, then clasping his hands above his head like a victorious boxing champion.

On 6 March, at Pittsburgh's Syria Mosque, Costa sat in the wings and enjoyed the show whilst Mario was accompanied by the city's symphony orchestra, under the baton of Vladimir Bakaleinikoff, a tetchy individual who insisted on an extra afternoon rehearsal. Mario complied, but with one condition: the paying public would be allowed inside the concert hall. Bakaleinikoff consented, hardly knowing what he was letting himself in for. The screaming and applause after each item in the programme seemed to go on for ever, but each time Mario left the stage so that the orchestra could rehearse the piece without him, all hell broke loose, with fans chanting Mario's name and booing the orchestra. When the conductor yelled for them to shut up and show him some respect, some threw coins and even shoes at him until he was forced to abandon the rehearsal and allow Mario to complete his recital, flaws and all. The venue seated around 3,300 people in those days, but all safety regulations were flaunted for the evening performance when, as a result of Mario insisting that everyone should be allowed in whether they had tickets or not, 4,700 fans crammed into the auditorium. To his consternation, chairs had to be placed on the stage – so close to him that their occupants ducked each time he swung his arms. 'Mario Lanza and the Pittsburgh Symphony Orchestra rocked the Syria Mosque last night and the building blew a fuse,' observed the *Pittsburgh Press*. 'About the only place you didn't see a face was in the huge chandelier above the auditorium.'

In Columbus, Ohio, on 9 March, Mario announced before singing 'Because' that it was Terry Robinson's 35th birthday, and that this evening the song would be dedicated to him. What was then seen as no more than an expression of friendship would today be viewed more cynically, particularly the sob in the voice which accompanied the line, 'Because you speak to me in accent sweet'. Compounding this, on 13 April, the last day of the tour, Mario presented Robinson with a 'little something' in appreciation of all that he had done for him: the keys to a brand new Chevrolet convertible. At least one wag read more into their relationship than there really was, dubbing the tour 'The Robinson–Caruso Extravaganza' when the 'birthday' dedication turned into a regular feature. Mario's parents also received keys – for an ocean-view home on Toyopa Drive, in Pacific Palisades. This was also his sixth wedding anniversary, but all that he gave Betty was a bunch of flowers.

In the meantime it was a case of counting one's chickens before they hatched, regarding Mario's 13 March recital at Philadelphia's Academy of Music. Much was made in the press of the local boy coming home after having made his fortune, his first return visit since the premiere of *That Midnight Kiss*. The sojourn started off well enough. Salvatore Cocozza had received a letter from one of Mario's biggest fans, an 80-year-old lady now residing in a nursing home in the northern section of the city. The concert had been sold out for weeks, and she had been unable to acquire a ticket. When Mario called the home and learned that she might not have long to live, he drove to see her personally, gave a 20-minute impromptu concert for the other residents, and personally escorted the old lady to the theatre.

The same dignitaries were here to welcome him: Sergei Koussevitzky sent him a telegram wishing him every success in the venue where he had supposedly shifted that grand piano just a few short years before. Mario's reception here was wilder than anywhere else on the circuit, but the broad smile soon faded when he reached his dressing room after the performance. Mingling with the fans and press was a lawyer dispatched here on behalf of one 'Mrs Arthur Jackson', and marching up to Mario, he shoved an envelope into his jacket top pocket. The lady in question was Irene Williams, Mario's first agent; he had completely forgotten about her. The envelope contained a writ for unpaid commission. The contract he had signed with her back in 1942 still held good: Williams was legally entitled to 5 per cent of his earnings if these exceeded $5,000 a year, 10 per cent if they exceeded $10,000. Mario was surprisingly gracious towards her lawyer, never challenged Willams's demands, and the matter was settled a few months later when the Los Angeles Superior Court ordered him to pay her $10,000. Four years later he would send a 'Good luck, don't worry!' telegram to Maria Callas, after she had been served with an identical writ after a performance of *Madama Butterfly* in

Chicago, a city which he said had also caused him grief. The lawyer here thrust the writ into her cleavage, and considering her ferocious temperament, he was lucky to get out of the theatre in one piece. Callas's 'error of judgement' would set her back a whopping $300,000, so in a way Mario was lucky to have got off so lightly. Since leaving Irene Williams he had earned an estimated $800,000 in record royalties alone. No one was sure exactly how much he had netted from his films so far, but a similar amount was suggested, and *Variety* reported that he was earning an estimated $25,000 a week on the tour circuit.

In Miami, a few evenings later, the air-conditioning failed just before the start of the performance, and Mario sweated through his first three arias before yanking off his bow tie and tossing it into the audience for the fans to squabble over. 'Singing's supposed to be fun,' he cracked. 'Why do they insist on us wearing these things?' The jacket came off next, and after receiving a standing ovation for 'Celeste Aida' he unbuttoned his shirt halfway down and announced, 'Guys, take off your ties and relax! You too, ladies – loosen your stays!' This earned him an almighty cheer which all but raised the roof, though the stuffier members of the critics' circle were horrified. 'This is not the sort of behaviour one expects from such an artiste,' one complained. Lucky then that these journalists were unaware of Mario's latest 'party trick' – standing on his hotel balcony in the dark, and urinating over the balcony to drench whichever unfortunate person happened to be strolling on the pavement below. *Ladies Home Journal* wanted to write a profile of Mario, and assigned one of their stuffier female reporters to trailing him around for three days, an exercise which was abandoned on the second day, on account of Mario's 'chicanery'. Terry Robinson recalled one particular interview over lunch, and the ensuing conversation which took place over dessert:

Mario:	Now, dear, you've asked *me* questions for two days. May I please ask one of you?
Interviewer:	Of course. Anything you wish...
Mario:	Do you give good head?
Interviewer:	If we don't hurry, I'll miss my plane!

Robinson's story might not have been believed – could Mario have really said such a thing to a *woman*, some fans would later ask? – but it was typical of his fun-loving behaviour at the time. My godfather, the revue artiste Roger Normand, spent several evenings on the town with 'Mario and the gang' during the early fifties, and was witness to some of these pranks:

> One particular waitress had a face like the back of a bus, and someone suggested that maybe if he sang to her, it might make her smile. She came back with the next course, and he lifted one leg and let out a loud, rasping fart. 'How was that for a perfect top C?' he asked.
>
> On another occasion he let one go and held his cigarette lighter down there – there was a flash of lightning and the whole restaurant gave him a standing ovation. I remember somebody once saying that Montgomery Clift radiated class, even when urinating in the gutter. Mario was just the same. He could be as lewd as he liked, and no one was ever offended because he did everything with a big wide grin, and with such impeccable humour.

Some critics denounced Mario's 'good deeds', such as spiriting his elderly fan in Philadelphia to the theatre, as cheap publicity stunts. Mario had insisted that these should not be made public, but someone had leaked them to the press. Before a show, he and Terry Robinson would drive past the front of the venue and if they saw any fans in wheelchairs or on crutches, he would insist that these people were given seats in front of the stalls. 'With all his faults,' Costa recalled, 'with all his hostilities and imperfections, Mario still managed to be one of the warmest, most sympathetic humans I have ever seen. I once saw him cry when he passed a blind man in the street.' The mother of Raphaella Fasano, a 10-year-old girl from Newark, New Jersey, called Mario's hotel one afternoon but it was Robinson who picked up the receiver. Her daughter was suffering from leukaemia and too ill to attend a concert, but would Mario have a few words with her just to cheer her up? He did better than this: he called Raphaella before the show and sang two songs for her down the phone. Later he invited her and her mother to Los Angeles for a week's respite. He paid for them and a private nurse to stay at a top hotel, and each day they visited him at his home. Mario promised to stay in touch, and was as good as his word, sending the little girl gifts and calling her every week until 31 January 1953 – his 32nd birthday – when he received word that she had died. Even then, he sent her one last present: an Immaculate Conception medallion which was buried with her.

Later that year, Mario also became unofficial patron of the Roselia Foundlings Home, in Pittsburgh. This came about in response to a letter and a batch of newspaper clippings which he received from Betty's aunt, who lived near the city. A newborn baby boy had been found abandoned in an apartment block vestibule, and taken to the home where staff had baptised him Mario Lanza on account of his lusty lungs. Touched by the gesture, Mario sent the home a cheque for $500 – money which he insisted should be put towards the child's education. Soon afterwards Mario Lanza II, as he became known and was eventually baptised, was found a proper home, but his adoptive parents decided not to change his name. Mario did not stay in touch with him, as he had with Raphaella Fasano, but he did set up the Mario Lanza Fund, based at the children's home – his first ever recognised charity – which would raise many thousands of dollars for abandoned children, and to which he made a regular monthly contribution.

Needless to say, Mario's benevolent nature would see other less honest 'causes' trying to take advantage of him: conmen who claimed they had gone to school with him and now needed money because they had fallen on hard times, others asking him to help finance bogus operations. 'As soon as the newspapers carried the story that Mario made a million dollars last year,' Betty told *Modern Screen's* Steve Cronin, 'he's become the target for every crackpot, beggar and confidence man in the country. It's gotten so bad we've had to hire someone to separate the legitimate requests from the loony ones.'

Meanwhile, Mario's aforementioned falling-out with Chicago occurred after his performance of 7 April at the city's Orchestra Hall. He had hoped to meet one of his favourite journalists, Claudia Cassidy, but she was out of town and the main review for the evening came from the teacher-composer Felix Borowski, writing for the *Chicago Sun-Times*:

> As a legitimate artiste, Lanza can make only the mildest appeal to a serious concertgoer. As one of his motion picture successes is *The Great Caruso*, there even has been controversy as to whether Lanza does or does not put his famous predecessor in the shade.

He does not. There can be no doubt about the natural magnif-
icence of Lanza's voice. A splendid voice is a notable asset but, alas,
there is more to singing than voice. Where an aria asks for the high
notes at the end and some kind of dramatic impact in the middle,
Lanza roars throughout like the Bull of Bashan. And in order to
underline the texts, even of the simplest songs, he indulges in the
arm waving that humbler tenors in small Italian theatres regard as
dramatic force. All this is a matter for pity, for there were moments
when Lanza did not shout, and his mezza-voice [*sic*] was ravishing
to hear. Given musical sensibility – even a better vocal production –
and Saturday's artiste may well achieve an approach to Caruso.

Mario was livid. May well achieve an *approach* to Caruso? In his eyes,
he was already better than Caruso. In the space of a few years he had
achieved more all-round fame than Caruso had achieved in his lifetime!
Regarding the actual comparisons with Caruso, however, the ultimate
tribute would come many years later from Caruso's tenor son, Enrico Jr
(1904–87), who could not praise Mario enough for portraying his father.
In *Enrico Caruso, My Father and My Family*, published shortly after his
death, he said of Lanza,

He imitated no one. His recordings of operatic sections are
original interpretations. Let it not be forgotten that Mario Lanza
excelled in both classical and light repertory, an accomplishment
that was beyond even my father's exceptional talents.

Chapter Seven

Metro-Goldwyn-Mario

Sure, I haven't sung at the Met yet. But the day I do, all hell
will break loose, the way it did in pictures. The world hasn't
heard from me yet. Wait till I develop!

Mario Lanza

With *The Great Caruso* riding on the crest of a spectacular
wave, in April 1951 Mario was informed by Dore Schary
that his next film would be *Because You're Mine* – even
before he read the script, in Mario's opinion 'a piece of shit' – which
again dipped into the Lanza biography: a popular singer, the idol of the
bobby-soxers, is drafted into the army, hates the experience, but comes
good in the end by falling for the sister of his best friend. For Bert Hicks
read Bat Batterson; for Betty, we have Bridget.

Initially, Mario refused to even entertain the idea. According to
Costa, he yelled at Joe Pasternak, 'Are you serious? How can you put
Caruso in the army? I don't think Mario Lanza will ever do it!' His army
days represented the most miserable period of his life, and he had spent
years trying to forget they ever happened. Pasternak was preparing what
promised to be a stunning screen adaptation of Sigmund Romberg's *The
Student Prince*, and Mario felt that he had enough on his plate –
recording his radio shows, besides rehearsing and helping Ray Sinatra to
arrange songs for a Christmas album – without taking several steps
backwards and making what looked like being an extension of *That
Midnight Kiss*. Also, he accused, in casting him as a mere private – the
least he expected was the rank of sergeant, or even general – MGM were

penalising him for being so utterly talented! To a certain extent, this was true. Both Schary and Pasternak believed that Lanza needed to be brought down a peg or two, and considered this to be the only way of doing it. Schary, not renowned for his interpersonal skills, vociferously reminded Mario that if he could have his way, this 'ersatz Caruso' would be washing dishes in a greasy spoon right now. Mario was offered an ultimatum: unless he completed the new film, MGM would find another actor for *The Student Prince*.

As usual, Mario threw a strop and pouted for a while. This time, however, he went over the top with his comfort eating – by the end of May his weight had reached 287 pounds, and even Terry Robinson could not get through to him that he was slowly killing himself. To Mario's way of thinking, if he remained obese, Schary would skip this film and wait until *The Student Prince* was ready to begin shooting at the end of the year. In fact, Schary was having none of this: in arguably the most foolish decision of his MGM career, he announced that Mario would begin the new film now, and lose weight whilst shooting was in progress. The studio's wardrobe experts and clever camera work would make Lanza appear slimmer, the mogul added. By the time shooting commenced, Mario's weight had dropped to 270 pounds and when the production wrapped in February 1952 he would be down to a record low of 160 pounds. As the scenes were not filmed in sequence, aside from the magnificent singing, the resulting film was little more than a joke.

Meanwhile, at the end of May Sam Weiler was approached by the Dairy Advertising Agency, representing the Coca-Cola Company, with a proposition he could hardly refuse. CBS Radio's *The Edgar Bergen Show*, broadcast on Sunday evenings and drawing some 20 million listeners, was taking a summer break, and the deal they had negotiated with a replacement had fallen through at the last minute. Would Mario therefore be interested in helping them out of a fix? Without even discussing it with his client, Weiler agreed, certain that Mario would jump at the chance to earn $5,300 a shot for just thirty minutes' work – and equally delighted that he himself would pocket a sizeable percentage of this, along with a weekly $500 fee for nominal 'production duties'. Initially, Mario hit the roof. Though his nerves had improved considerably over the years, he still disliked live radio performances because they brought back the horrors of his time working for Celanese

Hour. Weiler reassured him that in this respect he need not worry: though the shows would be publicised as 'live', their content would be pre-recorded at the Los Angeles Radio Recorders Studio, then introduced on each programme by Master of Ceremonies Bill Baldwin, with fake applause added to the tapes. In view of Mario's studio pranks and mother-in-law jokes, this was perhaps just as well. Next came the conditions. Having been put through the mill by Celanese Hour, Mario insisted that he would choose what to sing, and he would choose his conductors – Ray Sinatra fronting a 35-piece orchestra for the popular material, Costa taking up the baton for the arias and Neapolitan songs. CBS stepped in here and insisted that he be accompanied by Percy Faith, who had worked with many of the day's hit-parade stars including Tony Bennett and Guy Mitchell. Mario's response to this was, 'No Sinatra, no Lanza!' With no one else to fill the bill at such short notice – the first show was scheduled to air on 10 June – CBS capitulated.

Once the contract had been signed and CBS could not get out of it, Mario brought in more conditions. Each show had been allocated a special guest star, and many of these had already been hired when Mario announced that these would be female only, and very definitely no opera stars. This was his show, he declared, and not a showcase for inferior talents or would-be rivals – in other words, he was the biggest male singer in the world, which in a sense was true in his particular field: by now no one could touch him. Also, there would be no duets.

His first guest was Gisele MacKenzie (1927–2003), the gifted Canadian songstress he had met a few years earlier while touring with the Bel Canto Trio. Possessed of a voice which was both crystal clear and perfect-pitch, besides being a virtuoso violinist, MacKenzie was generally regarded as one of the finest female vocalists of her generation and had already enjoyed success in Canada with her own radio series, *Meet Gisele*. After working with Mario, she toured with Jack Benny and triumphed with musical theatre productions around the world. Mario liked her so much – the two socialised together, though they never became romantically involved – that he insisted that she alone guest throughout the series. She did, though there were times when she was unavoidably indisposed, when she was replaced by popular singers such as Kitty Kallen, Debbie Reynolds and Rosemary Clooney. Neither was MacKenzie, like her predecessors, exempt from Mario's devilish sense of humour – such as hiding a photograph of his penis inside her sheet music, to get her to crack up – though unlike Frances Yeend and Ethel Barrymore, she had a sense of humour and an ability to curse along with the best of them.

Those who have denounced Mario as coarse and vulgar should try and listen to the so-called 'Blue Tape'. Only the stuffiest of female fans – lovingly referred to by Mario as the DOPs, or dried-up old pussies – would ever take offence at this material, the real Lanza, letting his hair down and having fun with his friends. This was a retrospective of Mario's gaffs – mostly deliberate – which are so hilarious, they have to be heard to be believed. Similar tapes exist of Maria Callas and Elvis Presley, but even their outbursts are not as rib-tickling as Mario's. The tape was assembled by the 'unholy three' (Bill Baldwin, with technicians Jack Laddie and Kenny MacManus), and presented to Mario 'in the spirit of hilarity and a lot of laughs, and remembering good times', when the series closed. Baldwin explains in the tongue-in-cheek introduction,

> Just over a year ago, some fifty persons were introduced to this fabulous gentleman for the first time...musicians, directors, producers, engineers, tape engineers, librarians, a script girl and an announcer. This group of artisans, with Mr Lanza as their guide for enthusiasm, interest and hard work, sweat and slave to make this show one of the highest-rated programmes in radio. His warmth of heart and spirit was a constant reminder to us all to give our all, as he was doing, to do the best we know how, always, come what may. And many things came – and many things went.

Baldwin recalls Mario walking into the studio in June 1951, and includes Mario's taped 'shy' response when asked how he was feeling: 'I feel for the first time like a faggot feels when he gets his first cock up his ass!' In his 18 April 1952 show he almost gets through Frankie Laine's 'When You're In Love' – which would almost certainly have proved the definitive version had he finished it – when he forgets the lyrics and bellows, 'Aw, shit!' Next is his 'You'll Never Walk Alone', his opener recorded for the 16 May 1952 show, which he sings beautifully – until he stalls on the line, 'Walk on through the wind of your mother-in-law's ass!' For the 6 June show of that same year he announces, 'One of the loveliest and the most musical imports from South of the Border is "Besame mucho", introduced and made famous by Andy Russell. Literally translated it means, "Kiss me much" – which might not be a good idea if you're kissing your mother-in-law's big open snatch!' Then, when a laughter-creased Ray Sinatra misses his cue, Mario barks, 'Ray, you're jerking off!'

Another star who appreciated Mario's dry humour, and who like Gisele MacKenzie never missed an opportunity to get in a few four-letter words of her own, was the contralto Lisa Kirk (1925–90). Acclaimed for her performances in *Kiss Me Kate*, she would double for Rosalind Russell's voice in *Gypsy*, and for Lucille Ball in *Mame* – having a stand-up row with the latter when Lucy declared that no one could duplicate her singing voice because it was so bad. In an undated show of 1952, Mario personally introduced her: 'When I saw Cole Porter's *Kiss Me Kate*, I felt, as did everyone in the audience, that I was seeing the birth of a new star – namely, Lisa Kirk. Tonight she's honouring us as our guest, and for her first number Lisa sings a song which she recently recorded, "I Thought of You Last Night, and I Came in my Fucking Drawers"!' Next, Mario announces (but does not sing!) the song which Bill Baldwin is sure would get into the hit parade, if only he would record it: 'Baby, Go in the Bathroom and Wipe Me off your Face'. He then announces that after 'Fanculo' (Fuck off) he will close the show, as usual, with an aria from *Pagliacci* – 'Viva la fica!', which translates as 'Long live pussy'. Then comes his thank-you speech, 'With this broadcast we tenderly wave farewell to his [Baldwin's] sister-in-law's twat!' – and the whole thing ends with Kenny MacManus shouting across the studio, 'Be sure to get laid, Mario!'

'Even if you lean towards the Crosby kind of hooting, you should try Mr Lanza's singing for half an hour,' declared Jack Maple in the *Chicago Daily News*. 'How any human can sing so loud and clear with-out blowing a tonsil is a secret only Lanza can tell.' *The Mario Lanza Show* became an institution, running until June 1952. It has been suggested that it did not earn him a lot of money, that he was responsible for paying the musicians' overtime and even the cost of hiring the studio. This is untrue: no organisation such as CBS or Coca-Cola would have expected an artiste to cover their own overheads, though Costa's salary did come out of Mario's pocket because he acted purely in an advisory capacity, and was not on the original musicians' call-sheet. After its initial season, the show moved to a regular Friday evening slot at 9pm. There were 66 shows in all, with a total of 151 musical items from Mario. Some of the arias are sung slightly faster than written so as to fit them into the limited airtime, but this is a minor detail. Mario had sung most of them before, but rarely as well as during this period. Unquestionably, his vocal powers were at their peak. And though none of these recordings were intended for commercial release – indeed, they may not have been released at all had Mario lived – we are fortunate that almost all of them have at some time turned up on album or CD. Because of the very tight schedule, there was virtually no time for retakes, yet their quality is second to none, and rivals anything he ever did in the studio for RCA. Receiving its debut on 27 June 1952 – the day the radio show ended and Mario received a gold disc for one million sales of 'Be My Love', which also opened and closed each show – was 'Testa adorata', from Leoncavallo's rarely heard *La Bohème*.

Where Mario truly excelled, however, with the so-called 'Coca-Cola Shows', was in the show songs he never got around to recording for RCA: 'Among My Souvenirs', 'You Are but a Dream', 'Danny Boy', 'April in Paris', and 'The Rosary', an amazing piece composed in 1898 by Robert Cameron Rogers and Ethelbert Nevin within which he declares his profound faith. He also performed 'Roses of Picardy' with the verse, as introduced by Harry Pilcer in 1916. Especially good among the popular songs is Mario's reading of 'I'll Be Seeing You', which so moved Peggy Lee that she later used the arrangement to close her concerts. Then there were 'If I Loved You', 'Long Ago and Far Away' (which inspired Portuguese fado star Amália Rodrigues to cover the song for her only English-language album), 'My Wild Irish Rose' (which he still dedicated to Betty), the Jane Froman hit 'Somebody Bigger than You and I', 'You Are Love' from Jerome Kern's *Showboat*, and Cole Porter's 'Night and Day'. The list is endless, and what makes Mario's work at this time all the more remarkable is that so much of it was recorded while he was under the influence – after each song had been satisfactorily put down he would take a long swig from the thermos flask he carried around with him, containing his favourite tipple, Chivas Regal. He was taken to task by supposed music buffs for suddenly belting out a top C, if the mood took him, or for adding embellishments not on the printed page, though in many ways this only makes his work more thrilling. The Three Tenors, towards the end of their collective run, would similarly over-embellish to show off while performing songs they arguably should not have been performing in the first place – their attempts at Edith Piaf's 'La vie en rose' were truly lamentable – and make an absolute hash of it. This said, Mario warranted criticism when, before singing 'The Lord's Prayer', he asked his 'audience' not to applaud on account of the seriousness of the piece. There *was* no audience.

On 12 July and 2 August, Mario squeezed in two recording sessions for the new film. In the first he laid down new, more powerful readings of 'Mamma mia, che vo' sape' and 'O paradiso'; in the second a less convincing 'Lord's Prayer' than the one he had sung in his radio show, and Nicholas Brodsky and Sammy Cahn's title track, which would later give him his third million-seller. When Brodsky and Mario went out on the prowl, virtually no attractive woman is said to have been safe from seduction. One of the few people who could match Mario's drinking glass for glass, Brodsky, referred to by Mario as 'the gypsy' because of his Hungarian ancestry, had recently recovered from hard times. Their theme song was 'Play Gypsies, Dance Gypsies', from Kalman and Brammer's *Countess Maritza*, which they would belt out when drunk. After he had composed 'Be My Love' for *The Toast of New Orleans*, MGM had dispensed with Brodsky's services and, whilst waiting for the outcome of the film, he had found himself living hand to mouth. On 20 April 1951, Brodsky's 46th birthday, Mario sent him a package containing $2,000, with a note stating that this was to tide him over until they worked together again, such was his confidencing in talking – or rather bullying – the studio into to re-employing him. This had not been possible with *The Great Caruso*: there had been no scope for new material. Now, thanks to Mario, he was back on track.

On 6 August, Mario – with his alter ego Caruso keeping a watchful eye over his shoulder – appeared on the cover of *Time* magazine. In America, this was regarded as the ultimate accolade, though in this instance the emphasis was on mockery: instead of photographs, the publication chose caricatures of the two tenors with music staves wrapped around their necks. The caption, 'Would Caruso Fracture 'Em In Scranton?', gave readers a clear indication of what they would find inside. Three weeks ahead of the release, Sam Weiler had called the editor with Mario's demands that this time only the truth be printed about him. The accompanying feature, headed 'Million-Dollar Voice', took brutal pleasure in doing just this, so much so that the writer did not disclose his or her name. There have been claims that the culprit was the sports writer, Jim Murray, but there is no proof of this. With the Mario Lanza story unravelling under sensationalist sub-headings such as 'Tears Of Gratitude', 'Dead-End Kid', 'Breakfast In Bed' and 'Beer In The Berkshires', just about the only thing they got right this time, from Mario's point of view, was the place of his birth.

The rumours surrounding Mario's personal life were rife. When he had been invited to appear on Hedda Hopper's radio show in November 1950, the arch hack had only been interested in fishing for titbits, none of which had been forthcoming, and in getting one over on her rival, Louella Parsons, who henceforth would never have many good words to write about Mario. He would only make matters worse in February 1951 when awarded the Photoplay Gold Medal Award, along with Doris Day. Speaking from the podium at the Ambassador Hotel, he announced that he owed his success to three people who were in the room that evening: Frank Sinatra, for believing in him when he had first arrived in Hollywood; Joe Pasternak, for giving him his big break in the movies; and Hedda Hopper, for her 'unlimited support'. In one of her syndicated columns, Hedda had defended his decision to sing all night for friends if he wanted to, but to stop singing for free at Hollywood parties. 'These cracks against Mario are being handed out by the higher-ups at MGM,' she had written. 'His Caruso was one of the studio's biggest ever grossers, and now he's being punished for bringing home the bacon.' Louella, having witnessed Mario refusing to sing for some bigwig, declaring that he was not 'some circus act to be gawked at', had labelled him mean and uncooperative, and this had stuck. Louella was also one of those who, when Kathryn Grayson filed for divorce from her husband Johnnie Johnson in October 1951, hinted that Mario was 'the other man', when in fact no one else had been involved, and that he and Betty were about to file for divorce. The Lanzas' second daughter, baptised Elissa after Mario's grandmother, had been born on 3 December, since which time Betty had rarely been seen by her husband's side. News of a possible rift in their marriage had been brought to Louis B. Mayer on the eve of *The Great*

Caruso premiere, and one of his final acts as MGM's vice-president had been to offer Mario a compromise: he should announce his official separation from Betty and move out of the family home, or salvage what was reputedly left of his marriage. And whatever he decided, he should stop sleeping around.

The lengthy *Time* feature started off well enough, describing Mario as 'an exuberant young man with the face of a choirboy and the frame of a prize bull'. Adding that his was a voice which many experts ranked alongside the titans of opera, the editorial continued sucking up to him: 'The voice sells Lanza, but Lanza also sells the voice with curly-haired good looks and a paradoxical combination of beaming boyishness and hairy-chested animal magnetism.' Then, having placed him on the requisite pedestal, the writer proceeded to bring him back to earth with a suitable bump. Mario was no longer the strapping six-footer so described by other journalists, but a vastly overweight man of 'less than 5 feet 10 inches' who wore elevator shoes – something no one had known about until now. Neither had he always been fussy about personal hygiene, as attested by his former army buddy Johnny Silver, soon to be dismissed by Mario who was later so obsessed with cleanliness that he sometimes showered four times a day. Mario's attempts at losing weight, according to *Time*, were also a sham. Revealing that he had once polished off 40 pieces of chicken in one sitting, washed down by a quart of eggnog, the editorial added, 'Lanza's idea of dieting, based on his own theory that proteins add no weight, is to pile chicken legs, half-pound chunks of rare steak and a mound of barbecued kidneys on his plate, devour them and then heap on a second helping.'

On the subject of the undisputable Lanza ego, *Time* observed, 'When the mood is on him, Lanza can gorge his ego as freely as his stomach, and his studio bosses have sometimes tried needling him to deflate his head as well as his hide.' Mario was also reported as ruling his entourage 'like a comic-opera Latin American dictator'. Much of this was water off a duck's back. What upset Mario most of all, however, enough for him to want to meet this mysterious author and 'thrash the shit out of him' was the criticism of his voice, and the magazine's revelation concerning his persistent boasting that he would some day sing opera on the legitimate platform:

Lanza has frequently pictured the Met as showering offers on him, but the Met itself seems to know nothing abou them... He can sail up to D flat above high C with ease, and he has sung a low A that gives some baritones trouble. But he lacks musical taste, discipline, and the years of training needed to settle even the greatest voice.

Peter Herman Adler backed up this statement, declaring that Mario's too-swift success had added to his insecurity, and that all the boasting and showing off was his way of coping with this. 'Ten years with the right opera company, and no one could compare with him,' Adler affirmed, 'but who would expect him, after being a star, to go back to learning?' On the subject of his actual singing technique, *Time* took no prisoners by comparing Mario with an over-eager baseball player, in that he treated his voice like an athletic talent, swinging for a home run every time, but ultimately punching the ball out of the park:

> He overworks the Caruso sob. His Italian is rough. He tends to swallow his notes. His brilliant tone is often white – lacking resonance. Worst of all, from a singer's point of view, he is forcing his voice, especially in the abandon with which he hurls himself into high notes at top volume. Lanza's voice may be able to take this abuse for two or three more years before he hurts it, say the experts. Ultimately, he will burn it out.

This analysis was only partially true. Mario did overwork the Caruso sob: like most of the great tenors he was an emotional man – it went with the territory – but this only added to the quality of his work. Similarly, on account of this surfeit of emotion he *was* forcing his voice, and there was every likelihood that he would burn himself out, at the rate he was going, before he reached 50, as had happened with Maria Callas. Her downfall, however, related more to her personal life – in particular, her involvement with Aristotle Onassis, who treated her like any other costly acquisition and encouraged her to eschew those vital rehearsals in favour of yachting around the world with him. Mario's downfall, already forecast in the summer of 1951, would also be linked to the wrong lifestyle and a severe lack of self-discipline. His voice, however, was not lacking in resonance – far from it – and had he taken better care of himself, instead of rip-roaring through life with his finger firmly pressed on the self-destruct button, it would have served him well into his sixties. What was a blatant lie was the *Time* scribe's suggestion that, during his first two films, Mario's vocal pyrotechnics had been created by mechanical intervention: 'MGM's expert sound technicians, who now do virtually no tampering with Lanza's voice, can work wonders with their electronic gadgets.'

Time magazine could have divulged more, had it wished to continue its stance of tabloid journalism. Mario was fast heading towards dissipation, and appears not to have cared who knew this. Whilst Betty was drinking and drugging herself into near-oblivion – friends have attested that she took so many sleeping pills, she was frequently out cold for days, and on more than one occasion ended up in hospital after overdosing – her husband was painting the town red each evening after the Coca-Cola recording sessions, and according to Terry Robinson, sleeping with any female who fluttered her eyelids at him. If he could not get a woman to submit to his not inconsiderable charms, he promised her a nonexistent part in one of his films – or simply paid her hard cash. 'Often as much as a thousand dollars,' Robinson said. When Betty was not bombed out on her daily diet of uppers, downers and whisky, the rows at North Whittier Drive were sometimes so vociferous that they could be heard a hundred yards away. Though he never laid a finger on Betty, in a violent, drunken rage Mario would smash everything in sight – crockery, ornaments, even the furniture. 'His exceptional verbal skills made for volleys of obscene phrases that would have emptied the rowdiest saloon on the Barbary Coast,' Roland L. Bessette observed in *Mario Lanza: Tenor In Exile*. And if ever his mother walked in on one of these arguments, Mario would calm down at once and fling himself sobbing into her arms. Then he would rush outside, jump into his car, and drive off in search of sex – whether this be with an extra from the studio, a friend's wife or girlfriend, or a prostitute. He was not fussy. And if the husband or boyfriend wanted to watch, who was he to argue?

This psychotic behaviour accompanied him to the studio each day, with Mario drawing even more attention to himself than usual by his insistence on still wearing his Caruso get-up of spats, Homburg and walking cane. His antics resulted in the Hollywood Press Writers Association presenting him with their annual award for Most Uncooperative Star In Hollywood. By the time the film was in the can, virtually everyone involved with it swore that they would never work with him again. Mario would twice be suspended for antisocial behaviour – periods he spent wisely, heading for Palm Springs with Terry Robinson to lose weight with a vengeance until he reduced his frame to an all-time low of 160 pounds which for him was almost anorexic. Dore Schary had all but washed his hands of him, and claimed to be looking for the slightest excuse to fire him. This of course was not true. Lanza may have been an untamable monster, but he was one of MGM's biggest money-earners, and news of his inexcusable behaviour and inordinate demands never reached his fans, in whose eyes he could do no wrong. Schary and Joe Pasternak had private meetings with his friends, the closest of which was of course Terry Robinson; these friends were alternately cajoled and threatened into at least attempting to bring him into line. Invariably they failed – Robinson is known to have lost his temper at least once with Mario, and actually hit him. Lanza was a mighty star and knew it: he was surrounded by yes-men and spongers who submitted to his every whim, and so long as he was dipping his hand in his pocket, these people would have allowed him to get away with murder.

Costa recalled an incident when Joe Pasternak mentioned to Mario that he was putting his Bel Air mansion on the market. The asking price was $145,000, and Mario pulled out a $25,000 wad of banknotes out of his pocket because he was interested in buying it. When the producer advised him to discuss the matter with Betty, Mario promised that he would, but subsequently accused Pasternak of trying to steal his money. A few days later, a sozzled Mario rammed his Cadillac into Pasternak's mailbox, but the matter did not end there. In *Lanza, His Tragic Life*, Terry Robinson recalls how Mario asked him to drive him to Pasternak's home late one night, and what happened when they got there: 'He got out of the car, took down his pants, and had a bowel movement on the lawn. "Get me some leaves from those bushes," he said. "And I hope he's not growing poison ivy as a hobby."'

Nicholas Brodsky was one of the few people that Mario got along with on the set of *Because You're Mine*, which began shooting a few weeks before the *Time* feature appeared. Mario had insisted that his friend be hired to write at least one song for the score and Joe Pasternak, a fellow

Hungarian, agreed. Brodsky had come up with the stunning title track, which Mario delayed recording until 2 August, when he cut it alongside 'The Lord's Prayer', with Wesley Tourtelot accompanying him on a church organ. Regarding his part, that of pop star Renaldo Rossano, Dore Schary had listened to Mario's 'bellyaching', and had changed Renaldo's vocation to that of a famous opera star – sarcastically remarking that this would be the nearest Lanza would ever get to singing with the New York Met. Mario still hated every aspect of the film. 'The script stinks,' he told *Modern Screen*, 'and when a script's no good, I got a perfect right to say so. My whole life I've spoken my mind, been honest and told the truth. I was brought up that way.'

Mario complained persistently to Pasternak and director Alexander Hall, and more than once directly to Dore Schary himself, about the 'dirty habit' of his leading lady – at one stage threatening to boycott the production unless Schary fired her. Doretta Morrow (1928–68) was a New York-born actress who had recently triumphed as Tuptim, introducing the song 'I Have Dreamed' in the Broadway production of *The King And I* with Yul Brynner and Gertrude Lawrence. Lawrence had died three weeks into the show's run, 'And little wonder, with all that smoke around,' Mario had quipped. Morrow, the cousin of crooner Vic Damone, chain-smoked when not in front of the cameras, and this caused havoc with Mario's voice – in all he missed 25 studio calls through illness, which he mostly attributed to the smoke on Morrow's breath and clothes. Several times during shooting, too, she marched into Dore Schary's office and demanded to be taken off the picture because Mario kept addressing her as *fica* – that vulgar Italian word again. One reported incident, repeated by Roland L. Bessette, took place when they were in the studio, recording their duet of the title-song: Mario, sporting an erection through his trousers, asked Morrow if she could add a little romance to the occasion by getting herself wet and rubbing herself up against him. Not surprisingly, she fled from the scene in tears. Schary's response to this was to have a burly stuntman pose as Morrow's brother, and threaten to take Mario apart unless he curbed his libido and his bullying tactics. Mario reacted by going berserk in his dressing room, smashing every stick of furniture and even ripping out the wall panels. Then, declaring that he had got the frustration out of his system, he paid for the damage, but steadfastly refused to apologise to Morrow. Her experiences with Mario so shattered her confidence that, although she appeared in several successful stage musicals, including *Kismet*, she never made another film. Not surprisingly, she succumbed to lung cancer in a London hospital, shortly after her 40th birthday.

The farce begins within moments of the opening credits: $5,000-a-week opera sensation Renaldo Rossano turns up for his draft board medical, whilst the voiceover reminds us that no one over the age of 25 is ever recruited into the army (Mario was 31). To be truthful, he looks great clad just in his jocks – the best we will see him looking in this film – a pleasant V-shape, only slightly sucking in his stomach, and weighing in at an attractive 170 pounds. He is just as impressive in the next scene, singing a heartfelt 'Addio alla madre' in *Cavalleria Rusticana*, then making an announcement to the audience (which would never have been allowed in a Met production) that they will not be seeing him for a while because he has enlisted. Just as happened with Mario in real life his manager, Albert (Edouard Franz) tries but fails to use his self-inflated influence to get him excused from military duty. Renaldo says goodbye to his blonde bombshell soprano girlfriend, Francesca Landers (Paula Corday). In the next scene, 40 pounds heavier, he minces into his mother's parlour with a poodle to bid her farewell – and to be chided for spending money as fast as he earns it, another Lanza trait – before heading for the railway station. When the train reaches its destination, whilst the welcoming sergeant attempts a poor emulation of Jimmy Durante – who for some reason was present for the scene, but does not appear in it – and orders him to sing an aria ('Questa o quella'), a couple stroll by. She asks him for his autograph, while the man one assumes must be her father looks on. These were Mario's parents, and elsewhere Terry Robinson will make a brief, uncredited appearance in the fight sequence he was asked to stage.

At the army base, Renaldo meets his biggest fan – Sergeant 'Bat' Batterson (James Whitmore), whose fawning gives every impression that he may have a crush on the handsome young tenor. This becomes evident when Renaldo serenades him with 'The Song the Angels Sing': Bat promotes him to be his second-in-command, assuring him a hard time from the other recruits. Then we learn that he wants to fix him up with his kid sister, Bridget (Morrow), a character obviously based on Betty Hicks, save that here she is given a voice. Bridget is taking singing lessons and works for a radio station, so Renaldo calls her, throws in a snatch of 'Casta diva' from Bellini's *Norma* for good measure, and invites her to the barracks – obviously, this particular army base doubles as a holiday camp where some recruits can please themselves. However, just to hammer home the fact that soldiering is a serious business, the captain who nabs him coming out of the telephone box admonishes him with, 'You're not an opera star any more. You're a soldier, and from what I've seen a half-baked one. But you're going into the oven, and you're not coming out until you are well done!' It was a line which would not have been out of place in one of the later Doris Day–Rock Hudson comedies.

Naturally, when they meet it is love at first sight. Bridget performs her 'audition' piece – the jingle she does on air to promote indigestion tablets – whilst he blows her away with an impromptu jingle he has just made up for Fluffy Foam washing powder. He then tells her that she has all the makings of an opera star, and to prove this point she sits at the piano and sings Marlene Dietrich's 'You Do Something to Me' – and rather nicely, too. Renaldo tells her that she is ruining her voice singing commercials; he puts her through her scales, and a moment later she is singing 'Be My Love', far better than Kathryn Grayson ever could.

Happy and in love, Renaldo goes to the army chapel to sing 'The Lord's Prayer' – entering the building at 170 pounds, and gaining another 70 pounds by the time he reaches the altar. Joe Pasternak, after viewing the rushes, asked for the second part of this scene to be shot again, but by this stage Mario had had enough: his stubbornness would make him the butt of many jokes when the film was released. And no sooner have audiences stopped sniggering at his alarming change in shape than Renaldo comes up with the plum line, Mario's personal contribution to the script, 'The odd thing is that lots of people think that good music is only for the long hairs. But you know who my real fans are? The teenagers up in the gallery!'

Like Mario Lanza, 'Corporal' Rossano has a knack of getting what he wants, and he swings more leave to enter the recording studio with the by now jealous Francesca (whose singing is dubbed by soprano Peggy Bonini). He is starting to tire of her, and has used the occasion to have Bridget auditioned by Albert. Love goes sour, however, when Francesca convinces her rival that Renaldo is a louse who has used women all his life. Now, with Bridget walking out on him, he has her angry brother to deal with. All ends well, though from this point the story becomes even more ridiculous. Bat gives Renaldo a bad time, assigning him to garbage and spud-peeling duties, patrols in the rain, and military manoeuvres – with Mario once more vowing to walk off the picture because he claimed the mock shellfire was affecting his ears – whilst the other recruits mock him with cod-opera. The two former friends end up scrapping and are thrown in the slammer, allowing us a moment's grace from this nonsense while one Private Artie Pilcer executes a perilous dance routine in the barrackroom – Pasternak's private joke which sees Broadway hoofer Bobby Van repeating step-for-step the one perfected by fellow Hungarian dancer Harry Pilcer in 1911. Enter the general's wife (Spring Byington), a big Renaldo fan who wants him to sing for a visiting United Nations delegation. Her husband is not so sure, until Renaldo delivers an a cappella 'Miserere' from *Il Trovatore* through the prison bars, just as the French general he once sang to in Paris happens to be passing by. Freed, he wows the crowd with a rip-roaring 'Granada'. By now, both he and Bridget have seen the error of their ways: she turns up at the concert in time to reprise the title track with him. This scene enabled Mario to exact his revenge for having to put up with the stench of smoke coming from Doretta Morrow, which he claimed made him want to throw up: insisting upon there being only one take so that he would have to get it right first time, before kissing her he chomped on a raw clove of garlic.

Despite the mostly poor reviews – *Time* denounced it as 'under-nourished', which was probably being too kind – *Because You're Mine* fared exceptionally well at the box office: most fans were not really bothered about the paltry storyline, or whether Lanza could act or not. All that mattered was the singing, and as always this was second to none. In Britain, the film was chosen for that year's Royal Command Performance, the very first to be attended by the new queen, Elizabeth II, who is said to have been 'thrilled' at the prospect of meeting Mario Lanza. He stunned everyone at MGM by refusing to attend the 27 November premiere at London's Empire Theatre in Leicester Square, a rejection unheard of in those days. The American press denounced this as a snub to the queen, unaware that he had made a transatlantic call to Buckingham Palace explaining why he could not attend. With his abject fear of flying he had wanted to sail to England, but problems with the studio meant that he would not have been able

A star is born. Mario is mobbed by autograph hunters in 1949, during a return visit to his hometown, Philadelphia.

The Toast of Hollywood! On the set of *The Toast of New Orleans*, 1950, with 18-year-old Rita Moreno.

On the set of *The Great Caruso*, 1951, with Jimmy Durante, who had 'popped in' to supervise an emulation of him by one of Mario's co-stars. Despite numerous requests, Durante declined to make a cameo appearance.

WARNER BROS. STUDIOS
MAKE-UP & HAIR TESTS
FOR
"SERENADE" 824
MARIO LANZA
OF SARITA MONTIEL
MAKE-UP # 2-2
EYES
HAIRDRESS #
AGE
WB
9-2-55
WB

September 1955, on the set of *Serenade* with his co-star, gay icon Sarita Montiel. With them is director Anthony Mann.

Mario and his family arrive in Las Vegas in March 1955, ahead of one of the most disastrous failures of his career.

The great soprano Renata Tebaldi visits Mario on the set of *Serenade*, 1955.
Afterwards, the pair retreated to Mario's home for a 'sing-song' which went
on all night. Sadly, the event was not recorded.

Move Over Caruso! *This* is the world's greatest tenor!

October 1959. Mario lies in state at the Villa Badoglio, Rome. He suffered the ultimate humiliation of having his bones broken so that his body would fit into a lidless coffin two sizes too small.

to leave Hollywood until the 25th, which would have meant taking a plane. Reluctantly, he had had to stay home. Additionally, his wife was pregnant again and he felt that it was his duty to remain by her side. The British fans loved him all the more for his loyalty as a family man, unaware of how hellish the Lanza household could be at times.

On 28 and 29 September, Mario had taken a break from filming to record seven Christmas songs, and a reworking of 'The Lord's Prayer', for RCA. Ray Sinatra conducted the sessions at the Republic Studios in Hollywood, and the result was stunning. Despite his vulgarity and hugely controversial lifestyle, Mario was a spiritual man and approached religion very much like a child, always praying on his knees at the foot of his bed. He rarely attended church, not because he did not want to, but because fame had made this impossible. Though he would record all of these songs again, the versions he put down now when he was vocally at his most intense have become almost definitive, even taking into consideration that just about every star in the firmament has recorded at least one of them in their career. One could never doubt the choking sincerity of 'Guardian Angels', the childlike innocence he brings to 'Away in a Manger', the sheer powerhouse performance of 'The First Nowell'. The album, released in October 1951, sold 250,000 copies in its first week.

That same month, Mario was interviewed by Jack Wade of *Modern Screen*, a magazine he had learned to distrust since the 'Wonderful Madman' fiasco. Wade's quest was to defend him against the 'knife-throwers', those critics who over the last months had written only negative things about him, unafraid of litigation because most of their accusations had been true. The magazine's editor was still smarting from the after-effects of the earlier piece, and needed to get Mario on side with a good story to prevent circulation figures from slumping, as they had since Jim Henaghan had seemingly insulted half the populace of South Philadelphia. In the space of ten minutes, all the time Mario allowed him, a gullible Wade swallowed all the waffle his subject had to offer. 'Mario Lanza is not stepping out on his wife,' he wrote. 'He is not pulling a snob act on his old friends. He is not being difficult at the studio. His is the most stirring, beautiful and powerful voice ever placed on a Hollywood soundtrack. *And* he has a personality to match.'

Those who knew Mario and who had suffered in the process might have argued with this. And no one had suffered more than Betty, whose defence of him in *Movie Stars Parade* was nothing short of laughable. Refusing to be interviewed by a journalist, Betty insisted on penning the piece herself – and succeeded in shooting herself in the foot with every paragraph. Firstly she denied having a nurse to look after her children: 'I never could see myself handing my little girls over to a nurse and saying, "Here, you bring them up!"' Most of the time, Betty was in no fit state to care for anyone, and as her behaviour by this time was so erratic that employees rarely stayed beyond the end of the week, Colleen and Elissa must have been very confused youngsters indeed. Next, she painted a too well-balanced portrait of Lanza, the stay-at-home family man. Though there is no doubting that Mario doted on his daughters, his only truly happy moments when not singing were spent partying anywhere but at home, raising merry hell, and bedding women. 'When a man feels so intensely about his work, it takes a great deal out of him,' she wrote of his legendary temper. 'Yes, Mario is sensitive and easily upset at times. But then, would he be an artiste if he didn't have such powerful emotions?' Betty's biggest howler, however, came at the end of the piece:

> If it's true, as I've heard, that two careers in one family are often the stumbling block to Hollywood marriages, I am glad to say our family nurtures only one career. Not that I consider ours a 'Hollywood marriage' – whatever that may be. I consider it a good marriage – a lasting marriage.

From the substantial evidence we have, it was a *dreadful* marriage. And in true European 'You've made your bed, so lie on it' fashion, and solely for the sake of their children, both parties would struggle for another seven years to keep it afloat.

Chapter Eight

The Student Prince Fiasco

The voice is kind of like a sacred trust to me. If I don't use it
wisely then I feel I'm cheating the public, and that's one thing
I'll never do. They can sue me for fifty million dollars, a
hundred million. I'll declare bankruptcy before I
compromise the voice.

Mario Lanza

The Student Prince, with music by Sigmund Romberg and lyrics by Dorothy Donnelly, was based on the Wilhelm Meyer-Förster play, *In Old Heidelberg*. The most successful of Romberg's operettas, it had opened on Broadway in December 1924, and ran for over 600 performances. Then, its most popular and ironic song had been 'Drink, Drink, Drink' – America had been at the height of Prohibition. Ernst Lubitsch had filmed it (as a silent film) with Ramon Novarro and Norma Shearer, since which time there had been several Broadway revivals. The Lanza version finally went into production in June 1952, though he was already familiar with much of the score, having sung several of the songs on the radio and concert platform. 'If they thought I'd fractured 'em in *Caruso*, wait till they see me in this one,' he told one reporter. 'I'm sitting on top of the world right now – and there's going to be another December baby!' He had completely forgotten an interview he had given a few weeks earlier for *Modern Screen*, in which he had brought up the subject of retiring from movies altogether and concentrating on his recording and concert work – giving a hint that this time he might really be heading for the operatic stage. This interview was now published, and would only add to the confusion of the next few months.

Though his contract did not stipulate script, co-star and director approval, as happened with many of MGM's major stars, Joe Pasternak had kept Mario abreast of all the developments so far with the pre-production stage of the film, and informed him that any reasonable ideas would be taken on board. Had this sharing and developing of ideas continued, none of the mess over the coming months would have happened. Well aware of Mario's 'Johnny Opposite' character and his unswaying stubbornness, it was very wrong of the powers-that-be to persistently try to drag him back into line with endless threats of suspension just because his ideas for the production did not match their own. If this had been the case, then why had Pasternak invited his input in the first place? What also has to be said is that Mario was no less ebullient and demanding than Pasternak, Schary and any of the other MGM hierarchy. At the end of the day, few cinemagoers were interested in who had produced and directed a Mario Lanza film, who his co-stars were, who had written the script or even if the film was any good. Just about all that counted was the voice, and to keep the voice in good form necessitated its owner experiencing as little stress as possible – even if this meant giving him his own way when they believed him to be wrong. This was why great singers such as Callas, Piaf, Sinatra and Crosby retained greatness throughout their careers – they never allowed anyone to ride roughshod over them because, at the end of the day, their names were appearing on the billboards and record labels. Today, Lanza, like all these artistes, continues to sell millions of records every year and, like them, his popularity never diminishes. But how many of those buying the product can relate the names of those who managed and produced them, and who more often than not made the artistes' lives a misery because they were less interested in their stars than they were in lining their own pockets and boosting their already overinflated egos?

Briefly, Doretta Morrow had been considered for the part of Kathie, the servant girl who captures the heart of Prince Karl Franz and almost causes him to renounce his royal title. 'Over my dead body' had been Mario's response to this, although Morrow, Lana Turner, Jane Powell and several others had been approached, and refused to have anything to do with a man whose reputation preceded him. Then Mario told Pasternak, 'Fine, get me Ann Blyth!' So far, so good. She was contacted, and jumped at the chance to work with him again. The two had got along famously during *The Great Caruso*, and would do so again during what little time they spent on the production.

Mario also asked for George Stoll as the film's musical director: Stoll had worked his magic in *The Toast of New Orleans* with no complaints from the tetchy tenor, and he suggested Maurice De Packh for the orchestrations – he too had worked on the earlier film. This left just the director. Pasternak hired German-born Curtis Bernhardt, a man used to difficult actors – he had just 'suffered' *Sirocco* with Humphrey Bogart. The assistant director was Joel Freeman, who for some reason Mario loathed on sight. Another big mistake was Pasternak's decision to engage William Ludwig and Sonya Levien to write the script. These two had made an absolute hash of *The Great Caruso*: they would fare much better here, but so far as Mario was concerned they had messed up once, and he did not trust them. An ingenious idea, on the other hand, was Pasternak's commissioning of Nicholas Brodsky and Paul Francis Webster to augment the score with three songs: 'Beloved', 'Summertime in Heidelberg', and 'I'll Walk with God' – fine pieces of work which blend well with Romberg's uniquely European style. On the negative side, Webster was asked to change some of the lines in the original songs because, Pasternak believed, they did not fit well with Mario's persona. Mario would later accuse MGM of not having the decency to wait until Romberg was cold in his grave – he had died the previous November – before 'fucking up' his work. The rot had set in.

On 20 June, Costa conducted the first session for the film soundtrack. Organist Wesley Tourtelot, who had backed Mario on 'The Lord's Prayer', accompanied him on 'A Mighty Fortress' and 'I'll Walk with God'. The latter, which became Paul Francis Webster's best-selling composition until Doris Day recorded his songs for *Calamity Jane*, may make some cynics smile today. Back in 1952, when Jane Froman was topping the album charts with 'Faith', it was taken very seriously – some people actually knelt while Mario was performing it. Before entering the studio, he made a discreet visit to a church in Beverly Hills. He sang it with all the passion that was within his heart, and applied the same gusto to his on-screen character when he reported to the studio for rehearsals, six days later. This innate *joie de vivre* immediately got him on the wrong side of director Curtis Bernhardt. In the past, few had been able to get away with criticising Mario's singing to his face unless they were ready to receive a severe tongue-lashing, or worse. The Lanza voice was sacred: criticism was tantamount to blasphemy. Now, it seemed, they could not find fault with his acting either, though in this instance Bernhardt was right. Prince Karl Franz was not supposed to be a jovial, devil-may-care young man; he was heir to the Prussian throne and the script called for him to be suitably aristocratic, stiff-lipped and unsmiling. Mario disagreed. All of his characters thus far had carried a large element of his own persona, and with his fondness for rewriting history (though this prince was already a fictitious royal) he saw no reason why the scriptwriters should not make the young man a little more like himself. Pasternak and Bernhardt bawled him out on the set: he would play the part as he was told to play it, and the same would apply to his singing. Mario sent a message to Dore Schary: the least he expected was for the director to be fired. When Mario turned up at the studio for the first day of shooting, he got no further than the make-up chair in his dressing room. When Joel Freeman came to collect him for his first scene, Mario asked if Bernhardt was still supervising the film. When Freeman replied that he was, for once there was no tantrum. Mario simply asked Terry Robinson to drive him home.

Pasternak called Dore Schary, who had by now become so used to Mario's behaviour that he chose to ignore what had happened. Lanza had left the studio without turning the air blue, and would be back the next day, of this he was convinced. In fact, he did not return to the set at all. Each time Freeman, Pasternak or Schary called him at home, he slammed the phone down. Schary sent a message to his home, ordering him to report to the studio for 'make or break' talks on 14 July. When Mario told Schary in no uncertain terms what to do with his meeting, Schary put him on a two-week suspension. Mario's reaction to this was strange indeed. He had Terry Robinson fix up a meeting between Schary, Pasternak, MGM's legal department – and his parents, his theory being that if these people met the Cocozzas and saw for themselves that he came from decent stock, then maybe they might start showing him some respect. The truth is, Schary was hard put to respect anyone, and saw the move as yet more proof of the tenor's insecurity. Was Lanza so immature that he was incapable of fighting his battles without having Mama there to hold his hand? The Cocozzas were politely received, but the meeting achieved nothing.

Neither was this the only dilemma Mario faced at this time. A few days later, he fired Sam Weiler from being his manager, though without legal intervention he was unable to dissolve their partnership just yet. In truth, Weiler had been manager mostly in name only – he certainly had not brought that much work winging Mario's way. Mario's earlier tours had been organised by Columbia Concerts, his recording sessions had all taken place under the jurisdiction of RCA, and his contract with MGM had come about as a result of their organisation of the 1947 Hollywood Bowl concert. Over the years, Weiler had been used by both Mario and Betty as a prop and confidant – and as a bank to bale them out when things had got rough. Now, Mario no longer regarded Weiler as a kindly father figure but as a conspiring thief who had intentionally set out to rob him. Initially, he suspected him of misappropriating funds from their company, Marsam, and on most counts he would be proved right. When Weiler refused him access to the books, he and Terry Robinson waited until he was out of town before breaking into the offices with an MGM stills photographer. Mario knew little about money, other than how to spend it recklessly, but he was sensible enough to have every important document photographed. These pictures he handed to his lawyers, who immediately set about having Weiler investigated. While this was taking place, he appointed Fred Matsuo and later Rex Cole to handle his affairs.

On 29 July, with his contract reinstated, Mario and Costa returned to the MGM Studios to record three more songs for the film soundtrack. All were single takes. 'Summertime in Heidelberg' was a lovely duet with Ann Blyth. 'Serenade', the third of five songs Mario performed with this title, was undoubtedly the highlight of his recording career. Much more than a popular song, this is a *symphonie en miniature*, and a song that so many have wanted to take with them to that mythical desert island. Few poets could have come up with lines as poignant as 'Soft in the trees lies the echo of my longing, While all around my dreams of rapture throng.' Add to this Costa's atmospheric orchestrations and the murmuring choir, and what we have is a true masterpiece. Not so 'Beloved', which Mario sang during this session almost an octave above as written – nothing unusual in that, save that this time he injected a little *too* much passion, and in doing so veered slightly off-key. In *Lanza, His Tragic Life*, Terry Robinson recalled the extent of this passion, though of course we only have his word for what happened in the men's room after the session:

> The two men stood by the urinals and Lanza extended his penis and squeezed. There was an excretion of some sort. Terry panicked, 'My God, you didn't get yourself a dose, did you?' Lanza shook his head, 'No, I had an orgasm when I sang. That's what a song can do for me. I put so much into the song that my entire body gives.' He cleaned himself up and said, 'Let's go listen to the playback.'

Mario was in sparkling form two days later when he recorded 'Golden Days', and positively boisterous on 5 August when he cut 'Drink, Drink, Drink', arguably his most popular song in Britain in radio request programmes. Even so, the next day he contacted Dore Schary to say that he would not be returning to the set until Curtis Bernhardt had been replaced. The director, he opined, lacked sensitivity towards good music and should have never been on the picture in the first place. Then, without waiting for a response, Mario hurled himself into yet another period of dissipation. Most of the weight he had lost for *Because You're Mine* had been put back on, and though not as heavy as before – he was still over 200 pounds – he had been instructed to slim down to 170 pounds before shooting began on the new film. Now, even the loyal Terry Robinson was shunted aside as Mario kept the very worst company, hitting the Hollywood bars with questionable friends such as Nick Adams, often spending days away from Betty and the children. He was suffering from the shakes but extremely apologetic when he dropped in at the MGM Studios on 12 August to record 'Deep in my Heart, Dear' with Ann Blyth. Most of the songs for the soundtrack had been put down in a single take – the one the previous week for 'Gaudeamus igitur' had required four takes, and this second duet with Blyth took seven, with Mario still complaining that he had not got it right. Costa convinced him otherwise. Neither was Curtis Bernhardt happy with Mario's rendition of 'Beloved', when he listened to the playback. This, he declared, was too impassioned an interpretation to have come from the lips of a supposedly reserved Prussian prince raised never to show emotion, and therefore Mario would have to record it again. Mario grabbed the sheet music, and indicated the stanza, 'But try though I may, I cannot hide this passion inside that won't be denied – this is madness!' Why, he wanted to know, had Joe Pasternak included such a lyric, only to have his 'lackey' now denounce it as unsuitable?

Mario was quoted as yelling at Bernhardt in front of the whole set, 'How can a great singer take such ridiculous orders?' There then followed such a tirade of abuse that once Mario had all but been dragged out of the studio, the director petitioned Dore Schary – insisting that he would walk off the picture unless Mario underwent psychiatric counselling, or what would today be described as a course in anger management. Even more astonishing is that Mario agreed to this, or at least he humoured Schary by attending a preliminary session at the UCLA Medical Center with Dr Augustus Rose, who had helped established neurotics Judy Garland and Montgomery Clift. Rose, a big Lanza fan, spent most of the allotted hour talking about opera and listening to Mario's grandiose plans for the future, which did not include staying with MGM unless Dore Schary, Joe Pasternak and a whole host of executives suddenly dropped dead, and it was mutually agreed that there would be no more psychiatric counselling. At the end of August, Mario put some distance between himself and the studio by accepting an invitation to stay with his friend, the actor-singer John Carroll and his scriptwriter wife, Lucille, at their ranch at Chatsworth, in the Hollywood hills. Carroll (1906–79) was a former Western star and baritone who had appeared in several *Zorro* movies, but had fallen foul of studio chiefs on account of his own drinking and unsociable behaviour. It was whilst Mario was here, on 4 September, that he received official notification that work on *The Student Prince* had been suspended indefinitely.

By now, the press were taking sides over who to support in the dispute. Jimmy Fiddler, an acid-tongued hack whose dislike of Mario was on account of the tenor's friendship with Hedda Hopper and for no other reason, attacked him in his syndicated column: Mario was dismissed as ungrateful and belligerent because he had recently cancelled a recording session which Fiddler claimed had set the studio back $5,000. What Fiddler omitted from his attack was that Mario had made up for the loss out of his own pocket. Jim Bacon, writing for the Associated Press, set up an interview with Mario which was cancelled when Betty was taken ill with what appears to have been an accidental overdose of sleeping pills. He flatly refused to speak to any other reporters, declaring that this 'nasty business' was between himself and MGM, that it was unfair to foist his problems on the thousands of fans who had loved and supported him over the years. The *Journal American* agreed that Mario's behaviour of late had been irresponsible, but blamed this on his latest weight-loss programme. 'Anyone who has dieted strenuously can understand what a mental and physical ordeal this can be,' the editorial read. 'All of this is enough to get an elephant down. Actors are humans, not machines.' It was Costa, however, who hit the nail on the head when he later wrote, 'It always struck me as rather strange that so little effort was made to save this man from himself. The whole town moved in the name of money, and the victim was a simple, terrified soul named Mario.'

Even so, Mario was given one more chance to 'right the wrongs' he had been accused of inflicting on MGM (in fact, the root of the problem lay not with Mario but with Curtis Bernhardt, whose lack of tact had caused Mario to walk off the picture in the first place). This no longer interested Dore Schary, who was now more concerned with Mario's association with known troublemakers Nick Adams and John Carroll, and the fact that his increasingly lascivious conduct was bringing the studio into disrepute. On 14 September he found himself on the mat in Schary's office as the mogul read out a printed list of his misdeeds: drinking and brawling, potential sex scandals, gross indecency, on-set violence, wilful damage to property. He was told that unless he dragged himself back into line, his next suspension from MGM would be permanent. Mario might just have accepted such criticism, had Schary gone about it politely. He did not: several times he called Mario a 'dirty bum wop', or worse, and accused him of diminishing the pay-packets of those he purported to care about most – the extras, technicians, and other 'little people' – by persistently failing to turn up for work. Mario, like any other man, took exception to such racist slurs and reacted accordingly, storming out of Schary's office and slamming the door behind him. Major stars had been fired for less, but by this stage he was beyond caring.

The next morning, 19 December, Mario was served with a second suspension and two writs for projected breach of contract. The first was for $690,000, the amount Schary calculated had been lost on *The Student Prince* whilst Mario had been on suspension – a suspension which Mario himself had extended by refusing to return to the studio when summoned to do so. The second writ was for a staggering $4.5 million – the amount which MGM's lawyers speculated the studio would lose if the film remained aborted. Unless Mario returned to work at once, both writs would stand. To compound his misery, he also received a tax demand for $210,000.

Two days later, Mario's lawyers drafted a letter which was delivered personally to Ben Thau, 'vice-president of talent' for Loew's Inc (MGM's parent company) and liaison officer between the gods of the hierarchy and its ground-level stars. In it, Mario protested his innocence: he had not breached his contract, but taken a sabbatical because Curtis Bernhardt, a man with no knowledge of music, had criticised his singing. Mario ended the brief missive by declaring that he was ready to return to work – then blew the whole thing by adding a five-inch signature which took up half the page. Dore Schary reacted with equal sarcasm by writing to the Dairy Advertising Agency, who were handling Mario's radio show. Such were the terms of his MGM contract that, until a suitable agreement had been reached between himself and the studio regarding his future with them, Mario would not be permitted to work elsewhere – this included concert appearances and recording for RCA – until his MGM contract expired, fifteen months from now. In his rage Mario turned on Sam Weiler, blaming him for the whole mess because he had re-negotiated the MGM contract and permitted this to be linked to the Coca-Cola deal. Their next meeting, he declared, would be in court.

On the plus side, if indeed there was one, and earning him a pyrrhic victory, MGM agreed to drop their lawsuit in exchange for their right to use anything Mario had recorded between December 1948 and August 1952, not just for *The Student Prince* but for any film they chose. They also coerced him back into the studio on 20 May 1953 to re-record 'Beloved', the song that had sparked off the furore in the first place. Within minutes of his arriving at the studio, word spread like wildfire and every lot closed down when the 'little people' he had loved, and who respected him more than his peers ever would, downed tools to come and say goodbye. He recorded the song in a single take, and walked out of the booth to the cheering of 300 people, many of them weeping. 'I love you all, every last one of you,' he said, the tears streaming down his cheeks.

Mario did what he always did in times of stress – he fell back on his excesses. 'As part of his lamentable game of hide-and-seek,' Costa recalled, 'Mario was drinking and eating again with the same mad compulsion that characterized all his periods of emotional crisis.' Costa remarked that he grew so fat that, even if he had wanted to portray Prince Karl Franz, this would now have been physically impossible. It was the same with sex. By now he did not appear to care who he was sleeping with, or where the woman might have been beforehand. There were turn-and-turn-about sessions with Nicholas Brodsky, whose own excesses were rapidly burning him out. Terry Robinson recalled how he and Mario drove to the MGM lot after dark to clear out Mario's dressing room, and bumped into a tipsy Judy Garland, leaving the studio screening room. Ever the gentleman, Mario insisted on plying her with Chivas Regal and giving her a lift home, only to change his mind and have Robinson drive them up into the Hollywood hills. Here, their chauffeur got out to stretch his legs, but saw a sight for sore eyes upon returning to the car. 'Lanza was on top of Garland, her legs up in the air,' he recalled. 'They were both yelling encouragement at each other.' This anecdote does not appear in any files or archives relating to Judy, however, and it is possible (if the incident happened at all) that Robinson may have confused her with someone else.

It was not long after this alleged incident that Mario became convinced that Robinson was spying on him on behalf of MGM. The two even came to blows, when Robinson walked in on one of the Lanzas' more violent rows and attempted to defend Betty. 'Lanza, half-drunk, grabbed him around the throat in a half-nelson and began to choke him,' his co-biographer Raymond Strait writes in *Lanza, His Tragic Life*. 'They wrestled to the floor...Betty took off her shoe and began hitting Terry on the head, screaming, "Leave Mario alone! You'll hurt him!"' The incident resulted in Robinson thinking that it might be better to give Mario a wide berth for a while – a separation, regarded by some as almost akin to a platonic lovers' tiff (the first of many), which lasted all of three days, during which time they were hardly off the phone to one another.

In the midst of all this the Lanzas moved home, having decided that North Whittier Road was an 'unlucky' house. The move, in December 1952, took place shortly after the birth on 12 December of their son, Damon, so named after Mario's favourite writer, Damon Runyon. The new property was at 500 Bel Air Road, a star-littered neighbourhood which had a regular Hollywood Police patrol to control over-intrusive fans. No sooner had the family settled here than they were served a writ for $17,000 by their former landlord. This was for items damaged during their tenancy, including furniture and garden ornaments, as a result of their increasingly violent rows. This made the press, as did an incident involving a half-sozzled Betty and a young parking lot attendant at a Beverly Hills department store, three days before Christmas. Courtesy of a revenge feature by Louella Parsons to compensate for yet more praise from Hedda Hopper, the fans learned that Betty had spoken to the store manager and demanded that the attendant be fired for rudeness. It later emerged that she had been rude to him – not only this, that she had slapped his face, when all he had tried to do was help her with her shopping. Had this been anyone else, she would have been prosecuted for assault. MGM's police department intervened, as usually happened with such cases: the attendant kept his job, and received a handsome reward from the studio for not taking the matter further.

In the meantime, Mario was compelled to sit it out at the sidelines while *The Student Prince* went into production, with another actor lip-synching to his singing, whether he approved or not. The studio did not even have the decency to tell him the news personally – he read the announcement in *Box Office* magazine. Doubly wounding was the departure of pariah Curtis Bernhardt, owing to other commitments: Schary must have gleaned sardonic pleasure from replacing him with Richard Thorpe, with whom Mario had got along so well while shooting *The Great Caruso*. Now, the part of Prince Karl Franz went to 24-year-old English stage actor Edmund Purdom, who had recently appeared with Marlon Brando in *Julius Caesar* – after this film he would replace Brando in *The Egyptian*.

It is an excellent film. Purdom (1924–2009) is archetypally tall, dark and handsome, and it is a delight to see him develop as the story unfolds from stuffy, humourless aristocrat into a charismatic, totally sympathetic young man. Karl Franz has been raised by his grandfather, the king, and as heir to the Prussian throne is expected to marry Princess Johanna (Betta St John). The pair have been betrothed since childhood, but have only just met. Brought up to excel in military and governmental matters, the prince is severely lacking in people skills, and therefore he is dispatched to Heidelberg University to learn these essential skills. Here, he falls in love with the innkeeper's daughter, Kathie (Ann Blyth), who enters the proceedings in a scene which is today regarded as pure camp: as the 'commoner' students of the Westphalian Corps don their house caps and mince around the refectory, she encourages them with 'Come on Boys, Let's be Gay'. This is the first time Karl Franz has seen anyone having fun, and he drops his royal identity and joins their group. Cue the rowdy, infectious 'Drink, Drink, Drink', which leaves one with little doubt that Mario would have added lusty vigour to the thigh-slapping, though perhaps only in this scene.

Later on, when Karl Franz swears his undying love to Kathie during a moonlight promenade, we are presented with a scenario which is not only totally surreal, it is also sadly ironic – the most romantic scene in all of Mario's films happens in the one where he is conspicuous by his absence. Mario's acting abilities were not a patch on Edmund Purdom's, and he probably would have been the first to admit this, though perhaps understandably he always loathed the man who had replaced him in the film. Similarly, such a tableau between a well-educated royal personage and a serving girl would not have worked without a British crystal-cut accent, which was why the likes of Stewart Granger, Errol Flynn and James Mason excelled in such roles. There was also the fear that Purdom would unconvincingly lip-synch to what may well be Mario's best-ever non-classical song, his own personal *hymne à l'amour*. In fact, it is because of the tempered way Mario performs the piece that it works so well, dropping from Top C to rich baritone, then rising to near falsetto with such ease that, for one magical moment, it is possible to forget that Purdom is not the one singing. Where Mario would almost definitely have failed, certainly with the screenplay as it stood, is in the section after this scene when, his identity rumbled, Karl Franz is compelled to fight a duel with swords. In one's wildest dreams one cannot imagine a swashbuckling Lanza, or see him dancing as frenetically as Purdom does in the subsequent masked ball sequence.

The outcome of the duel and the fact that the prince is unharmed leads to another romantic scene, a misty morning where the lovers sing 'Deep in my Heart, Dear' – Mario dropping a tone, belying his bad state on the day this was recorded, so that his and Blyth's voices blend beautifully. With these two there was never competition to prove who was the better singer, no axe to grind – they were friends and would remain so for the rest of Mario's life. It is inconceivable that any Ruritanian prince will be permitted to marry a foreigner: even so, Karl Franz asks Kathie to elope with him, and her rejection of this allows us to hear the re-recorded 'Beloved', for which Mario very relucantly entered the studio in May 1953. This version (which would have been Mario's third pleading with a lover on her balcony) is much better, much more restrained, and makes one wonder what might have been, had a compromise been effected – if Dore Schary could have brought Richard Thorpe into the production earlier before tempers started flaring. The part of the prince would have been adapted to suit Mario's personality and he might have surprised us, even in the dancing and swashbuckling scenes. Then today we would not be making comparisons – after all, it was not Edmund Purdom's fault that he was offered the role, or that he played it so well. The ending, of course, would still have been the same. By serenading Kathie, Karl Franz gets her to change her mind about running off with him, but before this can happen, he receives word that he must hurry home because his grandfather the king is dying. And when the king dies and he ascends the throne, Karl Franz is back where he started, compelled to marry the princess he does not love, though en route to the wedding – having reflected whilst singing 'Golden Days' – he orders the train to stop off at Heidelberg so that he can say goodbye to the woman he really loves.

Musically, *The Student Prince* is second only to *The Great Caruso*. Because Mario was not in it, however, it did not do great business at the box office: the fans stayed away in droves, silently protesting and waiting for the album. As for Mario, he is reputed to have always refused to see the film or even talk about it.

Chapter Nine

Non Est Vivere
Sed Valere Vita

Many people are still convinced that Lanza is an unstable
character of little-boy moods, a sybarite who indulges himself
in Farouk-like pleasures, or a bellowing bull who sweeps
everything before him. Actually he is a kind, hyper-sensitive,
super-generous artiste with a great love of people and an
abiding sense of humility.

Jim Newton, journalist

The dispute with MGM raged on behind the scenes until 10
April 1953, when the studio 'finally and irrevocably' terminated
Mario's contract. Now, he was completely free to do as he
pleased. The world was his oyster: concert work, opera, recordings,
signing with any one of half a dozen studios who wanted him. And yet
he turned down every offer that came his way. He, the loquacious
extrovert who had seemingly feared nothing and no one, withdrew into
his shell and became a near-total recluse: shabby, unkempt, depressed.
Occasionally he emerged from his drink and barbiturate-induced stupor
to receive friends such as the boxer Rocky Marciano and Hedda Hopper,
and there was a half-hearted reunion with George London. His weight
ballooned to almost record proporions – 290 pounds – whilst he drank
and gorged himself senseless. Betty, far from attempting to support him,
was herself out of it most of the time. Worse still from a singer's point of
view, he was smoking two packs of Camel cigarettes a day as if

deliberately wanting to destroy the magnificent voice which had brought him acclaim. 'He had become a forgotten man years before his time, years before his career might have been expected to reach its peak,' Costa wrote, adding how Mario would flare up over the least little thing.

According to Terry Robinson, though it has to be said that he was frequently prone to exaggeration when recalling the more dramatic events in his friend's life, Mario developed suicidal tendencies, particularly when he was behind the wheel. One incident is supposed to have taken place on a narrow road between Beverly Hills and the San Fernando Valley. 'Think of this,' Mario is claimed to have said as they hurtled along at 90 miles an hour. 'If I drive off this mountain, you and I would die in a burst of flames and every damn newspaper in the world would headline, "Mario Lanza and best friend die in a flaming wreck." What an end for a tiger and a terror!'

Then there were other 'prima donna' moments, real or invented. A former maid with the Lanza household, who said she had been fired by Betty for no particular reason, told of how the cook had taken Mario's lunch into his room – a huge tray containing six plates which he had proceeded to skim off the balcony into the living room below because the cook had not added enough pepper to the sauce. Another report described how, to annoy the neighbours, he had set up a speaker system on an outer wall of the house so that he could let off several of those legendary top Cs – not so welcome at three in the morning.

Only one journalist was permitted to see him at this time: Ben Maddox. A hugely influential freelancer guaranteed to offer stars maximum coverage and, if they were on their way up or down, enhance their careers, Maddox had in his younger days used sex as a means of acquiring his scoops. His trick had been to interview his subjects, both female and male, over lunch or dinner – always at their homes where there was less chance of his coming unstuck – and, once they had fallen for his seemingly limitless charms, offer himself for dessert. As a cub reporter his earliest conquest had been Rudolph Valentino; other lovers had included Jean Harlow, Robert Taylor and the indescribably gung-ho Clark Gable. Maddox was 52 now, but still sexually active. Maybe, to his way of thinking, seducing the flagrantly heterosexual Lanza would have added an impressive notch to the score on his belt. It would never happen, of course. Sharing a bottle of his favourite Chivas Regal with

Maddox, Mario was optimistic about the future. 'For the first time, I'm experiencing the thrill of being able to do what I've dreamed of. Each morning I wake up quickly, eagerly,' he said. He was, he added, planning a concert tour for the end of the year, but with an opera-only repertoire, and something which would be an annual event. 'It's a medium of expression that is a total contrast to much of the stuff I'm doing now,' he told Maddox. 'But it's the one I began in, and I want to make a three-month tour part of my regular pattern.'

For a few more weeks, Mario kept up this enthusiasm. On 17 June he entered the Republic Studios and cut six songs for RCA: four for a planned album, and two for a single which the company planned releasing at the end of the summer. For once he agreed with their choice for this: Rimsky-Korsakov's haunting 'Song of India', which he put down in a single take. The magic appeared to have returned. This is an inspirational work, and in the arrangement by Costa it is the perfect companion piece for 'Serenade', lots of lush strings and beautiful, unstraining, harmonising backing voices. Notable previous interpretations of the work had come from artistes as diverse as Rosa Ponselle, and the Tommy Dorsey Orchestra. Mario effortlessly sweeps these away, and makes it impossible for anyone to tackle the piece without inevitable comparison and therefore harsh criticism. The new words were supplied by Johnny Mercer, who had recently adapted 'Les feuilles mortes' into 'Autumn Leaves' for Edith Piaf – one of the songs Mario planned to record during a subsequent session which was cancelled. 'Song of India' is perhaps the most prosaic non-classical song he ever performed, an ingenious juxtaposition of the then mysterious Third World and the one he knew, where:

> The turbaned Sikhs and fakirs line the streets,
> While holy men in shadowed calm retreats
> Pray through the night and watch the stars.
> A lonely plane flies off to meet the dawn,
> While down below the busy life goes on,
> And women crowd the old bazaars.

Backing this was Costa's composition, 'You Are My Love', with lyrics by Paul Francis Webster. He had offered this to Mario two years earlier but he had turned it down; therefore Costa, in his capacity as recently appointed musical director of the Highland Park Symphony Orchestra, had given it to a young soprano named Marcella Reale, who had performed it with him on the tour circuit. Now, Mario asked for it back – and paid his friend $2,000 for the privilege. Having expended what little energy he had left on 'Song of India', this one required several takes to get it right, as did 'If You Were Mine' and 'Call Me Fool', subsequent minor hits for Mario but poor by comparison to the Rimsky-Korsakov piece.

Mario's neurasthenia returned the moment he left the recording studio. This time there were genuine offers from some of the country's top opera houses, including San Francisco and Chicago, and Mario could have had his pick, but he wanted only the New York Met. However, Rudolf Bing did not want him. Offers came in from Las Vegas, one proposing $35,000 for six one-hour concerts. 'Opera and Vegas don't mix,' he told Rex Cole, the agent who stepped into the breach until he had settled the dispute with Sam Weiler, or found himself another manager. On 25 August, this dispute was brought one step towards closure when Weiler and his wife, Selma, were arraigned for fraud at the Santa Monica Superior Court. Mario's lawyers had done their research and discovered that Weiler had ploughed his client's and his own money into several bad investments – but whereas Mario had lost out, Weiler had recovered his own losses from Mario's bank account. Similarly, at times he had deducted his commission twice and even three times, or simply kept the 10 per cent he should have handed over to MCA as part of the company's part-takeover deal. It was estimated that he had fleeced Mario for over $300,000. Weiler was forced to cough up, but this enforced only a pyrrhic victory for Mario when Weiler counter-sued for $58,000 for what he claimed as 'past unpaid commissions' – the money he had used to bail Mario and Betty out of their many financial difficulties, mostly out of the goodness of his heart without ever expecting to be repaid. The court sided with him, awarding him 5 per cent of Mario's current and future earnings for life – which would amount to considerably more than the $300,000 Mario had won back from him.

Mario's first annus horribilis ended on 28 December. Outside of the music room in his Beverly Hills home he had not sung one note since the summer recording session, and his income had been restricted to revenue from record sales. Now, he and Costa entered the Warner Brothers Studios for what should have been the first of three sessions to cut the soundtrack for *The Student Prince* – further sessions had been booked for 30 December and 2 January. Mario was not just in poor shape, he had been drinking heavily and his heart was not in it because Ann Blyth's exclusive contract with MGM prevented her from recording with RCA. Therefore he was given another leading lady, someone he did not particularly like. Gale Sherwood was currently the singing partner of Nelson Eddy, who was no longer a major attraction in movies, with his glory days behind him, but still a sizeable pull on the nightclub circuit. Sherwood duetted with Mario on 'Summertime in Heidelberg' and recorded one solo, 'Come on Boys, Let's be Gay'. Both were cut in a single take, but when it came to 'I'll Walk with God', Mario encountered a problem in reaching his top notes. He recorded the number four times, accepted that two of the takes were 'about average', then decided to try again the next session. This proved a disaster. When he had to keep stopping the orchestra on account of 'phlegm agitation', Costa, calling the shots, stopped the session and the third one was cancelled.

A few days into the new year, and tired of being pestered by reporters wanting the latest on the feud with MGM, the Lanzas left Hollywood for Palm Springs, where they rented a $300-a-week bungalow at what was supposed to be a secret location. Terry Robinson tagged along, naturally, and Costa was asked to put himself on 'standby' just in case Mario needed him. No sooner had they settled in than Mario began suffering dizzy spells. A local doctor diagnosed high blood pressure and slight diabetes – and gout, a malady not usually affecting one so young, exacerbated in Mario's case by his weight. The doctor prescribed complete rest, but the leeches managed to get to him with all the barbiturates he needed to get him back on track, and he was soon up and raring to go.

In the two months that he was in Palm Springs, Mario ran up a $3,000 telephone bill, calling sick fans and singing to them down the line – his way, he said, of keeping his tonsils oiled. If the couple left the house it was in the early hours of the morning, when they would drive around the deserted streets of the town. Once, when Mario hit on the idea of entering a bar, they were shown to a table in what was promised to be a quiet corner. Within five minutes, the place was invaded by Lanza fans demanding the usual impromptu recital. Mario obliged, but it would be the first and last time during this particular sojourn.

In February 1954, the Lanzas returned to Bel Air, where Manny Sachs of RCA made a last desperate bid to get Mario back into the studio. Each time he called, Mario put the phone down on him. Sachs realised that drastic measures would have to be taken if the album was to be released ahead of the June premiere. Therefore an uneasy compromise was reached with MGM to release the actual songs that Mario had recorded for the soundtrack, rather than force him to record them again for RCA. This hit a snag when Sachs decided that he did not want the duets with Ann Blyth because he did not consider her suitably polished for his primarily classical Red Label. Sachs contacted Gale Sherwood and asked her if she would record 'Deep in My Heart, Dear' separately, so that her sections could be dubbed over Blyth's voice. Not surprisingly she refused. As a last measure, Sachs hired soprano Elizabeth Doubleday to record this song and 'Summertime in Heidelberg' – Sherwood's voice was removed from the duet she had recorded with Mario and replaced with Doubleday's, bringing a tirade of abuse from Mario. Today, of course, overdubbing is commonplace when we have current stars 'duetting' with long-dead ones – a profoundly unprofessional practice unheard of in 1953. Sachs was told by an irate Mario that he would never set foot in the RCA studios again, and for over a year he was good to his word. And just as he never saw the film, so he is believed never to have played the album, which became the first American soundtrack album to sell over a million copies.

Claiming he was tired of Mario's tantrums, his drinking, and above all his lethargy and time wasting, Costa headed for New York, vowing that he would never work with him again. There followed several lengthy, impassioned and tearful telephone calls from Mario, begging him to return to the ever-decreasing fold as more and more friends deserted him. His behavioural pattern was akin to that of the serial wife-basher: the insults and violence – though in his case this would be restricted to whatever ornaments or items were close at hand when he lost his cool – followed by the sobbing and pleading, often on his knees, for absolution. 'After each disagreement and tempest, his warmth towards me increased,' Costa observed. 'Invariably it was a repentant Mario who begged me to understand and come back. And it was always a drinking orgy that would set him off again on the same bleak, hopeless trail to nowhere.'

At around this time, Hedda Hopper reported an incident at the Players restaurant on Sunset Strip, then owned by the actor Preston Sturges, a man no less abrasive than Mario when rubbed up the wrong way. Hedda wrote how Mario turned up at the place fifteen minutes before the 2am curfew, drunk and demanding drinks after hours. With Sturges this never presented a problem – he would simply lock the doors, dim the lights, and booze with his friends until dawn. Two of these friends were the local state liquor inspectors, off duty but still wearing their uniforms. The mistake they made, so far as Mario was concerned, was in pretending that they were still on duty, and bawling that everyone was under arrest. Mario lurched to his feet, grabbed one of the officers, and smashed his fist into his face, knocking out seven teeth. He slammed the second officer against the wall, knocking him out. Sturges called an ambulance, whilst Mario fled. Incredibly, no charges were laid against him – or if they were, they were expediently dealt with by MGM's chief-of-police, as had happened so many times in the past to prevent the matter getting into the newspapers. Obviously, he had not reckoned on Hedda Hopper's spies being everywhere. Out of his own pocket, Mario paid the first injured officer $4,000 to cover his dentist's bill, and instructed his tailor to kit out both men with $200 cashmere suits.

By March, there was a faint glimmer of light at the end of the tunnel when Mario received another tax demand for $150,000 and Costa, in what appears to have been a last attempt to prevent his friend from destroying himself completely, suggested what could have been a groundbreaking project which might bring in enough money to pay off not just the tax demand, but also his other outstanding debts. Maria Callas had single-handedly revived the long forgotten bel canto repertoire by unearthing operas that had not been performed for over 50 years; now Costa persuaded Mario to at least think of doing the same. Scouring archives and opera house vaults, he unearthed 35 tenor arias, all from (then) obscure works. Amongst those which Mario taped in his music room, but which seem to have disappeared, were 'O mio piccolo tavolo' from Leoncavallo's *Zaza*, 'Storia ho di sangue' from Cilea's *Gloria*, and 'Apri la tua finestra' from Mascagni's *Iris* – Caruso had recorded this one. It was Costa's idea to have Mario rehearse these, but perform them on the stage before recording them as hopefully the first step towards that elusive operatic career. Maybe Costa was kidding himself that Mario, never less than paranoid when it came to learning new material, would succeed with such a taxing project. If so, he was to be disappointed. For once there was no pressure on Mario to lose weight – he still weighed 290 pounds – and he tackled his new repertoire religiously, working with Costa two hours every morning for two months. Then he woke up one morning, in a bad mood and suffering from a hangover, and announced that he was no longer interested. The tax demand would have to wait.

For once it was Betty – seven months pregnant with her fourth child, and in a rare moment of sobriety – who inadvertently came up with a solution to the Lanzas' rapidly increasing financial problems. For several years she had been buying her furs from Al Teitelbaum, self-styled 'furrier to the stars' whose clients at that time included Zsa Zsa Gabor and Marlene Dietrich. Teitelbaum, a shrewd businessman, operated from a plush store on North Rodeo Drive; he had recently clothed Joan Crawford in *Sudden Fear*, and was currently employed on television's *The Loretta Young Show*. Betty's initial idea was for Teitelbaum to buy back some of her furs. Cynics have suggested that she was terrified that, if Mario was suddenly declared bankrupt, she would have no money for her essential whisky and pills. Teitelbaum, who had known the Lanzas since 1948, agreed to help, but only on his terms. Mario, he declared was sick, physically and mentally, and needed urgent treatment unless he wanted to suddenly drop down dead. He therefore took him to see his own doctor, Clarence Agress, picked up the tab, and persuaded Mario to take Agress's advice: immediate hospitalisation at the Cedars of Lebanon Hospital, where surgery would be conducted to control his weight, the 1950s equivalent of fitting a gastric belt or, if they deemed more stringent measures necessary, intestinal stapling. The thought of this filled Mario with horror – eating for him was a pleasure which was equalled only by singing and sex. Agress therefore suggested psycho-therapy, and in the middle of April, registering as Alfredo Cocozza, Mario entered the Las Encinas Sanitarium, ostensibly for respite treatment and to dry out. Not that this did him much good, for in return for the odd impromptu recital the nurses obeyed his every command, sneaking alcohol into his room or keeping him company at night. Again, Teitelbaum picked up the tab, besides loaning Mario $60,000 towards his outstanding debts, though he did have an ulterior motive for this unexpected transformation into Lanza's Good Samaritan. Seizing a moment of weakness, he offered to be his manager. Regardless of Teitelbaum's complete lack of experience in such matters, Mario took him on and the contract was signed on 1 May, but with certain curious concessions, which Mario agreed to. Teitelbaum would be working alongside two lawyers – one handling Mario's personal affairs, the other his inland revenue claims. There would also be a business administrator who would ensure that the other members of the Lanza team were doing their jobs efficiently.

The downside of the arrangement with Teitelbaum, which no entertainer today would accept, was that contractually the new management team was not obliged to find Mario any actual work – a clause he casually brushed aside, declaring that such was his fame, engagements would find him. To a certain extent this was true: the concert organisers and fans as yet knew nothing about his failing voice, which in any case would soon be restored to its former glory. On a perpetual commission of 10 per cent (which would remain legal after both their deaths), Teitelbaum kickstarted Mario's 'comeback' by hiring celebrity lawyer Greg Bautzer, himself a controversial character. Like Ben Maddox, Bautzer (1911–87) mostly chose clients he wanted to have sex with: he had represented Joan Crawford (he was Uncle Greg in *Mommie Dearest*), Ava Gardner, Ginger Rogers and Lana Turner, to name but a few, and had had affairs with all of them. Dealing with Lanza, he declared, would be different only in that no sex would be involved – like Joan Crawford, Lana Turner and the rest, Lanza was just another temperamental hothead with money to splash around.

The deal with Bautzer meant that he too would receive a perpetual 5 per cent of Mario's income – the same as Myrt Blum, Jack Benny's brother-in-law, who would act as Mario's business administrator. Completing the team was J. Everett, on a 2½ per cent perpetual percentage. In all, with Sam Weiler still pocketing 10 per cent of Mario's income following the court case, from now on Mario would be forking out over one-third of his earnings after tax. The worst part of the deal, however, which proved that Mario was too trusting of these people when it came to business matters (or just plain stupid), was allowing the word 'perpetual' to be applied to the contract in the first place. Effectively, if Mario fired any of them, they would still be entitled to their commission.

More madness followed when Mario's RCA contract came up for renewal: he rejected a deal which would have guaranteed him a minimum $1 million for 100 recordings, to be cut at his leisure. Other artistes were being offered better deals, he complained, including Dinah Shore – and he was ten times better than all of them! RCA terminated his contract at once, though they were legally entitled to release any material remaining in their vaults – the 151 items which Mario had recorded for the Coca-Cola shows. These would subsequently be released on the company's Black Label – the royalty payment for each item would be less, but as this was an economy label RCA expected them to sell more copies, and therefore bring in the same revenue. It was a wily move. Many of these items were superior to the material Mario had recorded for the parent label, which was saying something. Two albums of these songs were released over the coming year: A Kiss and Other Love Songs, and Magic Mario.

On 14 May, Betty gave birth to the Lanzas' fourth child and second son, whom they baptised Marc. It had been a difficult pregnancy, largely on account of Betty's drinking and drug dependency. Twice she had been rushed into hospital – the first time when she had begun spotting, the second when she had suffered convulsions and almost gone into premature labour. The birth coincided with the press showing of The Student Prince, giving Mario an official excuse to extend his apologies for not attending – though by now he was so overweight and in such poor shape that he did not wish to be seen in public. The reviews were generally bad, for no other reason that the critics did not want to see somebody else lip-synching to Lanza's voice. This prompted Al Teitelbaum into contacting MGM and asking if they were interested in negotiating a deal which would see Mario facing the cameras again by the end of the year. Dore Schary hung up on him, and the response was pretty much the same from Warner Brothers and Twentieth Century-Fox. One man who showed tremendous initial interest was the reclusive tycoon, Howard Hughes, who arranged a bizarre middle-of-the-night meeting with Mario in the back of a photographer's studio on Melrose Avenue. Director George Stevens had recently announced that he would soon be filming the epic, Giant, in Marfa, Texas, close to where Mario had been based during his stint with the army. Elizabeth Taylor, Rock Hudson and James Dean had been cast in the lead roles, and

Hughes was planning something along the same lines, but with music. Mario spent two hours with Hughes, and left the building with the promise that Hughes would contact him within the next few weeks to discuss the project further. He never did.

One man who showed some interest at this time was the director-scriptwriter Leo McCarey, who wanted Mario to appear in his own adapation of Donn Byrne's biographical novel of Marco Polo. The score was to have been written by Harry Warren, but there was just one snag – Mario did not want to play the part. Soon after rejecting it he was contacted by Paramount, then planning a remake of *The Vagabond King*, Rudolf Friml's colourful musical set in 15th-century France. Kathryn Grayson had already been cast and she (and Rita Moreno) even put in a good word for him, not because she wanted to work with him again – quite the opposite – but because the previous Lanza–Grayson vehicles had brought in the plaudits. The director was Michael Curtiz, and one shudders to think of the fireworks there would have been between him and Mario had the project come about.

Hungarian-born Curtiz (1888–1962) was one of the most respected – and feared – directors in Hollywood. Many of his films were timeless classics: *The Adventures Of Robin Hood* with Errol Flynn, *Casablanca* with Humphrey Bogart and Ingrid Bergman, *Yankee Doodle Dandy* with James Cagney, and *Mildred Pierce* with Joan Crawford – all involving tetchy stars who needed firm directorial control, but who had only brought out the worst of Curtiz's volatile temperament. Despite his many years in America, Curtiz had failed or refused to master the English language, other than its profanities. His most famous gaff, as repeated by David Niven (*Bring On The Empty Horses*) had occurred during an argument with Errol Flynn, when Flynn had called him a 'thick as pig-shit bowl of goulash' – bringing the response, 'You lousy faggot bum, you think I know fuck nothing. Well, let me tell you something – I know fuck *all*!' Curtiz was looking forward to sorting out 'that fake-Italian, fat-assed crooner bum', and there is little doubt that he might have succeeded where others had failed.

Mario read the script. He would play the poet François Villon, the leader of the Vagabonds, a French Robin Hood who robbed the rich to give to the poor and supported the Duke of Burgundy in his attempts to overthrow the unpopular Spider King, Louis XI, only to pay for his treason with his life. Curtiz then threw a massive spanner into the works by informing Teitelbaum that if Lanza wanted to be tested for the part, then in view of his recent stay in a 'loony bin' he would first have to undergo a psychiatric assessment to prove that he was mentally fit to take on such a project; and also, he would have to take a voice test to assure Curtiz and the Paramount executives that he could still sing. Needless to say, Paramount were told what to do with their offer. The role of Villon was assigned to the Maltese tenor Oreste Kirkop, for what would be his only and not so memorable film appearance.

Mario denounced *The Vagabond King* as a huge con – yet the biggest con of all, according to the critics and perpetrated by himself, was waiting just around the corner. In August 1954, Al Teitelbaum was approached by L.L. Colbert, the chairman of Chrysler Motors, who were sponsoring *The Shower Of Stars*, a new light entertainment show for CBS. Until now, Mario had refused to have anything to do with what Rock Hudson had publicly denounced as 'that fucking oblong box in the corner of the living room'. Mario, like many of the top stars, quite rightly believed that television was robbing cinemas and theatres of their business, but he also thought that it was a 'new-fangled' concept which would never take off. Cynics had said the same, of course, when talkies had begun taking over from the silent films. The previous year he had told Ben Maddox, 'My answer to television offers is no, thank you. When I cannot present what I do in a theatre or on a wide screen, then I'll be ready to take that step. I won't settle for less, meanwhile, not for any amount of money.' By 1954, however, one in three American households owned a television set, and for Mario this particular offer was far too lucrative to turn down: $40,000 and two brand new Chrysler cars, all in exchange for three songs of his choosing. This was a massive amount: even top-liners like Piaf, Sinatra and Crosby could not command such fees for full recitals in those days. The first show was scheduled to air live on 30 September, and would be Mario's first public performance in over two years.

It was only after Mario had signed the contract that he was contacted by the IRS: unless he wished to be arrested for non-payment of taxes, his fee for the show would go straight into their coffers – not only this, he would be expected to sell both cars and hand this money over too. Mario managed to pull a fast one by declaring that he had already given one of the cars to Betty. Angry at the idea that he would be working for nothing, he was about to renege on the deal when he read what some of his detractors were saying, and panic set in. Louella Parsons opined that millions of people would tune in to the show, regardless of the fact that it would be up against the phenomenally successful *Dragnet* series, just to see if Lanza could still hold it together. Some of these hatchet-job articles featured photographs which had been doctored to make Mario look pasty and ill, and much older than 33. Additionally, they made much of his weight, currently at 230 pounds. In the past he had been given adequate time to slim down for a role, and with the exception of some scenes from *Because You're Mine* he had never been seen looking fat in public. However, would he wish to endure one of Terry Robinson's gruelling training schedules for a 15-minute appearance on a television show which the public would only see once?

In fact, Mario made too much of an effort and for a month virtually starved himself – some days he was reported to have eaten no more than a grapefruit and one boiled egg – and in the process became more irritable than ever. For the second time, even the ultra-patient Terry Robinson threatened to leave him, until Mario pleaded with him to stay. Until the show, unable to cope with Betty's moods, which in truth were no worse than his own, he slept in the music room whilst Robinson took the couch. The panic attacks became more frequent. Mario, who had previously only been afraid of forgetting new material, suddenly became convinced that his voice would pack in the moment he stepped in front of a camera – yet on the other hand he needed to prove to his detractors that he was still the Great Lanza. Once again he checked into the Las Encinas Sanitarium, with one gossip columnist writing that he looked so ill, no one would be surprised if he 'didn't go the same way as W.C. Fields'. The great star, who had hated children and Christmas, had died here on Christmas Day 1946 whilst children had played outside his bungalow.

This time around, the treatment was much more severe. Doctors at the clinic prescribed Antabuse, a drug which resulted in projectile vomiting and severe migraines if the patient ingested alcohol after taking it. The nurses were instructed to stand by his bed to ensure that he swallowed it. After his discharge from the clinic, Betty was given the task of making sure her husband stuck to his medication, which of course did not happen.

Much has been made of Mario's television debut, and the fact that he put in what critics called a non-performance. Absolutely no one criticised Betty Grable, whose contribution to the show is in parts lamentable. In England, 'Softly, Softly' singing star Ruby Murray, struck by laryngitis, had caused a storm by miming to her recordings during a televised concert at the London Palladium. Mario, despite emerging from Las Encinas 'beaming with confidence', elected to do the same despite the fact that his voice was in sparkling form. Even so, his innate charisma shines through. Though advertised as live, it was not. All the segments were pre-recorded, and canned laughter and applause added afterwards. The show opens well enough: a song and dance routine extolling the best and worst of Hollywood. Then comes a too-daft-to-laugh-at sketch, headed by Fred Clark. This nonsense runs into Mario singing 'Vesti la giubba' in what resembles a disused warehouse: the fake applause starts before he reaches his final note, which is cut off. Next we have Betty Grable, famed for her legs – though by this stage of her career she had become knock-kneed – whose mimed interpretation of 'Digga-Digga-Doo' only adds to the horror. Later she will fare better, legs covered, in another routine with bandleader husband Harry James, before Mario again steals the show with 'Marechiare'. Again, the applause cuts him off. Then after Grable's final selection, an excellent take on Frank Sinatra's 'One for my Baby', Mario closes with 'Be My Love'. The producers had not budgeted for a chorus, so they used the recording from Mario's radio show of 10 June 1951. The whole thing ended farcically, with host William Lundigan giving one last plug for Chrysler cars – and for the next week's drama programme, *Climax*. This tickled Mario, though he was not so pleased to learn that the producers had billed Betty Grable above him in the credits. This had not been part of the deal!

Mario's dilemma began immediately after the show's airing, during a reception at the Beverly Hills Hotel, when gossip columnist Jim Bacon asked him in front of the distinguished gathering why he had mimed to recordings he had made several years earlier. Today, of course, lip-synching becomes almost essential when some mediocre artistes are incapable of projecting their voices without the studio trickery which has been added to their recordings, but in 1954 it was unheard of. Mario admitted that he had 'cheated', gave no excuse as to why and added that, along with Betty Grable, he had made the recordings two days earlier.

Mario's supporters have suggested that, in order to know exactly when Mario had made these recordings, Bacon must have been tipped off by an insider. This may have been so. Equally, he had several days to see the rushes before the show was aired, and in any case the clear give-away came from the end credits: whilst these announced that 'Vesti la giubba' and 'Marechiare' were conducted by Costa, there is no mention of who conducted 'Be My Love'.

It mattered little that Betty Grable had also mimed – these hypocritical columnists, allies of Louella Parsons, had had an axe to grind for some time, and from their point of view there was no excuse for what Mario had done. Those critics who had watched the show and heaped the plaudits on his shoulders now changed their tune and went for the jugular, particularly after Bacon reported how Mario had rounded on him with, 'My voice is greater than ever!' Leading the assault was Sheilah Graham, who headed her piece, 'Mario Collects 49 Gs Pay Without a Song'. What made matters infinitely worse was that, rather than coming from Mario, a statement was issued on behalf of CBS declaring that Mario had mimed because he had been suffering from laryngitis. This had not prevented him from belting out a few of those top Cs at the reception.

Mario decided to put matters right himself. He had Al Teitelbaum draw up a list of those columnists who had insulted him – Jim Bacon, Sheilah Graham, Louella Parsons, the *New York Times*'s Jack Gould, who had denounced his performance as 'Zombie television', and 37 others – and on 4 October they were invited to a recital in the music room of his home. Accompanied by Giacomo Spadoni, he gave a 20-minute recital of such brilliance that every one of them was singing his praises the next time they applied pen to paper. Within days, CBS Television announced that Mario would be making his second appearance on *The Shower Of Stars* on 28 October. The fee was the same: $40,000, which this time he kept, and two Chrysler cars, which he sold.

Accompanied by Spadoni, who congratulates him after his brief performance, Mario insisted that everything be live this time – and no canned applause. The sketches and everything else in the show are no less tacky than before. Announced again by William Lundigan, Mario is still psyching himself up as the orchestra strikes up the introduction to 'E lucevan le stelle'. The embellishments may be slightly over the top, as are the hand movements, but the voice and timbre are faultless as he ends the piece almost in tears. Then, he announces that his next song is the one his fans have written in and requested since his first Chrysler show – not specifically true, but who cares? Mario's 'Someday' from the aborted *Vagabond King* is quite possibly the best version of this that has ever been sung – he puts his last ounce of strength into it, and makes us lament all the more that he never made the film.

Afterwards, Mario was approached by Chrysler's L.L. Colbert and asked if he would appear in a Christmas special of the show. He consented, upped his fee to $50,000 – there were no cars this time – and insisted on being paid up-front. Chrysler paid him the money, but he backed out at the last minute and even dared the company to sue him, in the light of the recent suffering they had caused him. They never did, and with the exception of a brief, previously filmed interview some years later on *The Ed Sullivan Show*, Mario would never appear on American television again.

Chapter Ten

'Call Me...Unreliable!'

Lanza is the greatest musical talent of America in our century –
a man who is bringing great music to the kids, the farms,
the ghettos and the palaces.

Lawrence Tibbett, baritone

The year 1955 started off well enough, convincing Mario that he had finally awakened from the nightmare of the last two years. Warner Brothers announced that they had been holding discussions with Mario for some months, and that it had been mutually agreed that his comeback film would be *Serenade*, based on the 1937 novel by James M. Cain. Mario had been interested in the project for some time, it is true, but he had only been informed that he would be doing the film – one of several he had been pencilled in for, including the aforementioned *Marco Polo* – a few days before Christmas. The press now reported he had signed a one-movie deal with Jack Warner – the man who had declared him 'too fat for movies' at the time of *Winged Victory* – for $150,000, plus a whopping 35 per cent of the profits. At the same time, Al Teitelbaum calmed the waters with RCA and renegotiated a three-year recording contract.

Mario's army friend, actor Edmund O'Brien, is accredited with convincing Mario that he would be the perfect choice for the role of tenor John Sharpe, which is rather odd. Cain (1892–1977), one of the creators of the *roman noir*, was famed for creating characters in his books who had social or psychological problems, and who more often than not came from the wrong side of the tracks. Amongst his successful transitions to the screen were *The Postman Always Rings Twice*, *Double Indemnity* and, perhaps most famously, *Mildred Pierce*. In the original story, Sharpe loses his voice, heads for Mexico, and hooks up with Juana, a local prostitute. Later they return to Los Angeles where they open their own bordello. What made the story even more controversial was the fact that Sharpe falls in love with his impresario, and spends much of his time trying to come to terms with his homosexuality. Was O'Brien therefore thinking of Sam Weiler, and of his obvious but unrequited attraction towards Mario when they had first met? All that we know is that the gay-friendly Mario would have been content to leave the story as it stood, and damn the critics. A few years on, cautiously crafted gay subplots would work well in the cinema: notable examples were Tennessee Williams's *Cat On A Hot Tin Roof* and *Suddenly Last Summer*. Jack Warner, however, decided that the world was not yet ready to accept 'Lanza playing a fag', and the story was given to Ivan Goff and Ben Roberts, who were asked to normalise Sharpe – in other words, to rob the scenario of its essential theme. The name was then changed, upon Mario's request, to Damon Vincenti. The Damon was in honour of his eldest son, the Vincenti after his actor-singer friend, Vince Edwards (Vincenti Zoino, 1928–96), who he insisted should have a part in the film. Like Terry Robinson, Edwards, the son of Italian immigrants, was an avid bodybuilder and fitness enthusiast, a former swimming champion who had turned to acting when an appendectomy had ended his career. Though he was believed to have been gay and, like Robinson, to have had something of an unreciprocated crush on Mario, Edwards would marry four times – the first marriage lasting just a few months. During the sixties he would become a heart-throb as surgeon Ben Casey in the popular television series of the same name.

In the meantime, with time on his hands and Warner Brothers advancing him $1,000 a week against his salary, Mario decided that he no longer liked living in Beverly Hills, and he and the family upped sticks and moved to another rented property at 481 Merito Street, in Palm Springs. As before, the landlord served them with a writ for damages they had caused during their ceaseless arguments – this time for $40,000, excessive even by their standards. The new house had been built for cowboy star Rex Bell, who had lived there with his wife Clara Bow. The place would tide them over, Mario declared, until he got back on his feet and was able to buy a home of his own. No sooner had the Lanzas moved in than Betty was admitted to Las Encinas, for rehab treatment against chloral hydrate addiction. She managed to kick the habit, but within weeks of returning to Palm Springs had become hooked on Butisol, and had to be readmitted. Her indisposition allowed Mario two weeks' respite from the fights and her nagging – and to have prostitutes brought to the house, once the children had been put to bed. Some things never changed.

From his new abode, Mario threw himself into yet another Terry Robinson fitness programme to get in shape for the new film – this time he would drop down to a comfortable 180 pounds, though not without almost driving himself into the ground for this and his more imminent project, a two-week stint on stage in Las Vegas. In the past, Mario had severely criticised everyone from Frank Sinatra to Marlene Dietrich for their 'greed' in wanting to play the gambling capital of the world, when the real stars there were the gaming tables and slot machines. The record-breaking $100,000 fee for 20 two-per-evening 50-minute concerts at the New Frontier Hotel enabled him to revise his opinion: 80 per cent of this would go to his management team and towards paying off his tax debts, but at last he would be solvent. The shows, he said, would contain more show tunes than operatic arias, but there would be some new material. Ray Sinatra would be conducting, and each show would contain a classical segment with just Costa at the piano. The opening night was fixed for 4 April, but such was Mario's reputation that bookmakers in the city were soon offering odds against him actually turning up for this.

The Lanzas and their 15-strong entourage had been scheduled to arrive in Las Vegas on 2 April, but arrived two days early hoping to avoid the press. A tip-off ensured that they were greeted at the railway station by a barrage of 500 reporters. Their pertinent questions and the chilly weather – Palm Springs had been sweltering in over 100 degrees – put Mario in a surly mood. Why had he mimed on television? Was he going to do so on stage in Las Vegas? Was he still having marital problems, and what had been the real reason for Mrs Lanza's admission to a sanitarium? And were the reports true that he was suffering from high blood pressure and an acute, potentially life-threatening type of diabetes? He became further agitated upon reaching the New Frontier. The Lanzas' early arrival meant that the suites they had reserved were still occupied, and so Mario, Betty and the children would have to share a room – putting a damper on the fun he had anticipated, having a suite to himself. The rest of the entourage –

the Sinatras, Costa and his wife, the Teitelbaums, Mario's hairdresser and the children's nurses – had been given rooms on another floor, which meant that for much of the time Betty, in whatever state she found herself in, would have to cope with the children on her own.

For three days and nights, Mario stayed in his room. CBS had joined forces with the hotel management and mounted a personal vendetta against him, he declared, forcing him to 'slum it' with the other guests. And all because he had mimed on account of his 'red-throat'. Now, he had Terry Robinson inform the press that he was inflicted with the condition again, and that his doctor had yet to decide whether he would be fit to sing. Journalists, who were hanging around in the corridor outside the room listening to Mario and Betty going berserk and throwing things at each other, totting up over $500 in damages, reported differently. Costa recalled, 'He swung at his terrified wife, seized any object within reach of his hands, kicked over the furniture, ripped at the bedspreads, smashed the bulbs.' Costa also remembered how Mario contacted 'a friend' who knew exactly what he needed to obtain quick relief from his anguish: 'He got it, he let Mario have it, and it wasn't liquor.'

Ray Sinatra called Mario constantly, but he flatly refused to attend rehearsals, claiming that if he did not know his repertoire by now he never would. Neither would he inspect the vast Venus Room, with its revolving stage and rocket-ship decor. If he saw this beforehand, he said, he would worry unduly about his performance. This was no great problem: like Edith Piaf, currently packing theatres on the American tour circuit, Mario rarely inspected the auditorium before curtain up, believing this to be bad luck. During the afternoon of 4 April, four hours before his first show, he moved out of the New Frontier (leaving Betty to her own devices) and into an apartment at the Sands Hotel, put at his disposal by scriptwriter Ben Hecht. He had previously spent a week with Mario in Palm Springs, discussing a film project which had seemed exciting at the time, an original idea by Hecht to be produced in England by J. Arthur Rank. Mario found this name fascinating – an English extra had enlightened him as to how 'having a J. Arthur' was Cockney rhyming slang for masturbation, that is, 'having a wank'. Hecht, however, was not in town this time, and as had happened with Howard Hughes, the project was never mentioned again.

Within thirty minutes of settling in, Mario was joined by Nicholas

Brodsky and two showgirls. Between them, in the space of four hours, the quartet knocked back a whole case of champagne, and by the time Al Teitelbaum and Betty arrived to escort him back to the New Frontier for his show, Mario was so wasted that he could hardly stand. Teitelbaum and Betty, assisted by a similarly sozzled Brodsky, managed to get him backstage at the Venus Room, where the first-night audience, just starting to arrive, comprised equal numbers of press, celebrity guests and fans who had paid way over the odds for tickets. Mario asked to be left alone in his dressing room. This had happened many times before, when as if by divine intervention he managed to sober up in preparation for an exemplary performance. Not this time, though. No sooner had they closed the door behind them than Mario swallowed half a bottle of Betty's Seconal pills. Thirty minutes later, Teitelbaum found him unconscious on the floor.

Mario later claimed that he had swallowed the pills 'to find peace of mind', although this did not stop the rumours in some circles that he had attempted to kill himself. Also, if the act had *not* been planned, some wanted to know, then why had Mario been in possession of Betty's pills in the first place? What is strange is that, rather than summon an ambulance or drive Mario to the nearest hospital, someone called the hotel manager, Sam Lewis who, terrified of the adverse publicity this would cause, elected to handle matters himself. Lewis brought in his own doctor, who in turn sent out for a stomach pump and an oxygen tent – wasting valuable time, during which Mario could have died. Outside in the corridor, the press refused to budge until Lewis told them what had happened, but rather than do this and have a scandal on his hands, he called the police and there was an all-out scuffle as the area was cleared. All this took place less than thirty minutes before curtain up. Finally, confident now that Mario was going to survive, Lewis's chief concern was to find a replacement act.

The situation was 'saved' by Jimmy Durante, who was dragged from one of the casinos and walked on to the stage to a mild applause which changed to loud booing when he announced that Lanza was too sick to perform. Even Sam Lewis's statement that Mario had suffered 'acute respiratory collapse' and was fighting for his life in an oxygen tent failed to settle them down – word had quickly spread that the singer was still in his room, sleeping off his excesses. Lewis tried to make amends with a further announcement that, until midnight, all drinks and meals would be on the house. This gesture, he later claimed, had set him back over $20,000. Most of the audience stormed out of the Venus Room, some vowing to burn their Mario Lanza records when they got home. Over the course of the next two weeks, two-thirds of those who had bought their tickets were given refunds; the remainder saw various acts who had been brought in at short notice to replace Mario, the most popular of which was Frankie Laine.

On the morning of 5 April, Sam Lewis marched into Mario's room – not to ask how he was feeling, but to present him with a bill for $2,000. His contract had stipulated free accommodation for the Lanzas and their entourage, but as Mario had broken his contract by failing to sing, he would have to pay for everyone's rooms as well as for the damage he had caused. Mario screwed up the bill, threw it at Lewis and refused to pay, and asked Terry Robinson to drive him, Betty and the children to the railway station. As had happened with Chicago, he swore never to set foot in Las Vegas again – not that there was much chance of this once word got around, for just about every entertainments venue subsequently blacklisted him. On the platform, he was challenged by reporters who knew by now why his shows had been cancelled, but asked why just the same. Mario pointed to his throat, and his lips bruised by the oxygen mask, and mouthed, 'Laryngitis!' By the time the party reached Los Angeles, he was back to his boastful self. When a female reporter asked if he did not feel just a little ashamed of himself for having let so many people down, he growled, 'If I had any feeling of guilt towards myself, it would be like feeling guilty towards God!' Whilst in Las Vegas, he had made the mistake of speaking to the one hack he hated most of all: Louella Parsons, who in that weekend's *Los Angeles Examiner* attacked him with all the spite she could muster. Thanks to Louella, the world now knew that the Lanzas were deeply in debt, and that Mario was paranoid about losing his voice. 'He *looked* like a million dollars,' she observed, 'very thin, handsome and fit. But when he opened his mouth to tell us about his sore throat, I knew the jig was up and that he wouldn't sing at his widely publicised nightclub debut.'

Two weeks after the Las Vegas disaster, the Lanzas moved into their first non-rented home, a 12-bedroomed house at 355 St Cloud, in Bel Air. The property had been built for Jack Warner's brother, Harry, in 1923 at a cost of $750,000. Since the cost of running such mansions had become almost prohibitive in recent years, prices had slumped and Al Teitelbaum secured it on Mario's behalf for $120,000, paying the $15,000 deposit out of his own pocket before Mario even saw the place – along with $17,000 for the damage his client had inflicted on the house in Palm Springs. Mario was delighted with his new home, which boasted marble fireplaces in almost every room, a private bar, a massive swimming pool, and an 80-seater theatre added by Warner. Yet no sooner had the dust-sheets been removed than it looked like the real-estate agents would have to be called in: Mario was served with a series of writs by Sam Lewis of the New Frontier Hotel. Lewis was claiming $15,000 for unpaid accommodation, $10,000 for ticket refunds, a sum yet to be determined for advertising and costs for the unused rehearsal room he had put at Mario's disposal, and a whopping $100,000 for 'loss of goodwill'.

Teitelbaum would subsequently contest the action, and Lewis would receive just the $15,000. The hacks, led into the affray by Louella Parsons, also hinted – and hoped – that Jack Warner would rip up Mario's contract and cancel *Serenade* on account of the adverse publicity. In fact, Warner had been among the first to call him after the scandal and beg him not to worry. The incident had sent sales of Lanza records shooting through the roof, with the genuine fans – those who had made him and who would carry on supporting him until the end – believing that an artiste of his quality should never have agreed to appear in Las Vegas in the first place.

During the first week of May, leaving Betty to look after the children, Mario and Terry Robinson headed for Tijuana, Mexico. This was supposed to be a quiet sojourn, one which would enable Mario to recuperate from his latest self-inflicted ordeal. Robinson later shared a typical Lanza anecdote, of how they ended up in a backstreet dive, with Mario hoping that no one would see through his feeble disguise of hat and glasses – until a young guitarist took to the floor and began strumming 'Granada'. Unable to help himself, Mario belted out the chorus, was recognised, and almost caused a riot when the place was invaded by fans. Before leaving with a police escort, he walked up to the young man and gave him a $300 tip – saying how he wished it could have been more, but that this was all that Robinson had in his wallet! Later that evening he answered the valid question of why he had recently thrown away $100,000 by failing to sing in Las Vegas, yet had been willing to play in this *cantina* for nothing: 'Even for all the money in the world I wouldn't jeopardise my voice. The people I sang for today are my people. They don't pick on me. They love me fat or skinny. They feel what I feel.'

On 28 June 1955, Mario entered the Warner Brothers Studio to begin working on the *Serenade* soundtrack. His first recording session in 17 months worried him unduly – there would be many more sessions in an 11-month period – though Costa was at hand to help him through it, and suffer a martyrdom when things went wrong. Accompanied by Dominic Frontiere on the jazz accordion, he cut just one track, 'La danza', before declaring that he had had enough. Two days later, with Jacob Gimpel on the piano, he recorded 'Torna a Surriento'; these two pieces, along with 'O soave fanciulla', which he set down during the same session, had been in his repertoire for so long that they were sure bets for single takes. On 7 July, again with Gimpel, he recorded two songs written by Nicholas Brodsky and Sammy Cahn for the film, their last collaboration for a Lanza picture: two versions of the title track with different lyrics and melodies (the first of which was scrapped), and 'My Destiny'. This session did not go too well. Mario hated 'My Destiny', and asked for the acetate to be destroyed – he re-recorded the song later in the week, along with 'Di rigori armato' from Act I of *Der Rosenkavalier*.

On 13 July, under the baton of Warner's musical director, Ray Heindorf, Mario recorded another tried and tested stalwart, 'Federico's Lament' from *L'Arlesiana*, as well as 'Amor ti vieta' from *Fedora*. These were put down in single takes, but he was dissatisfied with 'Qual occhio al mondo', from *Tosca*, and asked for this to be 'trashed'. He was also unhappy with producer Henry Blanke's choice of sopranos for the opera segments of the film, dismissing both Gloria Boh and Jean Fenn as insipid. Fenn made it to the screen, but Mario refused to duet with her on 'Ci lasceremo alla stagion dei fiori' – a problem the studio subsequently solved by recording her section of aria separately and, with a little technical trickery, adding this to the tape. Gloria Boh was not so lucky. Mario shook his head in disbelief when listening to the playback of their duet from *Otello*, 'Dio ti giocondi', but was willing to try recording it again a few days later. The result was the same, and Jack Warner agreed with him that she was 'not up to the job', but gave Mario the responsibility of telling her and finding a replacement. He suggested his friend, Licia Albanese.

Born in Bari, Italy, in 1913, Albanese had debuted at La Scala in 1934, singing Cio-Cio San in *Madama Butterfly*, her most acclaimed role which she would reprise over 300 times in a lengthy career. She had sung this at the New York Met in 1940, in what would be the first of 26 hugely successful seasons here until, like most of the great sopranos, she found herself on the wrong side of Rudolf Bing. She had appeared in the Met's very first telecast, *Otello*, so it was fitting that Mario should ask her to sing Desdemona in *Serenade*. The pair got along famously for a brief period; until she tired of watching him throw his life away, Albanese became a close confidante, almost a mother figure, and unlike most of his co-stars she has never stopped singing his praises, her theory being that Lanza was only difficult when people sought to make him so. This was at least partly true.

In the operatic field, Licia Albanese slotted Mario between Caruso and Giuseppe de Stefano, though she was being too kind to them – artistically and vocally, he was superior to both. Another great soprano who admired him – just about the only thing she and her bitter rival Maria Callas ever agreed upon – was Renata Tebaldi. Tebaldi (1922–2004) was in Hollywood at the time, and asked her agent to contact Anthony Mann. She was a great Lanza fan, and would Mario be interested in meeting her? He was over the moon, and they met in the Warner Brothers commissary on 15 December, after which Mario personally escorted Tebaldi around the *Serenade* set. The next evening she was invited to his home, where they stayed up until 4am singing duets from their favourite operas. How lamentable that no one thought of switching on a tape recorder! Tebaldi is on record as going one step beyond Albanese by saying that Mario was the greatest tenor she had *ever* heard, the only one aside from Franco Corelli who could move her to tears. There was even talk of them recording an album together, as happened later with Tebaldi and Corelli. Sadly, this would never happen, though they would meet again a few weeks later when the soprano was special guest at a screening of the musical highlights from the new film.

For *Serenade*, Mario was given two leading ladies: Joan Fontaine, who Dorothy Caruso had wanted to portray her in *The Great Caruso*, and 26-year-old actress-singer Sara (Sarita) Montiel. An undisputed gay icon, Montiel had appeared in the 1947 Spanish version of *Don Quixote*. She received much favouritism during shooting because she was Anthony Mann's girlfriend – not that this prevented Mario from trying it on with her. She and Mann would marry in 1957. Montiel later inspired cult director Pedro Almodóvar, who included her character in his 2004 film, *Bad Education* – she was played, in drag, by Mexican heart-throb Gael Garcia Bernal. Mann was a curious choice for director: aside from *The Glen Miller Story*, he was more widely known for his gritty Westerns. Mario was better behaved on the set of this film than he had been in its predecessors. Almost certainly Jack Warner took him to one side and read him the riot act, telling him he had been given far too much of his own way in the past; Mario also wanted to stay in Warner's good books, in the hope of having his contract extended.

We first see Damon Vincenti driving the tractor in the San Francisco vineyard where he works: he sports an exaggerated pompadour which reminds one of the camp, turn-of-the-century French comic, Felix Mayol. Indeed, there are times when this hairdo takes on a life of its own, like a badly fitting toupee that dances each time Mario furrows his brow, which is often in this picture. A car drives up and the driver asks him directions. Its occupants are socialite Kendall Hale (Fontaine) and her toy-boy boxer lover, Rosselli (Edwards) – he addresses Damon as 'peasant' and she eyes him up and down like a prime slab of beef, so we instinctively know they will soon figure again in the scenario. This is Damon's last day here: he has an audition for Lardelli's operatic cabaret restaurant, which naturally he expects to sail through. 'Your voice is from God,' someone says, when the workers ask him to entertain them one last time before leaving. But, does he need to save his energy for the audition? One almost expects the self-assured response to have been penned by Lanza himself: 'To open the trunk for one small diamond! How much can it hurt?' He sings 'La danza'; the voice has dropped half a tone, but retains its velvety warmth, despite the sound technician's insistence on recording him in an echo chamber.

Cut to the audition, and the maestro's cynical instruction to the pianist, 'Giuseppe, play for Caruso!' The high notes are restrained and even. In the next scene Damon is performing for top impresario Charles Winthrop (Vincent Price), a seemingly snide but actually sympathetic character who tells him after he has finished (with Jean Fenn) the aria from *La Bohème*, 'I enjoyed you, but not the duet. The soprano sounded like the brakes on the Rome express.' Winthrop just happens to know

Kendall Hall, and although there is no reference here to Winthrop's sexuality, his attraction towards the podgy tenor, currently 225 pounds, is thinly veiled as he tries to warn him off her. He tells Damon that as a child, Kendall enjoyed building only the most beautiful sandcastles simply because it was much more fun knocking them down again. Her relationships here appear more maternal than sexual – indeed, in Cain's novel she comes across as a Tennessee Williams-style fag hag. And now she wants a new caddy: Rosselli has just lost his big fight and she no longer has any use for him. To woo Damon, she fixes him up with an audition with the greatest maestro of them all, Marcatello (Joseph Calleia), to whom Damon pronounces whilst maintaining his humility, 'A man is born with a voice, but it takes a great teacher to make it blossom.' He sings 'My Destiny' – an insipid piece Mario tries his best with, whilst forcing the sound throughout and cracking a few notes. This was not in the script, and perhaps might have benefited from a retake.

There then follows a typical Lanza tantrum. Everything is happening too fast: Kendall has messed around with his head and he has become infatuated with her almost to the point of madness. He says he wants to get out of this exciting but alien new world and return to the vineyard, as Lanza once claimed he wanted to go back to Philadelphia. Truthfully, of course, and again like Lanza, he needs the adulation, and soon we see him fulfilling the Lanza dream on the opera stage: *Der Rosenkavalier, Fedora, Il Trovatore* – that echo chamber again, when he performs 'Di quella pira' in full costume, with oddly no chorus in sight – each segment more mesmerising than the last. Then, it is all downhill. Damon is hired to sing *Otello* with Licia Albanese – something which would never have happened to any tenor, no matter how exemplary, after just one year in the opera house – enabling Kendall to fool around with a young sculptor whilst Damon is forced to attend rehearsals. When she fails to turn up at his premiere, he walks out mid-aria, knocks down the first man who calls her a tramp, and heads for her apartment. Upon learning that she has gone overseas with her latest squeeze, he exacts his revenge by clawing the face off the bust of her that his rival has fashioned.

Damon flees to Mexico City, where he gets an engagement, but is demoted to singing the second male lead in *Don Giovanni*. Fired after breaking down in rehearsal, he heads for the picturesque town of San Miguel Allende. Here, he falls sick with a fever and is rescued by matador's daughter Juana Montes (Montiel), whose father died in the bullring. She witnesses Damon's mood-swings as she nurses him back to health in preparation for his return to the stage, and here we see a carbon copy of the actor playing him – the doubts, tantrums and idiosyncrasies which made life *chez* Lanza so frequently unbearable. A tender scene sees him playing 'Serenade' on the guitar, yet the next moment he goes to pieces again. 'You lived through the fever,' she remonstrates, 'but your heart is dead!' More histrionics follow during the carnival held each year to commemorate the great matador's death, prompting Juana to go to the church where she prays – aloud and in English, no doubt so that Damon will understand her when he follows to listen in – that he might sing again. And so he does, kneeling at the altar to deliver a poignant 'Ave Maria' with tears which are for real.

Damon's recovery is of course Juana's loss, for now he will return to San Francisco to resume his career. Before she drives him to the station, he treats the community to a ravishing farewell performance of 'Serenade': he wants her to accompany him as his wife, which she cannot do because she feels that he is still in love with Kendall. A sudden storm and another fit of hysterics persuade her to change her mind, and we next see them as Mr and Mrs Vincenti, entering Lardelli's, where it all began for him. Restored as the house singer, between entering the building and singing what must be regarded as the finest 'O paradiso' of his career, Mario/Damon has shed 40 pounds but who cares about such things when the voice is so mesmerising? And just as quickly as before, Damon hits the dizzy heights of fame when Winthrop gets him the lead in *L'Arlesiana*. Unfortunately, Kendall also appears on the scene: having dumped her sculptor, she wants Damon back and makes a play for him at the cocktail party she throws after he has wowed her society friends with 'Nessun dorma'. 'Anyone who is anyone in the international white trash set,' Winthrop observes of the guest list. From then on the storyline becomes silly. Juana finds an antique matador's sword in Kendall's apartment, and entertains the crowd with her bullfight speciality dance – using Kendall as the bull. Then, having failed to kill her rival, in a scene which is hilariously but unintentionally funny, she has another fit of pique, rushes out into the street and gets knocked down by a bus. For Damon, however, the show must go on and he again performs the by now weary title track, unaware if his wife is alive or dead – until someone whispers loudly from the wings, totally robbing the moment of its magic, that she is all right, though by now we are past caring about her.

The producer for *Serenade* was the German-born Henry Blanke, who had recently completed *Sincerely Yours* with Liberace, whom Mario could not stand. Several scenes of the Liberace film were re-shot whilst Blanke was working with Mario, who was incensed to learn that Liberace had once accused him of being jealous of arguably the most effeminate man ever to have stepped on to a stage. In his memoirs, the pianist would waspishly descibe Mario as, 'That remarkable singing star who lit up the movie horizon for a little while before, I think, he literally ate himself to death.' Every evening for a week, while these re-shoots were taking place, Mario, with his flair for mimicry, would call Blanke at home and pretend to be Liberace – then proceed to call him all the names under the sun while telling him what a rubbish producer he was. Liberace claimed that Mario had kept this up, even after Blanke had sold his house to an order of nuns, saying 'things that shocked the good Sisters right out of their quiet habits.' This part of his story is hard to believe. The sole object of the prank had been to humiliate Liberace; Mario was a man who took his faith very seriously, and would never have insulted anyone connected with the church.

The film premiered at New York's Radio City Music Hall in April 1956, and did well during its first season, even though it remains the least popular of all the Lanza films, and was the only one to show an actual loss during his lifetime. Hollywood was a fickle lady in those days: unless major stars were churning out at least one film every year, it was so easy to fall by the wayside. Having heard second-hand some of the comments passed during the press previews – mostly criticism about his fluctuation in weight, though this is not quite so obvious here as it had been in *Because You're Mine* – Mario boycotted the event. In fact, the reviews were quite good. The *New York Times*'s A.H. Weiler wrote, 'Mr Lanza, who was never in better voice, makes this a full and sometimes impressive musical entertainment.' *Newsweek* observed, '*Serenade* serves if nothing else to show that Lanza is still in possession of the God-given high C.' *Picturegoer* complimented him, but could not resist having a dig at his ego: 'The trouble with Lanza is that he can never forget he is Lanza. When he does – as in the magnificent *Otello* aria – he comes very close to being sensational.' Only Mario's old enemy, *Time* magazine, went out of its way to offend. 'He looks like a colossal ravioli on toothpicks,' the editorial remarked scathingly, 'the face aflame with rich living, having the appearance of a gigantic red pepper.' Even so, the anonymous reviewer could not justifiably fault Mario's voice, adding of the scene where Damon Vincent auditions for Marcatello, 'Lanza can still rattle a teacup at twenty paces with his C, and with this picture he seems sure to rattle the cash registers across the land.' Then he or she spoiled it all by concluding, 'This is not, as the tenor seems to think, operatic acting. It is just smarm.'

Shortly before shooting wrapped on *Serenade*, like his on-screen character, Mario appears to have suffered a nervous breakdown, during which he convinced himself that everyone involved with the picture, most especially Joan Fontaine, had been out to get him. Terry Robinson recalls him saying in one of his down moments, 'The voice. That's what they want, the voice. But what about me? That's me on the screen and I'm the one they pick on. I can't even get a sore throat without being crucified. Well, soon I'll be dead and then the truth will come out.' Whether Mario meant what he said, or indeed whether he had said it at all, may be a matter for conjecture, but during his latter years he certainly seems to have been burdened with a fatalistic if not actually suicidal streak. Fontaine, reputed to have been one of the nicest, most easy-going stars in Hollywood, confessed how working with him had been a nightmare; every time he walked on to the set, she had been terrified of him 'kicking off'. Mario had also reverted to his old tricks – exposing himself, urinating in full view of everyone on the set into whichever receptacle was close at hand, and pinching his leading lady's bottom, which she did not find funny at all. Nauseatingly, he always ensured that he had a mouthful of raw garlic when called upon to kiss her. Mann took Fontaine's complaints to Jack Warner, who issued Mario with a 'behave yourself or else' warning. Much worse would have befallen Mario, had Warner known that he was enjoying a liaison with a 15-year-old Mexican extra.

It was one of Mario's friends, the columnist Lloyd Shearer, who suggested taking him to see a psychiatrist he knew in New York, ostensibly for a friendly chat. It was not mentioned that this friend was a consultant at the Payne-Whitney Psychiatric Clinic (demolished in the early 1990s to make way for an extension of the Presbyterian Hospital). This much can be said for Mario's frequently almost childlike naivety, that he did not question Shearer and Terry Robinson's motives. Mario agreed, but refused to fly. Since Anthony Mann could only get away with closing the set down for the weekend, travelling to New York by any other mode of transport was not an option: a plane with a sleeper compartment was chartered for the overnight flight, and Mario was given some of Betty's sleeping pills to knock him out. He boarded the plane as 'Fred Mason', wearing his customary feeble disguise of hat and dark glasses.

The consultation, not surprisingly, went disastrously wrong, leaving Mario with the impression that whoever had set up this meeting – in his confused state the culprit could have been anyone from Terry Robinson or Betty to one of the Warner Brothers' executives – had the sole intention of having him sectioned to this 'nut-house', as he denounced it. The friendly chat was revealed to be a full assessment of his mental state. Mario took one look at the bars up at the windows, and was out of the place like a shot. Outside the psychiatrist's office, he searched for Lloyd Shearer to give him a piece of his mind – or worse – but Shearer had heard him yelling and cursing, and made a hasty exit. Robinson was the next to suffer his wrath. For the umpteenth time, Mario threatened to end their friendship, save that this time Robinson, who almost always carried Mario's money in his pocket, had the power – or pleasure – to leave him in New York to stew in his own juices. Robinson later described how Mario had calmed down just as quickly as he had exploded, and asked a cab driver to take them to Coney Island, where the three of them ate hot dogs in Nathan's Restaurant, staying there until dawn. Mere hours later, Mario endured more mental torture during the long flight back to Los Angeles.

On 23 November, in a back room at the studio, Jack Warner, his executives and a group of friends joined Mario and Licia Albanese to run through the soundtrack playbacks for the film. The final piece, the retake of the *Otello* duet with Albanese, had been recorded the previous afternoon. Everyone applauded wildly, and Howard Keel was heard to comment, 'Only a madman would ever sing *Otello* like that!' Mario, who hated Keel for no other reason than the fact that Keel's collaborations with Kathryn Grayson had been even more successful than his own, squared up to him and the two almost came to blows. 'Listen to me, buddy,' Mario growled, 'get mad, fuck up a lot, and maybe *you'll* be a better singer some day!'

The long descent into hell had begun.

Chapter Eleven

Arrivederci, Roma

Mario Lanza roared upward to fame and fortune like a 4th of July
rocket, then fell back to earth, a burnt stick lost in the darkness.

Hedda Hopper

Two days after the Christmas of 1955, Mario became entangled
in a drama which for once was not of his making. After dinner,
he and Terry Robinson headed for a meeting with Al
Teitelbaum at his shop, where the furrier-manager infomed them that
only minutes before he had been robbed at gunpoint of stock valued at
an estimated $250,000. Later, several vital issues would be raised.
Teitelbaum claimed in his statement to the police that Mario's hammering on the back door of the premises had scared the culprits away, just as
they had been tying up one of his assistants. Mario and Robinson, on the
other hand, swore that they had seen nothing, despite the fact that the
robbers would have had to pass them to get away from the place. And,
Teitelbaum's insurance company investigators wanted to know, why had
Mario and Robinson made a hasty exit immediately after the alleged
event, before Teitelbaum had called the police? During the subsequent
hearing it emerged that Teitelbaum, deeply in debt, had set up the
whole thing – including receiving a black eye to make the heist look
more authentic – with two friends, and that Mario had fled the scene so
as not to get his name in the newspapers for something he had had
nothing to do with. Teitelbaum was found guilty of fraud, and sentenced
to twelve months in prison – a sentence which, on account of numerous
appeals, he would not serve until 1959.

Mario spent much of the earlier part of the new year 'lounging around' – entertaining friends at his home, but rarely socialising outside its four walls. Warner Brothers were in no hurry to extend his contract, so he half-heartedly searched for new horizons. On the eve of shooting *Serenade*, he and Anthony Mann had founded their own company, Cloudam Productions, with the intention of making at least one more film together – or maybe even producing a Broadway review with Mario as its star. Like his other partnerships it would prove short-lived. It is doubtful that a man with Mario's ego would have been satisfied with sharing the limelight with anyone else and limiting his nightly output to a couple of showstoppers, although this idea almost achieved fruition when he considered *Golden Boy*, based on the 1937 play by Clifford Odets. This tells the ubiquitous story of Joe Bonaparte, the son of dirt-poor immigrants and a would-be surgeon who takes up boxing to pay for his college fees. Adding to his problems, he has an affair with his manager's girlfriend, and accidentally kills a man in the ring. Sadly, nothing came of the project, which would be completely rewritten to provide a smash hit for Sammy Davis Jr in 1964.

RCA had committed Mario to completing two albums by the end of their financial year, and as a sweetener had offered him carte blanche on their content. In May, he made his long-awaited return to the studio for the first of three major sessions that month, to be followed by five more in August and September. His contract stipulated a minimum of 50 songs – though he only did 39 – in what appears to have been a desperate attempt to get as much mileage out of his voice as possible, just in case he 'went off' again. In fact, the company had good reason to be worried about their investment: Mario was drinking more than ever, still hooked on barbiturates, doubling up on his prescription tranquillisers, gorging prodigiously, and on some days getting through three packs of cigarettes – yet still managing to hang on to his near-perfect breath control.

Much has been made of the 'poor quality' of these 1956 recordings, particularly those from the first session under the baton of Irving Aaronson for the *Lanza On Broadway* album. It was as if the critics, and subsequent biographers, had to follow each other like sheep and dismiss this as the worst body of work he had ever produced, which simply is not true. It *is* true that Mario's voice is not always as powerful here as it was three years earlier – but it has to be remembered that he is singing show tunes, and not opera, therefore one would expect fewer of those top Cs and a much more mellow timbre, which is exactly what he gives us. However, there are a few faults which could have been rectified were it not for Mario's persistent belief that the first take could rarely be improved on.

For the album, Mario chose numbers from current or recent Broadway shows, including *Lady In The Dark, My Fair Lady, The Boys From Syracuse* and *Carousel.* The first track to be laid down was Billy Rose's 'More than You Know', which the great showman had written for his wife, Fanny Brice. Barbra Streisand is said to have been so overwhelmed by Mario's interpretation that she insisted upon having it in the score of *Funny Lady*, against the producer's wishes. Mario sings it slower than written; otherwise it is an excellent, well-tempered piece superseded only by the later recording by Doris Day. 'Falling in Love with Love' is no less engaging, though in today's climate Mario's embellishments place it in the high-camp bracket. Another powerhouse performance comes with Rodgers and Hammerstein's 'Younger than Springtime', overdubbed by the Jeff Alexander Choir – Edith Piaf used them for the recordings she made in New York for Columbia a few weeks later, though for some reason they were not credited on the record label. A mistake perhaps was 'September Song', composed by Kurt Weill in 1938 and introduced by Walter Huston in *Knickerbocker Holiday*. This, like 'On the Street Where You Live', is forced and sung almost at a snail's pace, whereas Huston's version – along with the equally famous one by Weill's wife, Lotte Lenya, made a few days after Mario's – sounds more world-weary, as it should when performed by someone looking back on a long, eventful life. Mario also sails woefully off key towards the end of the song. On the other hand, its companion piece, Weill's 'Speak Low', also a hit for Lenya, is remarkable – as are 'Why was I Born' and 'So In Love'. Even better is 'This Nearly Was Mine', unforgivably denounced by one biographer as 'arguably the worst performance ever captured on record by a great singer'. And finally we have 'And This is My Beloved' and 'You'll Never Walk Alone'. All in all, pretty stirring stuff.

In August and September, though advised by RCA to record them one at a time, Mario laid down the tracks for *A Cavalcade Of Show Tunes* and a second Christmas album, as yet untitled. For the latter, Mario wanted to reprise the songs and hymns from his previous festive album, but RCA persuaded him otherwise. Besides the regular fare of 'Deck the Halls', 'Hark the Herald Angels Sing' and so on, there were simplistic but nevertheless stunning interpretations of 'Joy to the World' and 'O Christmas Tree', which thankfully we can still hear each year, wedged between those inferior Christmas pop songs.

Wielding the baton this time was Henri René (1906–83), the American-born German conductor, producer and arranger currently enjoying great success working with Eartha Kitt and Harry Belafonte. It was he who persuaded Mario to record two less familiar works which, though the single reached Number 56 in the Billboard Chart, are virtually forgotten today. 'Earthbound', originally a German song, has a dreamlike orchestration and choral accompaniment, and is almost the kind of mood piece one associates with Jane Froman. Backing this was Mario's own composition, 'This Land', which contains the auto-biographical line, 'The trees have grown, and the dreams that I've sown rest in the breast of this land.' Equally lovely and as rarely heard are 'Do You Wonder', composed by Henry Hill, brother of the better known Victor Young, and 'Love in a Home', written by Johnny Mercer and Gene Paul.

Like *Lanza On Broadway*, *A Cavalcade of Show Tunes* – Mario loathed the title and wanted to call it *Lanza On Broadway II* – was an innovation, no less remarkable than the Broadway album, but more critically acclaimed. The concept was almost the same, save that the musicals and operettas represented were less contemporary: *The New Moon*, *Naughty Marietta*, *The Firefly*, *Rose Marie*, *The Vagabond King*, *Maytime*, *The Land Of Smiles*. Mario also revived a few obscure works by recording songs from *Music In The Air*, *Very Warm For May* and *The Fortune Teller*. Words cannot express the sheer beauty of these interpretations. Therefore, rather than reviewing it here and spoiling the surprise for those who are yet to hear it, maybe it is better to offer a simple instruction. Search high and low if you have to, but buy it!

When Mario was not rehearsing or working in the studio he was creating merry hell, mostly at home, where he took his frustrations out on those around him. In 1956 he was treated for Benzedrine addiction, the side-effects of which sent him spiralling completely out of control. His antisocial behaviour had now extended to his personal life. 'We were in a restaurant, sitting near a group of attractive women,' Roger

Normand recalled. 'Halfway through the meal, Mario burst into an impromptu "C'est si bon", grabbed a bread roll, pretended that it was his penis, and waved it at them. Everybody roared with laughter, but the ladies were not amused.' Few of Hollywood's top clubs and restaurants saw the funny side of such antics, and some began showing him the door. Others, having heard of the way he sometimes liked to let his hair down, refused to even let him in. For a while, even Betty stopped being seen with him in public, though sometimes, when under the influence, it was she who humiliated him. Then there were the outbursts aimed at his peers, even though these were never less than deserved. During a meeting with top executive Harry Cohn, a difficult man at the best of times, Mario became so unpleasant – 'Forty filthy names in less than two minutes,' according to one syndicated report – that with one fell swoop he put paid to ever working for Warner Brothers again.

Al Teitelbaum did the rounds of the other studios, not one of which was even remotely interested in offering his client a contract. By steadfastly refusing to curb his behaviour, Mario had made himself unemployable and uninsurable. Working with him had never been much fun in the first place, but now there was no telling what he would do next. Some studios feared that, if they took him on, he might harm himself, or worse still he might harm others, during one of his tantrums. His system was shot through on account of all the eating binges followed by crash diets. His drinking and addiction was slowly killing him, something he appears to have been well aware of: Mario had often told friends that he never wanted to grow old, and whilst previously they had thought he was just clowning around, they now knew that he meant it. Then there were the professional problems, especially his steadfast refusal to accept any form of discipline or directorial control. Most of the directors who had worked with him had started off liking him but ended up declaring him a nightmare. His treatment of some of his leading ladies had entered Hollywood folklore, to the extent that hardly any actress in Hollywood wanted to be within a hundred yards of him. An exception was 22-year-old Swedish-American blonde bombshell Inger Stevens, currently going through a rough patch with her agent husband, Anthony Soglio – the couple had separated after four months of marriage, and would not get back together again. Stevens, who many considered incapable of acting her way out of a paper bag, had previously had affairs with Bing Crosby and Anthony Quinn, and fell for Mario in such a way that she boasted to friends that they would be married once he had divorced Betty – something his friends swore would never happen, if only for the sake of his children.

Inger Stevens's *truc* was to invite beach bums and extras to her apartment, then have sex with them whilst her friends watched. Terry Robinson spoke of the incident which took place at the beach house Mario sometimes rented in Malibu, his getaway from Betty and the children, where he would spend much of his time drinking and getting high. Having posed for publicity shots with the bikini-clad actress – what these were to publicise was never established – Mario was asked to sing, but promised to do something better than this. 'He got up and walked over to her, lifted her up on the piano, and slipped off her bikini bottom,' Robinson recalled. 'He spread her legs apart and said, "For the first time, Lanza's high note will come out of a woman's body." He put his mouth over her bottom and sang into her vagina. In his drunken state he couldn't understand why she wasn't particularly delighted with his performance.' Stevens's affair with Mario quickly petered out. Extremely unstable, she welcomed in 1959 with a New Year's Eve cocktail of sleeping pills and ammonia from which doctors miraculously saved her, but finally ended it all with an overdose of barbiturates in April 1970, aged 35.

On 31 January 1957 – Mario's 36th birthday – there was a final humiliation on American soil when he was hauled before a judge and charged with drunken driving. Twice over the legal limit, he had crashed his car into a cab driven by one Seymour Maslow. Found guilty by the jury, he evaded a prison sentence by way of his lawyer pleading for clemency – he insisted his client was under considerable stress right now and was on the verge of a nervous breakdown. Some of the newspapers picked up on this, claiming that the stress was related to the Lanzas' crippling debts, which they listed in minute detail. Seven local shops were suing the couple for a total of $16,000 because Betty had 'forgotten' to pay her grocery bills for the past six months – though why they had kept on delivering supplies to the St Cloud house when there was no money in the kitty was not explained. Two local pharmacies and a private doctor had also resorted to legal action to recover the $18,000 they claimed the Lanzas owed them for prescription drugs. Additionally, the couple still owed over $25,000 for damages they had inflicted on various rented properties. MCA also claimed that Mario owed them $25,000 in unpaid commission. Then there were the outstanding taxes, raising the total amount of debt to $150,000. Mario's response to these demands, and his new status amongst his peers as one of the most unpopular stars in Hollywood, was, 'To hell with 'em all. If they don't want me here in America, then I'll go some place where I'm appreciated!'

According to Terry Robinson, Mario was visited around this time by his boxer friend Rocky Marciano – nothing unusual in this, save that this time Marciano was accompanied by two cronies from the Mob, the idea being that if Mario agreed to 'work' for them, his debts would be settled at once. These are named in *Lanza: His Tragic Life* as a Mr Lombardo, and diminutive thug Tommy 'Three Fingers' Lucchese, an associate of Charles 'Lucky' Luciano, the Sicilian mobster recently deported to Italy. Lucchese (1899–1967) is said to have been Luciano's favourite killer, with at least 30 known murders to his credit. He was a great favourite amongst crooked politicians and show-business stars, though exactly what he was expecting Mario to do, other than split the proceeds of a record deal fifty-fifty, is not known. And neither, if Robinson's story is to be believed, did Mario give him time to explain:

> 'Get out,' he yelled. 'I'm no fucking puppet! This is God's voice! It passes through here!' He grabbed his throat for emphasis. 'I wasn't made with a finger, you assholes! I was made with a prick! You think I don't know your kind? When I was a kid, my uncle was shot down in the streets of South Philadelphia for getting mixed up with your kind. I watched him die. My grandfather chased bums like you out of his store when they came around offering protection!'

Lucchese's reply to this, Robinson said, was, 'Listen here, you fat slob. You don't know who you're talking to. Keep your big mouth shut or I'll shut it permanently!' Two years later, much would be made of this alleged outburst.

Mario was also faced with another threat: the dreaded *Confidential* magazine. For years, the studios had been feeding the press with mostly fictitious biographies of their stars, but as the power of the moguls and their press offices declined, a new form of exposé was launched for a public hungry for scandal and titillation: cheaply produced periodicals, precursers of today's *Globe* and *National Enquirer*, where fans could find frequently unflattering pictures of their idols accompanying lurid, no-holds-barred accounts of their indiscretions – all this wedged between advertisements for impotency pills, personal horoscopes, slimming aids and other generally useless paraphernalia. With titles such as *Inside Story*, *Tip-Off* and *Whisper*, and with self-explanatory headlines – 'The Wild Party That Helped Sinatra To Forget Ava Gardner', 'John Carradine's Other John', and so on – they were sold everywhere: supermarkets, gas stations, laundromats, and most of all outside cinemas where they were showing the films of whichever star happened to be on the cover of that week's issue.

Confidential was the most feared publication of them all: its motto, 'Tells the Facts and Names the Names', appeared on the cover beneath the title. The magazine had been launched in 1952 by Robert Harrison, who got the idea from top-rated television crime investigator and clean-up campaigner Senator Carey Kefauver. According to Kefauver, America was gripped by a wave of vice, gambling scams and organised crime, which was rapidly turning it into a mafioso state. Harrison therefore decided that he would make money by exploring the nucleus of this so-called den of iniquity – Hollywood – and until now had kept several steps ahead of orthodox scandalmongers Hedda, Louella and Elsa Maxwell by not always checking the authenticity of his stories before publishing them. At the height of its popularity, *Confidential* was selling over four million copies per issue. What everyone detested about Harrison was the devious methods he employed to obtain some of his exclusives: whores of both sexes were paid huge sums of money to coerce stars into compromising positions, while a tiny machine concealed in the bedroom whirred away, capturing not just the sex act itself but the all-important post-coital small talk. Jealous or thwarted stars were encouraged to rubbish rivals so that they could step into their shoes when important roles were up for grabs. For 'special' cases such as Rock Hudson and Elvis Presley (homosexuality, real or alleged), Lana Turner (sharing lovers) and Errol Flynn (two-way mirrors), Harrison supplied his 'detectives' with tiny, sophisticated infra-red cameras. 'We all read it,' Marlene Dietrich told me, 'not because it was any good – it was rubbish, worse than some of the garbage you get on newsstands nowadays – but to find out if we were in it. Sometimes you never got an inkling until it was too late.'

Harrison had been sniffing around Mario for some time: he was the supermarket rag's dream quite simply because he had always been so terribly indiscreet. There was his on-set behaviour, the tantrums, the horrendous way in which he treated women – none more so than his own wife. Harrison also had his suspicions about Mario's relationships with some of his male friends such as Nick Adams, Nicholas Brodsky, Sam Weiler, and most especially Terry Robinson, whom Mario gave every impression of caring for more than anyone else in the world. Then there were the 'shifty' characters, such as Rocky Marciano, and others known to have connections with the Mafia; and those women with whom Mario had enjoyed extra-marital affairs, reputed to have run into their hundreds. And finally there were those who had worked with him – or for him and Betty – and rued doing so, many of whom would have been more than willing to get even by selling some real or invented story to Robert Harrison. Had Harrison decided to completely fabricate a story – the one thing he was best at – there would have been little point in Mario denying it, based on the maxim 'no smoke without fire'. Some of those he had wronged chose not to protest, the theory being that attacking Harrison would only make him invent more stories which, like today's tabloid tales, the majority of the American public would have taken as gospel. The difference between then and now was that, in 1950s America, even the slightest indiscretion could put an end to a career.

By April 1957, the magazine had received so many lawsuits that Hollywood's public relations officer, Robert Murphy, warned the District Attorney that unless action was taken against *Confidential*, the major studios would all withdraw their support from the forthcoming Republican campaign. Despite the warning signs, Harrison remained defiant. One of his features, 'Mad About The Boy', concerning Liberace, had detailed the arch-camp pianist's seduction of a young male press agent in an Ohio hotel. Another which he was planning to run concerned Rock Hudson's very active but secret gay life. When the agents of both threatened to sue, Harrison told them to go ahead – he promised to reveal even more lurid details of their personal lives which he said would finish their careers. Exactly what sort of exposé he planned for Mario was not known, but the fear of this was one of the reasons that Al Teitelbaum and Greg Bautzer decided to throw out a few feelers overseas, hoping that their client's reputation had not preceded him on the other side of the Atlantic.

What Mario's team may not have known was that Robert Harrison was about to get his comeuppance. One by one, the stars he had wronged began taking action against him. The black actress Dorothy Dandridge, whom Harrison had accused of 'perverted antics' with a naturist group, served him with a writ for $2 million. There were further writs from Errol Flynn, Anthony Quinn, Maureen O'Hara and Eartha Kitt. Then Liberace, the one person Harrison had said would never dare sue him because his arch-effeminacy spoke for itself, denounced Dandridge's writ as 'a piddling little trifle', and served one of his own for a whopping $25 million. The proceedings, hailed by the press as 'The Trial of 100 Stars', took place in August – by which time Mario had left the country.

Harrison was ordered to submit his 'research files' for scrutiny by the court. The trial was a semi-farce, resulting in little more than a large number of out-of-court settlements, the largest of these being the $40,000 Harrison was forced to pay Liberace. Had Mario not left Hollywood when he did, almost certainly Harrison would have published his exclusive, and Mario would have been one of those compelled to stick by the other stars and sue Harrison. Almost certainly his career would not have survived the scandal, for unlike Liberace, whose star would never fade no matter what anyone wrote about him, by this time Mario was clinging to his movie career by the skin of his teeth because of his general unpleasantness towards everyone who had crossed his path.

It was actually Art Cohn, the scriptwriter best friend of Elizabeth Taylor's showman-producer husband, Mike Todd, who put in a good word for Mario with Franco de Simone Niquesa, the American representative of the Rome-based studio, LeCloud-Titanus. Todd, no less brash and vulgar than Mario, had wanted him to appear in his megabucks production, *Around The World In 80 Days*. This had boasted just about every major star in the Hollywood firmament in cameo roles, but Mario had been compelled to turn the offer down because of his contractual obligations to Warner Brothers. Now, Todd was planning a big-budget movie about a temperamental opera star, quite possibly with Elizabeth Taylor playing his love interest. The mind boggles to think how this would have turned out – with the almost guaranteed on-set eruptions between two stars as famed for their neuroses as for their talent – had Todd not been killed in a plane crash. In the meantime, whilst Cohn was writing the script, LeCloud-Titanus came up with a comparatively low-budget production, also scripted by Cohn, provisionally entitled *Arrivederci Roma* and based on a story by Giuseppe Amato, whose *La Dolce Vita* was about to begin shooting. The title of the Lanza film, his only B-movie and completed on a budget of less than $1 million, would subsequently be changed to *Seven Hills of Rome* – astonishingly because MGM, backing and distributing it, were worried that American audiences would conclude that it was in a foreign language and avoid going to see it. In fact, as will be seen, this was almost the case.

Mario's fee for making the film had been fixed at $150,000, along with 50 per cent of the profits, though a quarter of this would be deducted to clear his outstanding debts. His contract stipulated that he would be paid $50,000 up-front, and the balance once the film had been completed. The company's executives, well aware of his reputation, were covering their backs in the event of the inevitable problems they knew he would cause. Al Teitelbaum negotiated a similar package with RCA: 50 per cent of his royalties would be paid directly to the IRS. Mario also made it very clear, certainly in the present climate when he believed that everyone was against him, that if he was going to shoot the film in Italy, Betty and the children would be travelling with him – and none of them would be returning to America. For this reason, Mario asked Terry Robinson to accompany them.

In the meantime, Mario made what would be his last visit to an American recording studio. No one had taken his threat to stay in Italy seriously, and during his absence RCA planned keeping fans happy with the release of a compilation album of Lanza favourites, along with two singles. The first would be 'A Night to Remember', the theme for the film of the same name which told of the sinking of the *Titanic*, and this would be paired with 'Behold!'. The follow-up single would be 'I'll Never Stop Loving You', essentially a woman's song – Doris Day had sung it beautifully in the Ruth Etting biopic, *Love Me Or Leave Me*. On the flipside would be Sammy Cahn and Jimmy Van Heusen's 'Come Dance with Me'. Mario had seen Peggy Lee performing this on television, and Frank Sinatra's album of the same name had won him a Grammy award.

Mario was in a surly mood thoughout the 15 April session, this time with good cause: his grandmother, Eliza, had died two days previously. No matter how many times Mario attempted the Doris Day song, which he had dedicated to the old lady, his emotions got the better of him and eventually he gave up trying. The other three songs were not up to his usual standard, and rarely crop up in compilations – a poor swansong for Lanza's mighty American career, though of course no one had any way of knowing this at the time.

During the first week of May, the Lanzas had their sons Damon and Marc baptised at St Paul's Church in Westwood. Why this had not happened before is not known. If they were taking their children to Rome where there was every chance of them being granted an audience with the Pope, Betty declared – such were her delusions of grandeur – then they would not be entering the Eternal City as heathens. The next day, Betty and her brood boarded the train for Chicago, whilst Mario took the express to Las Vegas, the city he had sworn never to set foot in again. By travelling thus he was hoping he might evade the press, but in his usual disguise of large hat and shades he stuck out like a sore thumb, and the first conclusion drawn by most journalists was that the couple had split up. In Las Vegas he met up with Ray Sinatra and half-heartedly discussed plans for a season here which would make up for his faux pas with the New Frontier. Two days later he caught up with Betty, where they said their farewells to her family. At the last minute Terry Robinson, like Mario's father, elected to stay in Los Angeles, unaware that they would never see Mario again. From Chicago the family took the train to New York, where on 16 May they were greeted in the foyer of the Waldorf Astoria by RCA chairman Manny Sachs, who had organised a press conference. Mario refused to attend this, growling at Sachs that whatever he said would only be twisted by these 'lying bastards'. That evening he threw a no-expenses-spared party for whichever of his friends happened to be in town. The special guests were Maria and Salvatore Lanza.

Early the next morning, the Lanzas set sail on the *Giulio Cesare*. Never one to do things by halves, Mario had booked four staterooms – one for the children and their nurses, one for Betty, one for entertaining guests, and one for himself so that he could enjoy uninterrupted fun with whoever he might seduce during the crossing. He spent much of his time here laid low with sea-sickness. Nine days later the ship docked in Naples, where he was given a hero's welcome by hundreds of fans gathered on the quayside. Many of these accompanied him on his pilgrimage to Caruso's grave, where he sang a tremulous 'Because' before bursting into tears. 'I feel so humble, standing in this sacred spot,' he said. 'Hollywood is six thousand miles away, little more than an unpleasant dream.' Humility was not on the cards later in the day, though, when the Lanzas boarded the Rome express – travelling first class in a compartment to themselves. LeCloud-Titanus had reserved two suites at the Bernini Hotel: one was filled with flowers from wellwishers and gifts for the children, which meant that Mario would have to share with Betty. He suffered the 'cramped conditions' for just the one night before relocating to the Hotel Excelsior, one of the city's most expensive hotels, on the Via Veneto.

Mario was just as troublesome working in Rome as he had been back home. Whereas he had refused to speak to reporters before leaving America, now he could not stop talking, and some of his comments about Hollywood and those who had been instrumental in forging his career were quite venomous. Mario said nothing about the chaos he had caused on set, or the crude pranks he had played on co-stars. In his blinkered way of seeing things, since setting foot in Hollywood he had been the victim, cowering like a frightened puppy in his corner whilst these bullies had conspired to get him. Pretty soon, their Italian counterparts would be wishing that he had stayed there.

Initially, his demands were reasonable. Damon, his character in *Serenade*, had been renamed in honour of his eldest son, so there were no problems naming this new one Marc, after his youngest. Similarly, he asked that his love interest in the film be named in honour of his favourite Italian 'after Anna Magnani and the Pope' – Raphaella, the little girl who had died of leukaemia. And then, the rot set in. Mario took an instant dislike to director Roy Rowland, then best known for *Bugles In The Afternoon* (1952) and *The 5,000 Fingers Of Dr T.* (1953). Rowland got off lightly, however, compared with the way he treated his female co-stars. American B-movie veteran Peggy Castle (1927–73) would retire from the movies after her ordeal with Mario – later she became a household name playing Lily Merrill in the *Lawman* television series. He initially refused to work with 21-year-old Marisa Allasio, known as 'the Italian Jayne Mansfield', who had been contracted to play Raphaella. A few days after arriving in Rome he had seen *The Young Caruso*, and wanted Rowland to fire Allasio and replace her with Gina Lollobrigida. La Lollo, it is said, had heard too many negative reports about him and was not interested in associating with a man incapable of keeping his hands to himself or speaking without spouting profanities. Mario was told that he would work with Allasio – or find himself and his family booked on the next boat back to America.

On the other hand, Mario got along famously with singer-songwriter-actor Renato Rascel (Renatto Renucci, 1912–91), an engaging personality who had recently completed *The Monte Carlo Story* with Marlene Dietrich. Rascel's most successful composition would be 'Romantica', with which he represented Italy in the 1960 Eurovision Song Contest – Mario would sing it on the Rome club circuit. The song only came eighth in the competition (France's Jacqueline Boyer won with 'Tom Pilibi') but it remains a classic. Another was 'Arrivederci Roma', which, contrary to popular belief, was not written especially for the film: two years previously, as 'Arrivederci Darling', it had provided a UK hit for Anne Shelton. For Mario, Rascel merely commissioned new lyrics. During his brief stay in Naples, Mario had been fascinated by the *scugnizzi* – the thousands of homeless, under-age urchins living on the streets of the city who nevertheless made a lucrative living from organised petty crime and selling themselves for sex. Mario had asked Roy Rowland to hire some of these to add authenticity to the crowd scenes in the film. There was a similar occurrence in Rome when, upon seeing a crowd in the square outside his hotel, he flung open his window to hear a 10-year-old girl singing on a street corner. Her name was Luisa Di Meo, and after going outside to chat to her father, who was accompanying her on the accordion, Mario asked for her to be in the film too. A wily character, Signor Di Meo asked for the equivalent of $100 for his daughter's services, bringing the response from a kindly Mario, 'Ask for $1,000, and we have a deal!' Rowland initially refused the request, declaring that hiring such a 'creature' would only set an unwelcome precedent – it was bad enough having the cleaned-up *scugnizzi* in his film, he concluded, without inviting half the riff-raff of Rome as well. Mario raved, and got his own way: Rowland hired Luisa for $500, and Mario did not think twice about making up the deficit from his own pocket, though the director had his revenge when he refused to add Luisa's name to the credits.

Mario recorded the film's soundtrack in three sessions at Rome's Auditorium Angelico studios under the baton of George Stoll, the conductor he had worked with in *The Toast of New Orleans*. Known by the trade as 'The Pope's Theatre', this was a fussy establishment which had refused admittance to Callas and Toscanini, snippets of information which went to Mario's head: being allowed to record on 'holy ground', he boasted, was proof indeed that he had been sent to earth by God. The first session took place on 5 June 1957, and Mario was in fine vocal fettle throughout. Only 'Seven Hills of Rome' required more than one take: this was because Roy Rowland was unsure which of the two very different versions of the song he was going to use in the final cut. Like 'Arrividerci Roma', which Mario sang as a duet with Luisa Di Meo, the song had not been written for the film – its composer, Victor Young of *Around The World In 80 Days* fame, had died the previous November and Art Cohn wanted this to be used as a tribute to him. Mario also reprised two of the last numbers he had recorded in Los Angeles – 'All the Things You Are' and 'Come Dance with Me' – along with 'The Loveliest Night of the Year'. The second session took care of 'Lolita', which had been one of Caruso's favourites, and the film's two inspired (for once) novelty numbers, 'Ay-Ay-Ay' and 'There's Gonna be a Party Tonight'. 'Questa o quella', on the other hand, Mario denounced as not being up to scratch: with film producer Silvio Clementelli standing in for Stoll, Mario would re-record this during his final 15-minute session on 23 June.

The biggest thorn in everyone's side during the Lanzas' first month in Italy was Betty. In Hollywood, Mario had been content to leave her to her own devices, which was one of the reasons why she had been hospitalised 19 times for drink and drugs-related illnesses, three of these including attempted suicide. In Rome, she was like the proverbial fish out of water, and to save her from 'humiliating' him further – though much of the time he did a better job of this himself – he insisted on her accompanying him to the studio each morning, usually when both of them were nursing hangovers. When she fought against this, Mario designated her his personal assistant, a role she took way too seriously, particularly when she began shouting directions from the sidelines and overruling the director's instructions to the cameraman. Finally, on 6 June, roughly halfway through the shooting schedule, Roy Rowland barred her from the set. Mario's reaction to this was to get blind drunk and threaten the director with a fate worse than death unless Betty was reinstated. The director took his complaint to the LeCloud-Titanus executives: the next day they closed down the set and announced that production on the film had been suspended indefinitely.

Mario called Al Teitelbaum in Los Angeles. Could his agent fly him home? For once he was not entirely to blame for all of the production problems. When we begin watching the film we instinctively know that we are not in for an intelligent drama: the Italian actors all speak to each other with thick Italian accents and one is hard put to work out what they are saying. Indeed, Renato Rascel's English is so poor that in one scene we actually see him reading from the cue cards on the table. Because of this, perfectly good scenes had to be shot time and time again. Little wonder then that Mario was feeling fraught. Returning to Hollywood, however, was out of the question. He had no assets in America, his house had been sold and, loath as Teitelbaum was to tell him, his unsavoury antics had made him no longer welcome in the film capital.

Teitelbaum held an emergency meeting with Greg Bautzer and the rest of the Lanza team: within two hours he was headed for Rome, where he was met at the airport by Maurice Silverstein, MGM's Italian deputy head of production. Silverstein had been all for firing Mario and getting him out of his hair once and for all. However, he acknowledged the fact that there must have been something to salvage, otherwise Teitelbaum would not have gone to so much trouble, and an uneasy compromise was reached wherein Mario would be given one last chance. The pair headed for his hotel, where they found him in a lamentable state. He had barricaded himself in his suite, completely bombed on a cocktail of alcohol and anti-depressants, and was once again threatening to end it all. Teitelbaum moved in with him until he had sobered up, then read him the riot act. LeCloud-Titanus would take him to the cleaners, and unless he pulled himself together, when this happened he would be on his own with neither agent nor legal representation because the team, quite frankly, had had enough. Furthermore, RCA would cancel his contract, and he would end up in a debtor's prison. This was not specifically true, but Teitelbaum's harsh directive had the desired effect. LeCloud-Titanus agreed to give Mario another chance, and shooting resumed on 12 June with Teitelbaum accompanying his tetchy star to the set each morning and watching him like a hawk, whilst Betty was banned from going within 200 yards of him while he was working.

With calm restored to the set, the Lanzas still continued to cause problems elsewhere. Their persistent squabbling and rowdy parties brought so many complaints from other guests at the Hotel Excelsior that they were asked to leave, and as usual they were presented with a bill for damages. This was kept out of the press, otherwise the owners of the Villa Badoglio on the Via Bruxelles – which had former belonged to Mussolini – would never have allowed them to cross the threshhold. For Mario, this was a potential homewrecker's paradise: the Lanzas forked out $1,000 a month to rent the bottom floor of the five-storey building, which boasted exquisite marble floors, fireplaces and ceilings, and was filled with priceless glass and antiques. It also had a swimming pool, gymnasium and tennis courts, though by this stage Mario was no longer interested in keeping fit. To be on the safe side, LeCloud-Titanus hired round-the-clock security, not to protect the Lanzas but to keep the valuable contents of the villa from being destroyed. This being the case, this was the only property they ever rented which they did not wreck. 'This was where Mario took up his last stand against his fate,' Costa later observed. 'This was the villa where his final orgies were staged, his final battles staged!'

The film more resembles one of the later Elvis Presley 'travelogue' movies than a vehicle showcasing Mario Lanza's still superlative talents: its true star is the Eternal City itself. It opens with Chicago-born tenor Marc Revere – a super-slim Mario – singing 'All The Things You Are' before having a row with his girlfriend, Carole (Peggy Castle), who ticks him off for standing her up last night, gives him the elbow, then heads for Europe with her new beau. With little money, Marc sets off in pursuit and we next see him on the Rome express, a knight in shining armour to pretty Italian girl Raphaella who has lost her ticket whilst rushing for the train. Marc takes her to stay with his cousin Pepe (Rascel), who has never seen him before, yet has no qualms about welcoming them both with open arms. Neither is Pepe fazed when Marc says that he will only stay until he has earned enough money to continue searching for his snooty, philandering girlfriend. Next we see him behaving like a dizzy Pied Piper, leading the locals dancing through the streets whilst pronouncing, 'There's Gonna be a Party Tonight' –

without any doubt one of the daftest songs Mario ever performed, as well as being the most cringeworthy.

Cut to the party, where afer a nifty tarantella Marc-Mario does a complete volte-face and sings 'Come Dance with Me', beautifully delivered with lush strings and a pleasant backing from the crowd. Then it is back to the travelogue as a last-minute reveller takes Marc, Pepe and Raphaella for a spin in his helicopter – hence we get to see every monument in the city, for the benefit of Mario's American fans captioned 'Rome, Italy', just in case they wondered where it was. To make ends meet, Pepe sells cheap art and Raphaella shoplifts – a temporary measure as Marc is confident that he will get a job singing in Rome's most prestigious night club, whilst Raphaella will become a much sought-after fashion model. The character and actor become as one: no one here has ever heard of Marc Revere because Italy is famous for exporting tenors, not importing them. The first establishment he tries already has a tenor – one who murders 'Be My Love'. The voice is Lanza's, clowning around. Therefore he pouts for a while, wandering through the streets where absolutely everyone sings, from washerwomen to window-cleaners, all in perfect pitch, until he chances across street-singer Luisa Di Meo. Accompanied by her father, she belts out 'Sidoney'. Together, she and Marc sing 'Arrivederci Roma', a sublime blending of the flawless tenor voice and the raw, untrained tones of the child in what was undoubtedly her proudest moment.

Ever the optimist – the exact opposite of Mario at the time – Marc enters a local talent contest at the theatre where Pepe is resident pianist. He sings 'Questa o quella', wins the competition, and becomes artiste-in-residence, earning a pittance compared to what he used to make in the States. Art again mirrors real life when success goes to his head and he begins bringing women home, unaware that Raphaella has fallen for him. There is an amusing but very much over-rated sequence where, for the benefit of a bunch of trad-jazz kids out in the square, he does a few impressions: passable imitations of Perry Como ('Temptation'), Frankie Laine ('Jezebel') and Dean Martin ('Memories are Made of This'), and a not-so-hot take on Louis Armstrong singing 'When the Saints Go Marching In'. Otherwise, the second half of the film, aside from Mario's singing, is not just uninteresting, but downright boring. Suffice it to say that Marc finds Carole and decides to return with her to America – until he catches her with another man, almost a repetition of the scene with Joan Fontaine in *Serenade*, which results in one of the hammiest brawls ever seen on the screen. Then Pepe, who has fallen in love with Raphaella, realises that she is not in love with him and sacrifices his own happiness so that she can be with Marc, whose behaviour suggests that maybe he would have been better off getting deported – exactly what the LeCloud-Titanus executives were saying about Mario Lanza.

Chapter Twelve

Command Performance, Benders and Tantrums

I doubt if the Palladium has ever heard a tenor of such lung power...Lanza shows he can belt out those top notes without the benefit of commercial amplification.

Press review of Mario's appearance on the
Royal Variety Performance

Shooting on *Seven Hills of Rome* was almost complete when LeCloud-Titanus arranged for Mario to appear in a benefit concert – their idea being that if news of his bad behaviour on the set was leaked to the press, then at least he would be seen to have done good elsewhere, helping those less fortunate than himself. Initially, he refused, declaring that he was not a one-man charity. Then he was informed that the 'charity' was the Mafia, and that the concert had been arranged on behalf of Charles 'Lucky' Luciano – therefore attendance was obligatory.

Luciano (1897–1962) was the undisputed king of Sicilian organised crime, and the mastermind behind the international heroin trade, besides other nefarious activities. A thoroughly reprehensible individual, he had emigrated to New York's Jewish quarter in 1907, when he was 10 years old, which enabled him even at such a tender age to set up a lucrative operation mugging Jewish children on their way to school. By the age of 14 he had already served time in prison, and would do so many times in the future. Luciano draft-dodged World War I by deliberately contracting chlamydia. With the advent of Prohibition, he joined forces with the so-called Five Point Gang, netting an estimated $50,000 a year from bootlegging alone. He assumed his nickname in 1929 when ambushed by a rival gang – he survived, along with his trademark facial scar and droopy eye. During World War II he ran his empire from prison, and the authorities authorised his parole in 1946 with the proviso that he return to Sicily. Instead, he fled to Cuba, where he operated under the Batista dictatorship – until the United States issued sanctions against medical supplies to the island, forcing Batista to exile him to Italy. Here, he began running his empire from a 60-room mansion on the Via Tasso in Naples – dividing his time between organised crime and, oddly, raising funds for the city's *scugnizzi* and the poor. It is rather sad that Mario's only full-length Italian concert – there were others at receptions, and in various night clubs, amounting to a mere handful of songs and arias – should have been stage-managed by the Mob. The details are sketchy. After a dress rehearsal at the Via Tasso, it took place at the Teatro di San Carlo on or around 11 July 1957 before an audience hand-picked by Luciano and his associates. Other than 'Vesti la giubba' and a clutch of Neapolitan songs which included 'Tiritomba', Mario's programme is not known. Though no press were allowed inside the auditorium, the newspapers reported that Mario was nervous, hardly surprising given the circumstances, persistently mopping his brow and at times clinging to the microphone for support. After the recital, the Mayor of Naples made him an honorary citizen of the city, and Enrico Caruso Jr presented him with the Caruso Award, an accolade concocted for the evening.

After the Naples event, Mario embarked on the most staggering binge of his career – eight days of non-stop drinking, sex and drugs. The studio bosses were powerless to stop him. The Villa Badoglio was supplied with extra security to ensure that the place stayed in one piece, but when Mario finally returned to the set he was served with a $35,000 writ for holding up production. When he tore this up, LeCloud-Titanus chief Goffredo Lombardo merely shrugged his shoulders: by way of a fine, the money would be deducted from Mario's salary. In fact, he would have been better off paying the original demand – when the studio took the matter further in the wake of a few more Lanza tantrums, the fine was upped to $69,700.

There was a further dilemma on 21 July, when Al Teitelbaum

announced that he could no longer function as Mario's manager. This had nothing to do with the singer's behaviour. Teitelbaum had just received word that the latest appeal against his conviction for fraud had failed, and that he would have to return to Los Angeles to serve his suspended prison sentence. He took the first flight out of Rome, rushed to see his lawyer, and within days launched another appeal, which was successful. Even so, he decided against flying back to Rome, and so would never see Mario again.

On 23 July, Mario was hospitalised with a mysterious illness – some tabloids hinted at another suicide attempt, others that he had suffered a mild heart attack. The official statement issued by the hospital's American spokesman, Dr Pennington, declared that his patient was suffering from stress 'brought about by events of the last few days'. Whatever the malady, by 26 July he was back on the sound stage, reshooting those scenes deemed unsuitable by Roy Rowland on account of the Italian actors' problems with the English language.

After shooting wrapped, Mario did virtually nothing but party for two months. He was resting, he told reporters, before embarking on a major European tour, currently being assembled by Columbia Artists. Also, he had been made 'an offer he could not refuse' by London's Covent Garden Opera. The first part of his statement was true: the tour was to open on 25 November with the first of two recitals in Genoa, followed by dates in Turin and Milan, where his programme would consist entirely of Caruso favourites. This would be followed by an album of the same material. He was also scheduled to sing at the Palais de Chaillot in Paris, after which there would be concerts in Oslo, Copenhagen and Stockholm. The tour would close in Rome with gala concerts at the Teatro Adriano and Teatro New York on 16 and 18 December.

In September Mario received a call from Costa, in New York. 'I'm singing like ten tigers,' he told his favourite accompanist, who had recently separated from his wife: therefore, Mario offered, what better way of getting over this than by coming to Europe to pick up where they had left off? Costa, conducting with the New York City Center Opera, was granted leave from the season's last performance to travel to Rome. In the meantime, during the first week of October, Mario was visited by Ed Sullivan, doing overseas location interviews for his *Toast of the Town* television show. Sullivan had travelled to Rome, not to see Mario, but to interview Sophia Loren and Rossanno Brazzi. Naturally, when Mario learned that America's leading television host was in town he insisted on inviting him to the Villa Badoglio, and made arrangements for Marisa Allasio to be there too, regardless of the fact that they were no longer on speaking terms. Another guest should have been 19-year-old Austrian actress Romy Schneider, then involved with French heart-throb actor Alain Delon. Mario met Schneider, and was so unspeakably vulgar towards her that she refused to be filmed with him: her section of the show was shot elsewhere. Mario's interview with Sullivan went well enough: wearing a silk dressing gown, he spoke of how much he was missing his friends in Hollywood – in fact, he hardly had any – and sent his fondest regards to Rocky Marciano. Then he brought up the subject of which songs he would be performing on the *Sullivan Show* for his American fans. He had rehearsed five pieces, and did Sullivan want them all, or just two or three? When Sullivan responded that his section, like Loren's and Schneider's, would have *no* songs other than a monochrome clip of Mario and Luisa Di Meo singing 'Arrivederci Roma', Mario threw such a strop that in one fell swoop he ruined any chance of future appearances on *Toast of the Town* or any of its rivals, should he ever return to America. The clip filmed in Rome would air on 19 January 1958 when Sullivan had his revenge on Lanza 'for being such an asshole' by insisting that his name be left off the credits.

On 31 October, the Lanzas appeared in *The Christophers Show*, filmed at the Vatican. Apart from the wonderful singing, this is the most stomach-churning performance Mario ever gave, the epitome of hypocrisy with an approach only slightly removed from some of the cheesy interviews given by Liberace at around this time. The Christophers, founded in 1945 by Maryknoll Seminary priest Father James Keller (1900–77), was promoted as 'rooted in the Judeo-Christian tradition of service to God and humanity, whilst embracing people of every nation, religion and age level'. Based in New York, the organisation began broadcasting on ABC in 1952, and would continue until the early sixties, whence it transferred to several of the smaller cable channels. Its motto was, 'It's better to light a candle than to curse the darkness', and the song 'One Little Candle' was played over the opening and closing credits.

Many stars had featured on *The Christophers Show*, but few have proved more cringeworthy to watch than Mario and Betty Lanza. Mario, hyperactive on account of the uppers he had taken that morning, fidgets throughout the interview or toys with his cigarette packet – his hands flutter everywhere and he giggles a lot. He opens the proceedings with a stupendous 'Santa Lucia', before Father Keller leads him to one side to explain how he started out. As an altar boy, he says, he would enter his local church in South Philadelphia and, sitting alone in the huge building, he would stare at the flickering red light above the altar. In these moments, he adds, he witnessed his entire career taking place before it happened: 'Since I was simply and wholly the keeper of a gift [touches his throat], my job was to bring, let's say, greater beauty to the world in my own little way, since we all have a job to do, and in my way a little bit of beauty and contentment.' 'And the world needs beauty,' Keller interjects. Next Mario speaks of his parents, of the sacrifices they made for him – particularly his mother, who worked a 12-hour day to pay for his singing lessons. He sings 'Because You're Mine', then the scenario intensifies in its silliness when Keller introduces a decidedly giddy Betty. 'In life, to have a partner, a truly lovable partner, is so important,' Mario enthuses, wrapping his arm around her shoulder. 'And aren't I the luckiest guy in the world because I met a wonderful partner?... Looking back over thirteen years of marriage I can only tell you one thing. It is truly a thing of beauty, our marriage!' To which Betty chips in, 'We go through all the trials and tribulations with a smile!' The previous evening, Mario had left Betty in their hotel suite and, whilst he had been combing Rome's red-light district, she had drunk herself into such a stupor that the children had been confined to their room by their nurses, when they should have been appearing on this programme and completing this 'perfect family' portrait. Next comes the most hypocritical statement of all when Mario pronounces, 'We have a great life of beauty, and I just wish that everybody could enjoy and experience the great, great happiness that I do!' He then rounds off the charade with 'Ave Maria' – before Father Keller advises his viewers, presumably by now gagging, to seek contentment by following the Lanzas' example, advice he would have been reluctant to dish out had he known what they were really like.

Costa flew into Rome three days after *The Christophers Show*. Rather than put him up at the Villa Badoglio – there was more than enough room – Mario paid for him to have a suite at the Excelsior. He had sworn over the phone to his friend that he had stopped drinking, and did not wish him to be witness to the nightly dissipation at the villa. Costa had also arrived too late to be involved in the recording session at Rome's Cinecitta Studios, where Mario cut four tracks for RCA – wielding the baton once more was George Stoll. 'The Loveliest Night of the Year' was given a stunning new arrangement and, dissatisfied with the version recorded the previous year, Mario re-recorded 'Younger than Springtime'. There was also a solo reading of 'Arrivederci Roma', mostly in English, and 'Never Till Now' – the music from this had featured in the recent film, *Raintree County*, starring Montgomery Clift and Elizabeth Taylor.

Most of the dates for Mario's European tour had sold out already, and he was now invited to participate in the *Royal Variety Show*, then the high spot of the British show-business calendar when (as opposed to now, when commercialism and winners of second-rate pop competitions rule the day) the royal family had a say in who would be appearing. Topping the bill would be the legendary Gracie Fields, who lived on Capri and shared several hits with Mario – her recordings of 'Come Back to Sorrento', 'Mattinata', 'September Song', Toselli's 'Serenade' and 'The Lord's Prayer' had actually outsold his, something which he resented. Gracie, arguably Britain's greatest-ever entertainer and as unpretentious and down to earth as they came, would be supported by a veritable pantheon of stars, including Judy Garland, Joan Regan, Harry Secombe, The Crazy Gang, Winifred Atwell, Vera Lynn, Alma Cogan and Count Basie – every single one of whom would end up detesting Mario Lanza.

Firstly, Mario objected to anyone but himself topping any show that he appeared in – unless Gracie was 'dropped down the ladder', he said, he would be staying in Rome. He made such a song and dance about this whilst on the phone to the organisers, Britain's premier entrepreneurs Lew and Leslie Grade, that they elected to take no chances. Gracie was understanding. She was a bigger star in Britain than Lanza would ever be, and the Grades assured her that her fans would understand. 'Lew Grade told her, "Let the hot-headed bugger have his own way – we'll soon have him out of our hair,"' her stepdaughter, Irene, recalled. The Grades then dispatched their representative, Peter Prichard, to Rome to assess the situation at the Villa Badoglio and report back whether, in his opinion, Lanza was suitable material – given his off-the-cuff outbursts – for presenting to Queen Elizabeth and Prince Philip. Obviously, if

Mario was out of shape or if Prichard found him too hard to handle, he would be given his marching orders and Gracie would be moved back up the bill. In fact, Mario treated Prichard like visiting royalty and during his two-day stay in Rome behaved impeccably.

Prichard travelled back to London with the Lanzas and Costa – the only awkward moment thus far being when Mario refused to get on a plane. Instead, they travelled via steamer and the Golden Arrow Express, arriving at Victoria Station on 14 November, where Mario was mobbed by 2,000 fans, most of them women, and several rather rude reporters. One of these barged to the front of the crowd, knocking Mario off his feet and almost under the train, forcing him to retreat to his carriage until the police restored order. The same reporter accosted him as he was descending the steps, and for a moment it looked as if Mario might hit her with his cane. Haughtily, she demanded to know what he would be singing for the Queen. Smiling graciously but cursing under his breath, Mario told her that she would have to wait and see.

One of Mario's conditions for doing a 'free' show – then as now, the event raised money for the Artistes' Benevolent Fund – was that the Grades pay for him to stay at the Dorchester. They obliged, and the Lanzas were installed in the Oliver Messel Suite, then the most expensive the hotel had to offer. Peter Prichard was instructed not to let Mario out of his sight for a moment: though well-behaved thus far, he was very highly strung, drinking heavily – two bottles of champagne with his breakfast – and hooked on amphetamines. A press conference had been arranged, with reporters given no restrictions over what they might ask. In these days when transatlantic news was relatively slow, few knew about Mario's antics on the film sets, or about his other 'ungentlemanly' conduct. Therefore most of the initial questions centred around his children, who he was happy to talk about – and his 'blissful' marriage, which he was happy to lie about. He lost his cool, however, when a reporter commented on how fit he looked. 'And I didn't look fit *before*?' he growled back. 'I'm the biggest recording star in the world, so why do you want to talk about my weight? I'm here to sing for the Queen of England, not to fight in a boxing match!' Their hackles raised, the press became merciless – henceforth, all their questions concerned his fluctuating weight, until Mario grabbed a glass of champagne from one of the attendant waiters, toasted himself and downed it in one gulp, and pronounced, 'Tomorrow I concentrate on the singing, tonight I concentrate on myself!' He then walked out of the press conference, shut himself in his bedroom with a bottle of Chivas Regal, and proceeded to get plastered. The headlines the next day were amongst the worst he had ever received: the words 'fat', 'gluttonous', 'drunk' and 'rude' were used to describe him. One aggrieved journalist denounced him as 'the tubby, temperamental tenor', whilst another called him 'a musical Farouk' – referring to the immensely fat Egyptian king, Farouk I.

The show was to take place at the 2,300-seater Palladium, then as now the most prestigious entertainment venue in Britain, on the evening of 18 November, which left little time for rehearsals. Mario refused to go to the theatre on the Friday afternoon as planned: the 200 fans waiting outside the stage door were told that he was 'unwell but resting'. Early the next morning Costa visited him at the Dorchester. 'The dead magnums of champagne surrounded him, so many miserable relics of his personal battlefield,' he observed. The accompanist recalled how Mario had told him, *'La vita e breve, la morte vien'* – life is brief, death is coming, which he appears to have adopted as his personal credo. Predicting a repeat of the Las Vegas fiasco, bookmakers in the city began taking odds-on bets that he would not show up for the actual performance – he had snubbed the Queen once, and would do so again. He failed again to turn up for rehearsals on the Saturday and Sunday, and almost certainly would have skipped the Monday session had he not received a call from Leslie Grade with the ultimatum that he should 'move his backside', or head for home. A second visit from Costa left him with little doubt that, unless he pulled himself together, he would have to find another accompanist. He finally made it to the Palladium late that afternoon. 'If it was something I had said or done, I will never know,' Costa wrote. 'But something – fatigue, shame, disgust with himself, physical pain – had broken through to him.'

By now, tired of setting out on a wild-goose chase, only a handful of fans were at the stage door to greet him. Even so, he stood chatting to them for half an hour before striding into the theatre and creating immediate chaos by insisting on rehearsing on a 'closed' stage – in other words, the other artistes would have to remain in their dressing rooms until he had finished. The theatre staff were also banned from the auditorium, to avoid anyone taking photographs or sneaking in a tape recorder. If this did not earn him their enmity, the event which took place in Mario's dressing room afterwards certainly did. A press photographer had managed to get in unobserved, and now began snapping away whilst Mario cursed and threatened to tear him apart. When Peter Prichard tried to intervene, Mario punched him in the face. Had the Grades been told of this before the performance, there is no way that they would have allowed the bad-tempered star to continue with the show. Producer Val Parnell, however, begged Prichard to say nothing, and not for the first time in his career Mario was able to get away with what was effectively ABH.

The show itself went well. In those days it was not televised, but broadcast on the BBC's Light Programme a few days after the event. Introduced by Bob Monkhouse, Mario walked on to the stage to thunderous applause, and signalled for the technician to 'suck' the microphone back into the floor. 'You're damn right I'll be great,' he had boasted to Costa, 'I'll sing like those British have never heard anyone sing before.' The three songs he had chosen for tonight had been in his repertoire for some time, yet still he was terrified of forgetting the words – he had not sung on the stage for six years. Costa had agreed to mime the words and prompt him from the orchestra pit. 'It suddenly became apparent that Mario Lanza couldn't sing a note without his conductor guiding him through the sequence,' the event's musical director, Cyril Ornadel, later observed in BBC Radio's *The Mario Lanza Story*. 'But when you stopped looking at that, you just listened to this gorgeous, natural voice singing so beautifully.' Mario opened with 'Because You're Mine', rattled the rafters with 'E lucevan le stelle', and closed with the number he claimed was his most requested ever, 'The Loveliest Night of the Year'. It has to be said that despite all the recent criticism, he had rarely sung so well. He was not, however, permitted to lead the ensemble in the singing of 'God Save the Queen' – this honour went to Gracie Fields, who was accorded the biggest applause of the evening.

It has always been a tradition after the *Royal Variety Show* for the royals to meet the artistes after the performance. Initially, Mario refused to augment the backstage line-up: if the Queen wanted to thank him, he said, then she could do so in the privacy of his dressing room. Val Parnell persuaded him otherwise: he had snubbed the Queen once by failing to attend the premiere of *Because You're Mine*, and would be blacklisted and his forthcoming tour placed in jeopardy if he did so again. The press and some biographers have variously reported how the Queen lingered whilst shaking Mario's hand to pronounce something along the lines, 'I never knew that human lungs could produce such power and volume!' In fact, she said no such thing because she could not get a word in edgeways. For reasons known only to himself, Mario also took exception to Prince Philip's comment, 'I hear you're on a European tour at the moment. I hope it's proving successful?' To which Mario rudely shot back, 'If you call $5,000 a night successful, yes. So, what's *your* story?' Philip gave as good as he got by retorting, 'Oh, my story is about as interesting as my voice!' – before moving down the line to felicitate Joan Regan.

Mario repeated this programme on 24 November when he topped the bill on *Sunday Night at the London Palladium*, then one of the most watched programmes on British television. Introduced by Hughie Green, who erroneously labelled him 'a star of many opera stages', he gave a recital which, though lasting just twelve minutes, remains one of the most remarkable performances of his career. Cynics and critics who had accused Mario of being all washed up were made to eat their words. Blowing kisses at the audience – bread-and-butter fans who were there to see *him*, his time, as opposed to a 'royal' crowd that would have been there no matter who was on the bill – and almost in tears because of the reception they gave him, he launched into 'Because You're Mine' and brought the house down. He had barged through professional life stomping on toes and being obnoxious to many, but where the fans were concerned he had never been less than the perfect gentleman whose sincerity could never be doubted: he loved them as much as they worshipped him. Standing under a canopy, he sang the *Tosca* aria, and finished with 'The Loveliest Night of the Year' – this time, he said, because this was really what it was. And as he repeated the refrain, he was surrounded by a bevy of dancing lovelies, two of whom, when emotion got the better of him, escorted him to the back of the stage in preparation for the customary revolving platform finale.

Two days later, the Lanzas and Costa returned to Rome. Mario had completely exonerated himself of all the things that had gone wrong during *The Great Caruso* tour and the Las Vegas disaster. He was looking forward to the new tour, he said, and was preparing a repertoire which would drive the fans crazy. Costa, ever the Job's comforter, had his doubts. 'He would never recapture the past, no matter how hard he tried,' he observed. 'But I knew that it would be useless [to argue], that I was dealing with a sick man, a man incapable of saving himself from tragedy.' To a certain extent, Costa would be proved wrong, although the initial prognosis was not good: no sooner had Mario settled back in at the Villa Badoglio than all his old problems resurfaced. Following the elation of London came the 'black dog' depression which saw him drinking more than ever. The rows with Betty, quelled whilst they had been in London, started up again. On 5 December she was rushed into a clinic with 'suspected appendicitis' – a regular show-business excuse when a studio or an artiste's management did not wish the public to know the real cause of the malady, in this instance malnutrition. Mario had been too wrapped up in his own problems – and off his face most of the time – to notice that his wife had not been eating properly, though to his credit he never left her side for a moment, sleeping in her room until she had regained her appetite and strength. During her incapacity she fainted several times, and Mario took advantage of her absence by having the marble floors of the villa carpeted so that she would not fall and hurt herself. As a result of her illness, Mario cancelled his forthcoming tour, then changed his mind and announced that it had been rescheduled for the new year, but with different venues to the ones that had been sold out for weeks. Because of this, some critics accused him of 'bottling out', afraid of being torn apart by hypercritical Italian audiences who never really appreciated him for the great star that he was.

Now, instead of singing in Italy, Mario would return to Britain where he was more appreciated, and he would visit France, Holland, Belgium and Germany, where he had a massive fanbase. Effectively, it was a wise decision, though he would encounter more than his share of problems on the circuit. He also trimmed his repertoire. Though he had lost none of his vocal power – his voice had dropped half a tone, but the pyro-technics were still very much in evidence – he was still terrified of fluffing his lyrics, and even more so of cracking one of those famous top Cs. Therefore he dropped set-pieces such as 'Nessun dorma', 'Di quella pira' and 'Granada', and resurrected several numbers he had once vowed never to sing again. A few days before Christmas, to enable the programmes to be printed in time for the first concert of 4 January 1958, Columbia Concerts announced Mario's set-list. The venues were asked to add something along the lines, 'Mr Lanza reserves the right to amend the order of his programme', but the list supplied by Mario would be rigorously adhered to. Like Marlene Dietrich in her later concerts, he never once diverged from the order of this list other than to miss out one or more items, depending on his mood – even the anecdotes beween songs were word-for-word the same:

First Half	Second Half
Lamento di Federico (Cilea)	Mama mia che vo' sape (Nutile)
Lasciatemi morire (Monteverdi)	A vucchella/Marechiare (Tosti)
Gia al sole dal Gange (Scarlatti)	Softly as a Morning Sunrise
Pieta Signore (Stradella)	I'm Falling in Love with Someone
Tell Me O Blue, Blue Sky (Giannini)	Because You're Mine
Bonjour ma belle (Behrend)	It's Pretty Soft for Simon
The House on the Hill (Charles)	Seven Hills of Rome
E lucevan le stelle (Verdi)	La donna e mobile

Columbia Concerts were desperately worried that the tour might be cancelled again when, a few days before the Lanzas should have left for England, Betty's doctors advised her that she was not well enough to travel. Though they argued incessantly and gave every impression of hating each other, and though Mario serially cheated on her – sometimes right under her very nose – he was loath to venture far without her, and did so now under tremendous duress. He left her behind only when assured that, if she took care of herself, she would be able catch up with him on the road. There was also a dilemma with Costa, himself not averse to throwing the occasional tantrum, particularly if he believed he was being taken advantage of. On the eve of the first concert, the accompanist had a blazing row with John Coast, Columbia's British representative who was responsible for the smooth running of the tour, not an easy task when the client was Mario Lanza. In the past, Coast had been used to handling 'easy' stars such as Jussi Björling. Costa's very valid argument was that, as Mario would not function professionally without him, he should be paid accordingly. For years, Columbia had been paying him a pittance, and Mario had frequently upped his fee from his own pocket. Now, he demanded a minimum $750 for each concert, plus a weekly retainer of $250 for 'unspecified' duties – in other words, for coddling the star. The request

was not unreasonable: Costa had temporarily given up his conduc-
torship with the New York City Center Opera to be with Mario, and he
had wasted enough time already, hanging around in Rome and doing
nothing in the wake of all the cancellations. Coast's initial reaction was
to bring in a standby pianist willing to work for $100 a show – Geoffrey
Parsons (1929–95), who would famously accompany some of the great
classical names of the day, including Victoria de los Angeles and
Elisabeth Schwarzkopf. Mario opposed the decision, and as before an
ultimatum was delivered: if Costa could not play, then Lanza would not
sing. Parsons travelled with his entourage throughout the British leg of
the tour, in the event of Costa becoming indisposed, but Mario would
have nothing to do with him.

The tour kicked off on 4 January 1958: tickets for the 3,000-capacity
Sheffield City Hall had sold out within two hours of the box office
raising its shutters. Many of the fans here tonight would follow Mario
around the country, and he frequently chose one or two die-hard
admirers to share his train carriage. Tears filled his eyes as Costa began
the introduction to his opening number time and time again, only to be
stopped by whooping and stomping of feet, which lasted five minutes.
Here, as elsewhere on the tour, he eschewed being introduced – 'They
know who I am, so why bother!' – often walking on to the stage whilst
the stragglers were still entering the auditorium, causing them to freeze
in their tracks or kneel on the floor. This was adulation at its most
profound, and well deserved. Though he refused to rehearse between
concerts, Mario had rarely been in better vocal form, despite the fact that
physically he was falling apart. His performances had their flaws, of
course – a few wobbly or cracked notes – but these he transcended in
singing of the highest order. The fans witnessed none of the anguish his
entourage had getting him into the theatre, which was less to do with his
drinking than with his doctors having recently diagnosed phlebitis (now
known as deep-vein thrombosis), a potentially life-threatening condition –
Orson Welles would die from it – which he did his utmost to ignore.
Here and at his subsequent concert in Glasgow, Mario even made light
of his illness during his first curtain call, hobbling back on to the stage
aided by a 'Caruso cane', and rolling up his trouser leg to show off his
heavily bandaged leg.

On 14 January, Mario received word that Betty was fully recovered, and en route to London. They were reunited at the Dorchester the following afternoon, and during the evening they attended American tenor Richard Tucker's Covent Garden debut, singing Cavaradossi in *Tosca*. Tucker's wife, Sara, had invited the couple to share her box, with the proviso that Mario did not attempt to steal her husband's thunder – that he sat behind her and stayed out of sight during the performance. He later congratulated Tucker in his dressing room: but while photographs of the pair show Mario smiling radiantly, there is no doubt that he was tormented by his inner demons. For years he had dreamed of singing on the legitimate opera stage, and had been prevented from doing so by MGM's greed and his own shortcomings. And now he had witnessed an artiste of lesser status than himself achieving something he had not.

Fortunately, the highlight of this tour and one of the great moments of Mario's career took place the next evening, with an appearance at the 8,000-seater Royal Albert Hall. Only one recital had originally been planned for here, but when all the tickets sold in less than four hours, the promoters added another concert for 20 January, and a third to take place in February. Mario walked on to the stage, tripped over a wire, and laughed this off. 'Wow,' he exclaimed, surveying the massive domed concert hall for the first time, 'is this for real?' Blowing kisses at the audience, he nodded to the three waist-high microphones. 'You're being recorded,' he joked, 'otherwise why would *I* need three mikes?' This first show lasted almost three hours, with Mario taking a break after every third item – he needed to do so now to recover his strength – and during these intervals, Costa played solo piano pieces, much to the consternation of the fans, who were only really interested in Mario. Though there have been many subsequent 'live' Lanza compilations, apart from the 1947 Hollywood Bowl concert with Frances Yeend, to date this is the only complete Lanza recital to have been released commercially. Minus one song, 'It's Pretty Soft for Simon' from Victor Herbert's *Naughty Marietta*, it was issued as *The Mario Lanza Program*, and later under the more apt title, *Lanza In London*.

On 18 January, Mario topped the bill on ATV Television's *Saturday Night Spectacular*. The producer had wanted him to repeat his Palladium programme, but he insisted on a lighter repertoire: 'Softly as a Morning Sunrise', 'Marechiare', and 'I'm Falling in Love with

Someone'. Towards the end of the last song, he attempted a little dance and winced. That afternoon, he had lunched with Lana Turner at her Hampstead home (he was still carrying a torch for her), and whilst walking around her garden had slipped on the stone steps leading down from the patio. Then, he had laughed off the incident, but on the morning of the 19th he awoke with an excruciating pain in his side, and a doctor summoned to the Dorchester diagnosed a cracked rib and advised him to cancel his next concert at the Royal Albert Hall. He refused to even consider this, rightfully declaring that doing so would only earn him the enmity of those critics 'out to get him' following his disastrous London press conference the previous November. He also refused to have the injury strapped, arguing – again rightly – that this would hamper his breathing. In fact, he sang so well that, had he not joked with the audience that he had cracked a rib whilst attempting a particularly lengthy top C, no one would have been any the wiser.

On 25 January, under considerable duress, Betty and Costa coaxed Mario on to the plane for Munich. He downed an entire bottle of Chivas Regal en route in an attempt to calm his nerves, and afterwards told reporters in the airport lounge, 'Never again!' The brief German tour opened the following evening at the city's Congress Hall, and was reminiscent of the reception usually given to the likes of Tommy Steele and Johnnie Ray. Mario had scarcely finished taking his curtain calls when dozens of screaming fans invaded the stage, forcing him to flee into the wings. Amidst the confusion he lashed out at what he thought had been a burly male admirer wrapping his arms about his waist, knocking him flat on his back – in fact, it was a German security man. The next day, Mario visited him in hospital where he had been admitted with suspected concussion: it had been an easy mistake to make, and the man told him that no apology was necessary – that it had been a privilege to have been 'decked' by Mario Lanza. There was similar pandemonium in Stuttgart, three evenings later, when Mario sustained a top C at the end of 'La donna e mobile' for fifteen seconds. The audience stomped and yelled for him to sing the aria again, and he obliged – the only time during this tour that he did this, though long before the applause had died down he took one look at the crowd of people heading for the stage and fled to the safety of his dressing room, locking the door behind him.

The German critics, on the other hand, were not so enthusiastic. The journalists reviewing Mario's concert at the Royal Albert Hall had wanted to know why he had sung just two operatic arias. The German promoter had picked up on this, and asked Mario to amend his programme and include those arias from *La Bohème, Otello, Tosca* and *Pagliacci* that he was famed for. He refused, and now the detractors had their revenge. Reading their needlessly barbed and even occasionally poisonous reviews, one might be excused for thinking they had attended a totally different concert from everyone else. Almost all of them drew comparisons with Caruso's stage performances – which none of them had seen, of course. It really was a case of attacking for attacking's sake. The Stuttgart concert also proved too much for Mario – that one extra rendition of 'La donna e mobile' completely robbed him of his strength and no sooner had he reached his hotel than he collapsed from exhaustion. The next morning, a doctor was summoned and the tidings were grim: the phlebitis in his leg was worse, and his blood pressure was sky-high. The specialist who examined him next, a Dr Fruhwein, told him point-blank that if he continued working there was every chance of him dropping dead on the stage. Mario might have been content to ignore such a warning, but when Dr Fruhwein's diagnosis was relayed to John Coast, Columbia Concerts – terrified of how much they would have to fork out in compensation if anything happened to their biggest star – had no option but to cancel the next 12 concerts. These were the five that remained in Germany, the two at the Palais de Chaillot and the Royal Albert Hall, and five more elsewhere in England and Ireland.

The Lanzas returned to Rome, where Mario remained hospitalised for two weeks. He received a stream of visitors – mostly reporters and fans, though Lucky Luciano dropped in from time to time – and made plans for a future in which he, but few others, was confident would soon see him returning to his old form. A film was in the pipeline, he said, and he had been discussing plans to re-record the soundtrack of *The Student Prince* with busty soprano Anna Moffo. The tabloids reported that he needed to work to pay off his ever-mounting debts and continue his luxurious lifestyle: from the $40,000 he had earned from his January concerts he had around $12,000 to fork out in commission to various agents, $15,000 to the taxman, $3,000 to Costa, $4,000 in medical bills for himself and Betty, and $4,000 rent on the villa – the $2,000 he owed already, along with $2,000 which the owners were now demanding in advance. He therefore had to press on, regardless of how he felt, or sink like the *Titanic*. He was at his lowest ebb when a South African promoter offered him a brief tour of the country: his fee would be an unprecedented $36,000 for six tax-free, no-commission concerts in July – two each in Pretoria, Cape Town, and Johannesburg. Mario merely shrugged his shoulders and said that he would think about it.

On 2 March, the Lanzas and Costa returned to London to pick up where Mario had left off. On 6 March he received a five-minute ovation when he walked on stage at the 6,000-capacity King's Hall, in Manchester's Belle Vue district. Towards the end of the concert he forgot the words to 'Softly as a Morning Sunrise', and had to be prompted by Costa. He laughed off the gaff, telling the audience that emotion and the pain from his bad leg had got the better of him, which was at least partly true. 'He kicked around quietly, now and then,' observed the critic with the *Manchester Guardian*, who knew nothing of Mario's malady. Later in the week he sang to packed houses in Newcastle and Brighton. Somewhere en route he had picked up a new admirer, very much in the stamp of Terry Robinson, though many were soon denouncing him as a cross between an obsessive fan and a leech. Alex Revides was a failed Shakespearean actor who attached himself to Mario like a limpet. Like Robinson at the beginning of their friendship, Revides almost certainly had a crush on him, though unlike Robinson he does not appear to have given much in return other than bad advice, rubbing Betty and the rest of the entourage up the wrong way.

It was Revides who inherited the 'mothering and factotum' duties from the long-suffering Peter Prichard, who had elected to throw in the towel. When the Lanzas travelled back to Rome on 14 March – having cancelled concerts in Bradford, Croydon and Birmingham – Revides tagged along. By now, Mario and Betty were so engulfed in their self-inflicted problems that even the children had been forced into the background – causing havoc by riding their bicycles around the villa's marble corridors whilst their parents entertained, or simply drank themselves into oblivion. Every now and then they would be summoned into what one journalist described as 'the throne room': sitting in huge chairs placed six feet apart, Mario and Betty would receive each child one at a time, and feign interest in the scrapes they had got into since their last audience. Another visitor received here was Lucky Luciano, still demanding that Mario should sing for him and his Mafioso cronies, and more likely than not receiving the sharp end of Mario's tongue. In the haze of dissipation it may not have crossed his mind that he had been threatened by these people before leaving America, and that there was the very real danger of Luciano or one of his cohorts exacting his revenge by kidnapping one of the children unless he did as he was bid.

Ten days later, the show was back on the road with Mario's entourage laying odds-on bets on how long it would all last – such was his state of health and his steadfast refusal to cut himself any slack. The vitriol and tantrums that had driven everyone else to distraction were now aimed at himself. On 25 March he sang at Edinburgh's Usher Hall, and two evenings later gave a trimmed-down concert in Dundee. Alex Revides seems to have had little trouble getting him on to a plane – aided by a bottle of best Irish whiskey – and he thrilled over 10,000 fans at Belfast's King's Hall where, for the first time, he insisted on security men standing in the wings, purposely visible to the audience in the hope of avoiding a stage invasion. Tonight, there was to be no curtain call. On 31 March he sang at Leicester's De Montfort Hall, and two days later flew to Paris for what should have been one of the crowning glories of his career – a recital at the Olympia.

Chapter Thirteen

Je n'en connais pas la fin

Hell, I've got a strong constitution. I'll beat this thing. No
goddam pills are going to kill Mario Lanza!

Mario Lanza

T he Paris Olympia will go down in history as one of the biggest
mistakes of Mario Lanza's entire career. The Olympia was – and
still is – the most prestigious music-hall in France, if not in
Europe, and its audiences were notoriously difficult to please. Reopened in
1954 by Bruno Coquatrix, until the impresario's death in 1979 its red neon
lights boasted every major star on the planet – any artiste not invited to
appear at the Olympia simply was not worth their salt. Mario was booked
for a single concert on the evening of Wednesday 2 April – the only gap in
his busy schedule – which in itself caused Coquatrix an almighty headache.
The date was smack in the middle of a sell-out season by Edith Piaf, then
the highest-paid female entertainer in the world and, like Mario, a
legendary figure who burned the candle at both ends and lived way beyond
her means. Piaf had opened on 17 January for four weeks – itself twice the
length of a regular Olympia season – but had proved so popular that her
run had been extended several times. She would stay here until the
beginning of May. Coquatrix was even contravening fire regulations by
selling folding seats in the aisles. Under normal circumstances, a one-off
recital such as Mario's would have taken place on a Monday, traditionally
the *jour de relâche* when the big theatres in Paris either closed or put on
inferior fare – dropping their admission fees to make up for this. Piaf was
asked to do a 'swap', and did so – then promptly left for Deauville with her

latest flame, Georges Moustaki. The house capacity at the time was 2,300, and all the tickets for her impromptu Monday performance were sold within a few hours. Those who had bought tickets for the Wednesday were given the opportunity to have their money refunded, and did so when informed that they would on average have to cough up another 80 francs to exchange them for Lanza tickets. Coquatrix placed an advertisement in the evening paper, announcing that the Piaf–Lanza recitals had been swapped around, and this resulted in a huge queue forming outside the theatre before midnight on 1 April. The fans' excitement turned to anger, however, once the box office opened. Lanza's management had demanded $2,800 for his performance (Piaf was getting the equivalent of $1,500), which meant that Coquatrix had been forced to raise the average ticket price from 150 to 300 francs – a phenomenal amount – to break even.

The Olympia recital could have figured amongst Mario's greatest triumphs, but it ended up his biggest failure. Only 1,600 tickets were sold on account of the huge enforced hike in ticket prices. Piaf was performing 23 songs every evening, besides the Sunday matinee, and Bruno Coquatrix was expecting nothing less than the programme which Mario had adhered to this far in his tour. The Lanza entourage encamped at the best hotel in town – the George V on the Champs-Elysées – where Mario was officially welcomed by Coquatrix and his business partner, Jean-Michel Boris. Here, there was an altercation between Mario and Coquatrix – 'He did all the cursing and yelling, we just listened,' Coquatrix recalled – during which he declared that the fee he was getting for the Olympia concert was inadequate. Coquatrix, a gentle man, argued that the contract had been signed, and that Mario would have to take up the matter with the promoters. The showman explained what happened next:

> Lanza yelled that unless we coughed up *double* the amount he'd signed for, then he would perform pro-rata. The first song was great – not a massive applause. The second and third were much better, the fourth earned him a standing ovation. Then, after the fifth, he just threw up his arms and said, 'That's it, folks. I'm out of here!' Some people had paid 300 francs to see him, and he just walked off the stage. Any cheers were quickly drowned by the boos and the stamping of feet and the calls of '*Remboursez!*' We had no

option but to put out an announcement that anyone returning their ticket stubs to the box office would be reimbursed, and there couldn't have been more than a dozen spectators who didn't ask for their money back. The house lost a fortune. And worse was to come when I got to the dressing room. Never in forty years in this business have I come across a character so positively vile and dirty-mouthed. Until then, the bad boys of the music-hall were Gilbert Bécaud and Charles Trenet. Compared to Lanza, they behaved like saints. The fact that he actually spat in my face gained him the accolade of never being permitted to sing in France again.

Such, effectively, was Coquatrix's influence in the music-hall.

This blacklist extended beyond France. Mario had been scheduled to sing in a live television special in Brussels on 28 April, which was to have been relayed across the Continent via Eurovision. As such, this would have been the only full-length Lanza concert ever captured on celluloid. When Mario learned that this had been cancelled, he trashed his suite at the George V and was presented with a $1,000 bill for the damage, along with a second hefty bill for transatlantic telephone calls. When he refused to pay, the manager sent for the police and the gendarmes who attended the scene ordered him to hand over the cash – or be arrested and spend the night in a cell.

From Paris, jeered by former fans as they departed from the Gare du Nord, the Lanzas travelled to Ostend where, after a full concert this time, Mario received a cool reception and refused to take any curtain calls. A few evenings later in Rotterdam, he sang under extreme duress to a 25-per-cent capacity audience; news of his behaviour in Paris had preceded him, and the management neatly executed a volte-face on what Mario had done at the Olympia – they paid him pro rata, just $1,000 of his $4,000 fee. This put him in an absolutely vile mood, and the next morning Betty, having caught the brunt of this, announced that she had had enough – later that afternoon she flew back to Rome, telling reporters that one of the children was ill.

On 11 April, he sang 12 of the 16 items from his programme at the Neidersachshalle, in Hanover. Here, the critics were more interested in how he looked, rather than in how he sounded. Indeed, whatever he did in Gemany, there would be no pleasing them. Mario had never liked performing in a tuxedo, and tonight he went on in a perfectly smart lounge suit and, halfway through his set, removed his tie and unbuttoned the top three buttons of his shirt as he had during *The Great Caruso* tour. In America, female fans had screamed their delight – here, the stuffy audience booed. One critic wrote scathingly, 'It's no good having a great voice if the singer looks slovenly.' Mario was even pilloried for pausing between songs to take a sip of water. Two evenings later, despite suffering from a heavy cold, he put in a sterling performance at the huge 7,500-seater Ostseehalle, in Kiel. 'His voice, darker and richer than I have heard it in years, thrilled me,' Costa recalled. 'Its volume and substance rivalled any male voice I had ever heard in my life.'

The next evening Mario, Costa and Alex Revides travelled by car to Hamburg, where Mario was scheduled to sing on 16 April. Revides had booked suites at the Hotel Vier Jahreszeiten, but Mario announced that he wanted to take advantage of his wife's absence – not that it would have made any difference, had Betty been with him – by sampling the Reeperbahn red-light district. Costa had by now restricted his time spent with Mario to the rehearsal room and concert platform. 'I wanted discreetly to absent myself during the drinking bouts, the brawls with women, the wild and destructive rages,' he recalled. It was therefore up to Revides to persuade him to stay in his suite, and 'buy in' instead, though what happened when he did this would provide the hotel staff and other guests with enough ammunition to attack Mario for years to come. Mario was entertaining a Chinese prostitute when John Coast arrived with the German promoter – and Mario promptly demanded that she 'blow' them in front of him, seeing as he had paid, he said, way over the odds for her favours. They were acutely embarrassed, and when the young woman also voiced her disapproval Mario shoved a crumpled $100 bill down her cleavage, hit her and knocked her to the floor, then dragged her to the door, whereat she was reported to have yelled, 'To think that this is the great Mario Lanza. I feel sorry for you!' Neither did the matter end here. Half an hour later she returned to the hotel with her boyfriend, who initially only demanded an apology. When this was not forthcoming – Mario threatened to break his back – the police were called. Before they arrived, however, Mario and the boyfriend had reached an agreement – the prostitute was paid on-the-spot 'damages' of $1,000 and the matter was dropped.

Mario clearly had not learned his lesson. The next evening, after entertaining another prostitute, Mario and Revides got drunk in his suite and ended up in a heated debate about *Otello*, which he claimed he would soon be singing for one of the major houses – another Lanza tall tale, of course. The other guests at the Vier Jahreszeiten were therefore treated to an impromptu performance of some of Verdi's most dramatic arias, repeated time and time again until the early hours of the morning – prompting so many complaints that the hotel manager came close to evicting them. The next morning, Mario awoke with laryngitis, and a Doctor Schaake from the Hamburg Opera administered painkillers and a vitamin shot, sprayed Mario's throat, and assured him that he would be fine for the evening's concert providing he rested completely until it was time to leave for the theatre. Mario did as the doctor advised, but to alleviate his boredom, quaffed three bottles of champagne. The alcohol reacted badly with the medication: Doctor Schaake visited him again two hours before curtain-up, and informed him that his vocal cords were in such poor shape that if he sang tonight he ran the risk of permanent damage. Mario deliberated until twenty minutes before the performance, when most of the audience and invited guests had arrived, before contacting Costa – who was already at the theatre – to inform him that the concert was off.

The Germans reacted in pretty much the way the French had after the Olympia fiasco, save that this time Mario was not present to hear the boos, and the whistling – in Europe in those days a sign of extreme derision. The theatre manager had such a hard time controlling the crowd that Costa volunteered to have a go at calming them down by announcing that, this time, Mario was genuinely ill – though now having spoken to the doctor he was not sure whether he was ill, or just throwing another strop. The accompanist had barely opened his mouth when dozens of irate fans stormed the stage, chasing him and the manager into the wings and stopping only when beaten back by security men. Costa later observed how he had seen everything in the way of obnoxious behaviour during *The Great Caruso* tour, but that he had had to travel to Hamburg to experience his first concert-hall lynch mob. Their hatred of Mario saw hundreds of people heading for the Hotel Vier Jahreszeiten. Some were armed with albums and programmes they had brought along for Mario to sign – instead, they burned these out in the street whilst chanting, 'Mario, go home!'

Very early the next morning, Mario and his entourage left the hotel via the service entrance, and headed for the airport: there is newsreel footage of him arriving in Rome, limping across the tarmac and flinging himself into Betty's arms before hugging each of the children. The remaining tour dates had been cancelled, though he said he was very much looking forward to singing in South Africa: the promoter there had upped his fee to an unprecedented $10,000 a show. The 'wronged' German venues later attempted to sue for breach of contract, but achieved nothing when Mario's doctor confirmed that this time he had had a genuine excuse. Mario himself promised to return to Germany as soon as he could to fulfil the engagements.

Two days after the Hamburg disaster, Mario received a transatlantic call from Hy Gardner (1908–89), the bitchy, acid-tongued gossip columnist with the *New York Herald Tribune* who also had his own television chat show, *Hy Gardner Calling!* In this, the interviews were innovatively conducted by telephone. The programmes were broadcast split-screen, with Gardner sitting behind a studio desk and guests ensconced in a nearby hotel because most of them could not stand the sight of him – though pride was invariably swallowed because of mass audience exposure. Maria Callas would call Gardner 'son of a bitch' over the air for being unspeakably rude when asking questions about her personal life, and Elvis Presley – denounced prior to the show as 'a dope' – also got the better of this obnoxious man, who had a fondness for drawing attention to himself by being condescending or trying to catch out less knowledgeable guests.

Gardner's plan was to set up a similar studio in Rome, then deluge Mario with impertinent questions about his weight, his personal and marriage problems, his on-set traumas, and his bad-boy reputation. Mario was having none of this, but did agree to be interviewed for the *New York Herald Tribune*. Gardner promised to be in touch, and Mario jokingly told him, 'How's about coming over to the little castle I call home? Do that and I'll cook you a ton of fettuccine and chicken cacciatore, and answer all your foolish questions!' Gardner took him at his word, and on 26 April arrived in Rome hoping to get Mario to change his mind, or maybe submit to an 'informal' interview with the two of them facing each other in rocking chairs – a *truc* he sometimes adopted for tetchy guests such as Montgomery Clift. Mario refused to be swayed, insisting that Alex Revides be present so that he would not be misquoted, and very quickly changed his mind about putting Gardner up at his 'castle' once he started laying into him.

Gardner immediately wound Mario up by quoting from the enemy – the numerous *Time* and *Newsweek* features which had gone out of their way to offend him. Referring to the Hamburg cancellation he said, '*Newsweek* reported your failure to show up as "the old theatrical bromide" that you were suffering from a cold.' To which Mario angrily chimed in, '*Time* and *Newsweek* should report facts, not fantasy. I caught a cold so bad that I sounded like Andy Devine – and people were paying to hear Lanza.' He added that the doctor who had examined him in Hamburg had concluded that, although he had advised Mario against singing, the decision over whether to sing or not should ultimately be left to Mario himself, and the singer had wisely decided not to risk permanent damage to his voice. Gardner did not believe this, quoted *Time* again, and rebuked him for his previous cancellations, which brought about more expletives than Gardner had heard since getting on the wrong side of Maria Callas:

> Does *Time* think a kid from South Philadelphia could have grossed more than $5,250,000 in five years and paid Uncle Sam more than $4 million in taxes if he didn't sing? What do they think – that I'm a ventriloquist!

This was the cleaned-up version of Mario's outburst, and signalled an abrupt ending of the interview. Six months later, Gardner would observe, 'Mario was one of the nicest, brightest and most spirited persons I ever met, the antithesis of the picture painted by the press.' The truth is, he had not been particularly nice that afternoon in Rome. And who could blame him?

Eager it would appear to squeeze the last ounce of strength out of him, Columbia Concerts announced that Mario would resume touring in the late spring, and pencilled in more concerts for England and Ireland. The tour of South Africa was very definitely on, they added, though Mario was not sure that he would be honouring requests from as far afield as Australia and New Zealand. The fees discussed were staggering for a man whose career was supposedly on the slide: $6,000 for each one-hour recital. In 1958, only Frank Sinatra and Edith Piaf were earning this much for their concerts. Strangely, there was no interest in him from the United States: he had well and truly blotted his copybook on the other side of the Atlantic, though MGM were still willing to part-finance and distribute any films he made there – they just did not want him back, and no one was more to blame for this than Mario himself.

The Villa Badoglio had now become Mario's refuge from the world, from which he rarely emerged. Betty was out of it most of the time – her latest addiction was Seconal, washed down by a tumbler of whisky – and even the children had become too much for him as he retreated to the villa's downstairs kitchen. Once again he was convinced that someone was out to get him – indeed, he may have been genuinely under pressure to perform again for Lucky Luciano or one of his Mafia cronies. Whenever the phone rang, Alex Revides took the call, and the reply was always the same: Mr Lanza was not at home. 'I'm sick to death of spending twenty dollars a time to hear the arrogant and aggressive nonsense of a man like Revides,' John Coast is quoted as writing in a letter to Bill Judd, in New York. Others were not quite so polite: Revides was invariably referred to as 'that fucking Greek'.

In May, Mario booked himself into the Valle Giulia clinic after complaining of chest pains, and the prognosis was not good. His weight was up to 260 pounds, and although he had cut down on his beer and Chivas Regal intake, he now had a new tipple – neat Campari, which he drank from the bottle, by the bottle. Tests taken that day revealed extensive liver disease, though not too far advanced to effect a cure. Mario was told to stop drinking and smoking, to reduce his food intake by at least half, and to take gentle exercise. Doctors here administered mercurial diuretic injections which led to temporary mild incontinence, and prescribed Antabuse, the drug which, when mixed with alcohol, induced vomiting. Within a week, Mario had become immune to it: he began mixing it with amphetamines, became addicted, and when the doctors stopped prescribing it he simply bought it privately – when the client was Mario Lanza, there was never any shortage of suppliers. There were of course the inevitable side-effects: palpitations, shortness of breath, panic attacks and bloated, purple features. Had Terry Robinson been there, he might have badgered his friend into shape. Without him, Mario was a loose cannon. Doctors at the Valle Giulia pulled no punches with their prognosis: unless he drastically changed his lifestyle, he would not live to see 40.

Also in May, quite possibly at the clinic, Mario signed a contract with the Munich-based Corona Films to play yet another tetchy tenor in *For the First Time*, a German–Italian co-production which would be shot mostly on location in Capri and prove considerably better than its predecessor. Mario, who accepted the role only after tenor Franco Corelli had rejected it, insisted that his character's name be changed to Tony Costa, in honour of both his father and his favourite accompanist. He demanded a $200,000 fee for the film, along with a hefty percentage of the profits, and producer Alexander Gruter readily agreed – he had been about to offer half as much again. As a special request, to assist him with 'ongoing expenses' – Mario was still living way beyond his means – Corona agreed to advance him $8,000 a month, with the balance of his salary to be paid on completion of the film.

Rather than stay at a hotel on the island, Mario asked if he could stay at Gracie Fields's complex, La Canzone del Mare. 'He'd spouted off at the Palladium,' Irene Bevan said, 'and so had Gracie. Lanza's manager called Bert [Aza, Gracie's manager] and asked for her number. They talked on the phone for half an hour, and she gently explained why this might not be a good idea. He was very understanding – an absolute joy to talk to, Gracie said.' A little of their conversation was repeated by Gracie to her childhood pal from Rochdale, Mary Whipp, 'I told him, "Where are we going to put you, love. If there was just you and your family, that'd be fine. But I can't have all those bodyguards and hangers-on traipsing all over the place. I had enough of that with King Farouk. But Mario did come to the restaurant a couple of times with his wife, and I found the two of them delightful company."' A few years earlier, Gracie had allowed the infamous Egyptian king to stay in one of her private apartments – the complex was not a hotel – and with his huge retinue of retainers he had taken over the whole complex, driving the essential tourists away. Other hoteliers on the island followed Gracie's example: they did not object to Lanza, just to the hullabaloo which surrounded him; therefore he was forced to stay at an (unspecified) hotel in Naples, and commute to the island on a daily basis.

Next came the time-honoured tradition of getting the star into shape before the production began. As before, Mario wanted to record the soundtrack first – he still believed that it was obligatory to have this excess weight to push his voice forwards. But before the album, there was the South African tour. The tickets for all six shows had been sold out for weeks, and Mario was interested in extending the tour, providing the organisers would permit him to sing to all-black or non-segregated audiences. Under current apartheid legislation, this would never have happened: the British star George Formby had been ordered to leave the country for doing just the same thing. As a gesture of goodwill, unaware of his reputation, the promoter had deposited $30,000 in Mario's bank account (which had long ago been spent), and made arrangements for Mario and Betty to fly first class so that he would be as comfortable as possible throughout the flight. It was apparently only when he reached the airport with Costa that he learned that this flight would take 20 hours, and when the air traffic controller announced that a great deal of turbulence was predicted, that was it: within minutes he and his entourage were on their way back to the Villa Badoglio. 'I was crushed,' Costa recalled. 'I had been relying on the fees from the South African tour to regain solvency. Now I was left without a penny.'

The rows with Betty intensified, if such a thing was possible. Indeed, Mario had turned into a living nightmare for everyone who came into contact with him. On one occasion he was arguing with conductor Paul Baron over the proposed re-recording of *The Student Prince* soundtrack, and in his rage hurled a heavy Bakelite telephone across the room. This missed Baron and hit Costa, damaging his knee and sending him sprawling backwards, twisting his back. In her desperation Betty is believed to have called Terry Robinson in Los Angeles, who was in her opinion the only person capable of sorting Mario out once and for all. Robinson, probably thinking himself best out of it, refused to fly out to Rome. Since leaving America under a darkened cloud they had barely spoken. MGM would have put Mario on a crash diet, but Corona had a more relaxed attitude to getting things done – besides which, they were advised by Mario's doctors that a Robinson–MGM regime in his present state of health would probably kill him. On 28 May he was dispatched to the sanatorium at Jachenau, close to the shores of Lake Walchensee, 50 miles south of Munich, an establishment known for treating obese and/or alcoholic celebrities.

Mario's target was, in his own time, to lose 45 pounds. The doctors at Jachenau effected a sleep cure by injecting him with Megaphen and inducing a semi-coma for several days at a time, so that he could be fed intravenously. He was successfully weaned off Campari, but his swims in the lake during breaks from the treatment only increased his appetite. He also developed a passion for German beer, offering impromptu recitals and getting sozzled at the local bierkellers and bars. One German newspaper reported that it was not beyond him to down a one-litre stein without pausing for breath, and that on good nights he could quaff half a dozen of these. He also further endangered his health by throwing weights and going for early-morning runs, activities which were strictly forbidden on account of his phlebitis. Even so, by early August he was down to 190 pounds and up to receiving visitors. Betty and the children moved into a guest-house in nearby Wallgau so that they could drop in on him most afternoons, and Mario spent his mornings with Costa, rehearsing the numbers for the new film. On 23 August, declared 75 per cent fit, he was discharged from the clinic. When he arrived home, to his disappointment – but to Betty's delight and that of everyone else who had found his presence unsettling and a negative influence on Mario – the hated Alex Revides was gone.

On 28 August, walking for the first time in months without a cane, Mario entered the Rome Opera House studio to cut the first five tracks for the soundtrack album. Costa, remembering their last recording session in 1953, was naturally apprehensive – and so was Mario, particularly when he read in a newspaper how the studio had 'leaked' the news that he sounded good on his records only because clever American studio technicians had 'twiddled knobs to manufacture the Lanza sound'. 'This is like facing a firing squad,' he was heard to mutter as he glanced through the window of the recording booth at the 200-strong audience he had attracted – technicians and personnel from other studios, theatre managers, journalists, and the 160-strong Opera House ensemble hired to accompany him – most of these people waiting, and more than a few hoping, for him to die on his feet.

Mario was shaking and sweating profusely before the orchestra struck up the introduction to his first song. His agenda that day comprised 'I Love Thee' (Ich liebe dich), the 'Grand March' from *Aida*, the Trio from Mozart's *Cosi fan tutte* and, for the umpteenth time, 'Vesti la giubba'. He had however elected to get the most difficult piece out of the way first: 'Niun mi tema', the death scene from *Otello*. He sang this so precisely and with such unbridled passion that he received a standing ovation from the detractors in the other room. The next day, the same journalists who had been hoping to tear him apart enthused that he had been born to play the role. Sadly, however, it was not enough for them to base their assumptions on what they had just witnessed. The Lanza voice, though still almost faultless, was but part of the equation where playing Otello was concerned: even when younger and at the zenith of his powers, Mario would never have had the stamina to carry such a demanding role through a full-costume performance, so there was no chance of this happening now. Ricardo Vitale, the director general of the Rome Opera, was confident that he would be capable of singing Cavaradossi in *Tosca*, and offered him a contract to sing with Maria Callas in the company's 1960 season opener. What a delight this would have been for opera lovers! Sadly, Mario was by now too tired to take on what would have been a massive, groundbreaking challenge.

The details of Mario's argument with Costa after this first session are sketchy. Maybe the accompanist was feeling frustrated after hanging around doing nothing in the wake of all the cancellations: he confesses to having been broke, so maybe he packed his bags and flew to New York – effectively leaving Mario and RCA in the lurch – where he was assured of a guaranteed income. Or maybe the incident with the telephone had unnerved him. The situation was saved by Mario's friend, George Stoll, still working in Rome: he shared baton duties with Carlo Savina, who later conducted the soundtrack for *The Godfather*. Savina does a sterling job with the title track, written by Vincenzo di Paola and Sandro Taccani for Italian crooner Tony Dallara, though the most successful interpretations were by Dalida and Dominico Modugno. In Britain, Malcolm Vaughan recorded it one month before Mario, and took it into the Top Ten. Technically, Mario's version overrides them all.

It was Savina who suggested that Mario use an Edith Piaf song in the new film. 'Je n'en connais pas la fin', in its English adaptation, 'My Lost Melody', was Piaf's signature tune in America. Disappointingly, he sings just the refrain and it is over almost as soon as it has begun. Mario had met Piaf twice. The first time had been at the Versailles in New York, the second at the Mocambo in Hollywood, when she had closed her show with the song and afterwards, over dinner with Rocky Graziano and Rock Hudson, Mario had told her how one day he hoped to sing it. In February 1960, following the film's French release, Piaf called him from Paris. 'Hey, Mario,' she shouted down the phone, 'you did a good job with my song. We'll have to get together the next time I'm over there and I'll teach you how to sing the rest of it!' Sadly, Piaf's health was failing, and she would never visit America again.

Also recorded during this session were two takes of Schubert's 'Ave Maria', a not so sparkling 'O sole mio', and as a novelty item, 'La donna e mobile', which works well with just an accordion accompaniment. The album would be completed on 14 November in Berlin when Mario recorded 'The Hofbrauhaus Song' and George Stoll's composition, an oddity called 'Pineapple Pickers', of which the least said the better, though Elvis Presley loved the song enough to ask Sid Tepper and Ray Bennett to come up with something similar for *Blue Hawaii*. They did so, though it has to be said 'Beach Boy Blues' is much better.

Mario's confidence in his abilities was restored, certainly for the time being. He moved out of the villa kitchen, back upstairs with Betty and the children. Betty was still banned from the set of the new film – Corona were having none of the fuss she had caused during the shooting of *Seven Hills of Rome* – but he was given permission for the children to be there, providing they were kept under control. The film was directed by Polish-born former cameraman Rudolph Maté, one of the most respected men in Hollywood: recently he had completed *Miracle In The Rain* with Jane Wyman. Maté told the Italian press that he was apprehensive about working with Lanza, given his reputation, but there were no reported on-set problems during this one – the star simply did not have enough energy to be difficult. This job was left to 43-year-old fag hag par excellence Zsa Zsa Gabor, then as always knocking five years off her age and ordering the technicians around. Gabor had just finished her lamentably acted, 'so bad that it's good' camp-fest, *Queen Of Outer Space*, and she is no better here, swanning into every scene like an over-gesturing Queen of Sheba. With her ceaseless 'darlinks' she is without any doubt the hammiest co-star Mario had the misfortune to work with. Initially, she was also reluctant to work with him. 'We'd never met, but I had already had an unfortunate experience that didn't endear Mario much to me,' she wrote in her memoirs, *One Lifetime Is Not Enough* (whose title had cynics suggesting that neither was one marriage – she went through nine husbands). 'In the middle of the night he had once called me and, in explicit terms that left nothing to the imagination, informed me that he wanted to make love to me.' Actress-singer Johanna von Koczian is, on the other hand, a delight to watch: Mario admired her for her recent work with Lotte Lenya, sharing the honours in a new recorded production of Brecht and Weill's *The Threepenny Opera*.

'He's world famous, he has a magnificent voice, women throw themselves at him, he's got everything! Why doesn't he have some consideration for others?' This is how the theatre manager in the film describes 'mad genius' tenor Tony Costa, Mario more or less playing himself once more, and this time having a joke at the expense of all those fans he had let down in England and Germany. Tonight's performance at the Vienna State Opera may have sold out, but he keeps the society snobs, including girlfriend Gloria (Gabor), waiting until he has had a drink and entertained his kind of people – perched on top of a taxi in the pouring rain, he sings 'La donna e mobile' to all those fans who could not get tickets, and sings for so long that the show inside is cancelled and Tony finds himself forced to flee the country to evade a scandal. This is not as ridiculous as it sounds: in January 1958 Maria Callas had done the same when illness forced her to abandon a performance of Bellini's *Norma* in Rome after the first act, leaving the Italian president in the lurch. The film develops into another travelogue when Tony ends up in Capri, with Gloria trailing after him, insisting that he move into the mansion she has rented there. He, however, still prefers his own class, such as the crowd of girls outside the local café who, having rumbled the traditional Lanza disguise of hat and dark glasses, insist that he sings to them. Interestingly, the leader of this group is played by Christa Päffgen (1938–88), the German actress-singer-model who later achieved fame under the pseudonym Nico, one of the Andy Warhol clique and a founder member of the Velvet Underground.

The song is 'Come prima', which Tony sings beautifully and directs to one girl alone: Christa Bruckner (von Koczian), treating her harshly when she fails to react to his voice – until he learns that she is deaf; though unlike many deaf people, for Hollywood's benefit her speaking voice is unaffected. Pretty soon they are in love, and from this point in the film he takes a leaf out of the *Magnificent Obsession* book with his determination to make her hear again – accepting a European tour, but performing only in those cities where the best ear specialists practise. This permits us to see and hear Lanza's definitive *Pagliacci*, where in full costume he lives his favourite aria, along with the most electrifying *Otello* death scene one can imagine – sadly, though the voice is a near-perfect baritone, in this scene Mario looks ill, and considerably older than 37. In the end, it is Christa herself who finds a reputable surgeon, which leads to emotional kitsch as she sobs that she is willing to risk being operated on so close to the brain because she is in love, and she will lose everything if surgery does not take place – giving us the impression that if Tony cannot accept her disability, then maybe he is not worth bothering with. Gloria is jealous, of course, though we instinctively know long before the final credits roll that he will come to his senses and ditch this neo-pantomime dame for the girl he truly loves.

The reviews for the film were mostly indifferent. *Time*, Mario's foe of long standing, denounced him as 'an unpredictable, erratic, self-centered American singer', which was of course true, and drew attention to his 'aggressive smile, athletic nostrils, orbiting eyeballs and quivering poundage' – which was just downright mean. The film bombed at the box office, and this saw Mario illegally penalised by Corona. When the film wrapped, he was owed around $60,000 of the $200,000 the studio had contracted him for and, suspecting that they would never recover their investment, Alexander Gruter concocted the story that Mario was responsible for putting the production $100,000 over budget. In fact, the 'culprit' was Johanna von Koczian, who had been working on several theatrical and musical projects at the same time as the film. Gruter had known this before hiring her, but suddenly the tabloids were full of stories detailing Lanza's 'reprehensible behaviour' and 'permanent drunken state' which had necessitated the set shutting down for days at a time. This was blatant invention on Gruter's part to rob Mario of the money he owed him. For once – indeed, for the only time in his film career – Mario had behaved impeccably: no drinking, no crude pranks on his co-stars, no arguments. Even Zsa Zsa Gabor, who seems to have forgotten his earlier outburst over the phone, later went out of her way to defend him:

> I'd heard so many terrible things about him, that he was rude, that he used foul language. I spent six months [sic] with him and his

family in Rome and Capri, and in Berlin, and I thought he was the nicest, kindest man I ever met. He was a sweet, darling man...and if [MGM] would have let him be the peasant, the simple American boy that he was, he would still be alive. But they wanted to make a Clark Gable out of a man you can't make a Clark Gable out of. He was a fat, fudgy American with a blessed voice.

Gruter, however, still filed a suit against him, and even had the audacity to tell one German newspaper that he would get away with it – such was Mario's reputation in Germany in the wake of the cancelled concerts, he argued, that no court in the land would ever side with Mario Lanza. Mario's lawyers counter-sued, and though both he and Betty would be dead before the matter was settled, Gruter would lose his case and be ordered to compensate their estate.

On 30 October, Hedda Hopper ran an 'exclusive' in the *Los Angeles Times* reporting that Mario would begin shooting *Tales of the Vienna Woods* on location in Austria in February 1959. By 16 November, Mario was in Berlin, having just completed the soundtrack of *For the First Time*, when he learned that his friend Tyrone Power had suffered a fatal heart attack the previous day while shooting a duelling scene on the set of *Solomon And Sheba*. Power, a heavy drinker and chain-smoker, had like Mario been warned countless times to slow down, and had similarly ignored the advice of his doctors. Though only 44, he had looked much older. Earlier, at the Jachenau sanatorium, Costa had attempted to scare Mario into curbing his drinking by recounting the story of his friend, the baritone Lansing Hatfield, an alcoholic who had died at 38 of cirrhosis of the liver. Mario's unfeeling response to this tragic tale had been, 'I'll have that beer now.' Back in Rome on Christmas Day, he and the family were about to sit down to their dinner when he received more shocking news from Los Angeles, informing him that his close friend and former 'fuck buddy' Nicholas Brodsky had died of an alcohol-related illness, aged 53. And *still* Mario was of the opinion that death by one's excesses was something that only happened to other people, that he was somehow invincible.

Chapter Fourteen

Vissi d'arte...vissi d'amore

For me, Mario Lanza was the greatest tenor who ever drew breath.

Maria Callas, 1975

During the autumn of 1958, Mario signed a new five-year contract with RCA which would guarantee him a minimum annual income of $200,000. The deal was clinched when the company's New York representative, Alan Kayes, flew to Rome and spent several days with the Lanzas at the Villa Badoglio. Over the next nine months, Mario's studio work would be at its most prolific since his Coca-Cola sessions of 1951–2. It was as if RCA – and he himself – had already sensed that time was running out. The first session took place on 24 November at Rome's Cinecitta Studio, the last on Christmas Eve, when he achieved his ambition of recording an album of Neapolitan songs. *Mario!* included firm favourites such as 'Funiculi, funicula' and 'Na sera 'e maggio', along with lesser-known gems such as 'Dicitencello vuie'. Wielding the baton was acclaimed conductor-composer Franco Ferrara, and some of the arrangements were by a 30-year-old musician named Ennio Morricone. Mario was introduced to the future composer of the soundtracks of *A Fistful Of Dollars* and other soon-to-be-classic films by Renato Rascel. Mario may have been very ill – almost moribund – but he does not sound it here: the voice is molasses-rich and mature, the diction perfectly pronounced, the timing and delivery spot on.

Early in December, Ben Hecht turned up at the Villa Badoglio. He and Gottfried Reinhardt had scripted *Granada* some time before – the film had first been mentioned at the time of the Las Vegas fiasco, since which the script had been amended several times, always with Mario in mind. Mario was still disgruntled with the storyline – a tenor, unable to find work, pretends to be blind so that he can busk on the streets of Granada and hopefully be rediscovered – though he did sign the contract. Because Hecht was a friend, there were no harsh or impossible demands. The studio assigned to the project was the Berlin-based CCC Films and its producer-head, Artur Brauner, advanced Mario $50,000 of a reputed $250,000 salary. Pencilled in for co-star and support were Zsa Zsa Gabor and Eric Fleming, her gay co-star from their recently completed camp-fest, *Queen Of Outer Space*. Gabor would later drop out of the production, and Fleming (1925–66) would be assigned to the role of Gil Favor in the *Rawhide* television series, which made him a household name. Mario planned to record the soundtrack during the late summer, ahead of the shooting schedule pencilled in for November. Four further 'living stereo' recording projects were also set up: Lehár's *The Merry Widow*, Sigmund Romberg's *The Desert Song*, an album of sacred songs, and a re-recording of the soundtrack of *The Great Caruso*.

Sadly, aside from *The Desert Song*, none of these projects would see the light of day, though two potentially exciting new ones were heralded in the new year. Instead of *Granada*, Mario would be shooting what was described as a cross between *Pagliacci* and a remake of the 1928 Lon Chaney–Loretta Young silent classic, *Laugh, Clown, Laugh*. The new version, produced by Al Panone, would have him singing 'Vesti la giubba' – what else? – in full costume, which may or may not have been a good idea seeing as he had just done this in *For the First Time*. His co-star would be French-born (to Italian parents) Caterina Valente, a true polyglot capable of singing fluently in a dozen languages. The lyrics were by Bob Russell, the music by Mischa Spoliansky, who had composed for a young Marlene Dietrich in Berlin before fleeing Nazi persecution to work in Hollywood. Panone had already booked the recording sessions for the soundtrack album, the first to take place in London on 17 September, with Valente and Ted Heath's orchestra. Immediately afterwards, as a follow-up to his two travelogue films, he would be filming *Mario Lanza's Rome*. He had been allowed to choose his own material, which he would perform live in front of tourist hot-spots, again of his choosing. 'Three Coins In The Fountain', naturally, would be sung in front of the Trevi Fountain. Elsewhere there would be

'La danza', 'I've Got You Under My Skin', and 'Giannina mia' – this would be sung at the Canzone del Mare, Gracie Fields's complex on Capri. 'If I Loved You', 'One Alone' and a juxtaposed 'Be My Love' and 'Because You're Mine' were to be sung in the centre of the Coliseum. 'E lucevan le stelle' would be performed under the stars at the Trastevere, 'Vieni sul mar' in the Piazza di Spagna, and the film would close with Mario singing 'O Holy Night' in the Sistine Chapel.

Early in December, Mario was contacted by the Opera de Paris – not to sing there, but to augment the society-celebrity guest list for Maria Callas's Paris debut on the 19th of the month. The roster included the French president and most of his cabinet, the Secretary General of NATO, Jean Cocteau, Brigitte Bardot, Juliette Gréco, Gérard Philipe (whose death, seven weeks after Mario died, resulted in national mourning), the Duke and Duchess of Windsor, Aly Khan, Aristotle Onassis, and the ambassadors of Great Britain, the Soviet Union and Italy – Mario was to travel with the latter's party. The establishment had offered Callas $5,000 for the concert, a benefit for the *Légion d'Honneur* which was televised and broadcast throughout most of Europe; she demanded twice this amount, got it, and donated the lot to the charity. Mario was enthusiastic about meeting her, though not so happy about travelling to an 'enemy' city which he had left with boos ringing in his ears. He called her – the only time the two ever made contact – to offer his apologies, and promised to raise money in his own way for the *Légion d'Honneur*. Good to his word, on the evening of the concert he threw a 'Callas Party' at the Villa Badoglio, where the guests were charged for the privilege of quaffing bottles of 1947 Moët & Chandon champagne – a good vintage, he declared, for this was the year that his career had truly begun, with the Hollywood Bowl concert. Half a dozen television sets were placed around the villa so that no one missed a single second of what many consider to have been Callas's finest performance. Following her stunning entrance, wearing a gorgeous Biki gown and $3 million of rented diamonds, her programme included 'Casta diva' from *Norma*, the 'Miserere' from *Il Trovatore*, and the whole of Act II of *Tosca*, which Mario is reported to have watched with tears streaming down his face, particularly when Callas sang the 'theme song' which could just as easily have been his own: 'Vissi d'arte'.

There has been much speculation over whether Maria Callas

considered Lanza the greatest tenor of all time – and additionally, whether one of her greatest ambitions was to sing with him. Had this ever happened, of course, it would have had to be grand opera. Callas is unique amongst opera singers in that she never once performed anything that was not from her very extensive operatic repertoire. Lord Harewood, with whom I part-hosted a celebration marking the 20th anniversary of Callas's death in September 1977, declared that she had made such a statement to him – so too did her secretary, Nadia Stancioff. A close friend, Alan Sievewright, elaborated on this by recalling how Callas had said, 'For me, Mario Lanza was the greatest tenor who ever drew breath – but oh, how that man fucked up his life! But I could never have worked with a man so hell-bent on killing himself, even if I had wanted to! So I had to content myself with singing along to his records.' Montserrat Caballé, who wrote the introduction to my biography of Callas, put it more eloquently: 'Maria absolutely adored Lanza. She told me that he was the best, better even than Caruso, Corelli or di Stefano, and she was not a person to offer compliments lightly.' Another close friend, one of the last to visit her apartment before she died, was Roger Normand, who recalled that she had told him:

> Lanza was in my opinion the best tenor in the world, period, but sadly the least disciplined. Much as I regretted never having sung with him, because of this lack of discipline, any partnership would have been a nightmare. He had a ferocious temper, he was afraid of no one, yet he allowed everyone in Hollywood to treat him like shit. He would have made a fine Cavaradossi – maybe the finest ever. But he had also become used to the Hollywood lifestyle, which I don't think he would have given up to sing opera, not even at La Scala and the Met – even if this always had been his greatest dream.

A few days later, Mario treated his family to a holiday, which would prove temporarily therapeutic for himself and Betty – their first true vacation since their trip to Ginger Rogers's ranch in Oregon. Little is known of their stay in St Moritz, Switzerland: the family travelled incognito, with neither entourage nor nurses for the children, and spent six weeks at the resort far from the eyes of prying reporters. Only a handful of friends, including Mario's doctor, were given his contact details. One of the guests at the hotel was the Hungarian writer-producer, Alexander Paal (1910–72), who Mario had occasionally socialised with in Hollywood. Many years later, Paal recounted an anecdote to his British columnist friend, Donald Zec, which typifies Mario's fussiness regarding the way he liked his food to be served. One morning, Mario ordered beef for breakfast, only to complain to the waiter that it was not rare enough. Twice, according to Paal, the waiter returned from the kitchen, and still the beef was not to his liking. Zec observed, 'Finally, the enraged tenor grabbed a carving knife and cut his arm until it bled. "This is what I call rare. Now bring me something with blood in it!"'

Photographs taken in St Moritz show the Lanzas apparently having a whale of a time, and for once there were no rows. Mario wrote to his parents in Los Angeles, declaring that he was in tip-top health and happier than he had been in years. 'I feel like going on forever,' Terry Robinson quotes him as telling them. 'Now I know what I want. I want to live!' He added that he had plans to fulfil the aborted concerts in England and Germany, and that there had been offers to sing opera all over Europe and as far afield as the Middle and Far East, even Soviet Russia. For once, he was not making this up.

At the end of April, Mario complained of shortness of breath and dizziness, and was admitted to the Valle Giulia. His phlebitis had grown worse: though his heart was strong, doctors told him, there was every chance of the blood clot in his leg breaking free and causing a fatal coronary. His blood pressure was also high, and he was 60 pounds overweight for a man of his height. Yet again he was told to cut down on his drinking, smoking and food intake. And as usual he pleased himself. The two films were still in the planning stage, he said, so as before he would have plenty of time to get back into shape before shooting began. He would film *Mario Lanza's Rome* as he was – after all, it was traditional for tenors to be hefty. The film and television companies, however, were not willing to take the risk of having Lanza die on them – and no one would insure him until he had lost weight and been given a clean bill of health. All three projects were cancelled, although Mario was able to keep the advance from CCC.

Even so, there was still plenty of work to get through for RCA. In April, Mario entered the Cinecitta Studios to record the long-awaited

Student Prince album in the new medium of 'living stereo' – he was going back to the show's roots, he said, by singing the original Dorothy Donnelly lyrics before MGM had messed around with them. Anna Moffo was no longer available, and as Mario was not interested in working with anyone else, RCA recorded his solo voice for the duets whilst deciding who his 'co-star' would be. Eventually they would plump for the less illustrious Norma Giusti, whose voice was added to the tape a few months later. Compared to the original film soundtrack, the production was poor, though not lamentably so as some detractors have said. The main problem with the album was that Costa was not at the helm to gently badger Mario into top vocal form – having left New York, he was currently conducting with the Athens Symphony Orchestra. Therefore what had started out as an exciting prospect Mario very quickly found boring: there were far too many first takes, quite simply because he wanted to get it over with. There were also problems with Paul Baron – Mario found it near-impossible to take direction from a man he disliked. Baron was the conman who had made a fortune from 'composing' the Andrews Sisters' 1945 smash hit, 'Run and Coca-Cola': the real composers had recently won a $150,000 plagiarism suit against him, and he had subsequently been fired from his position as orchestral director of the CBS Network.

Much better, though no less fraught to work on, was a new seasonal album, *Lanza Sings Christmas Carols*, which he put down in two sessions at the end of May: these new arrangements on 'Guardian Angels' (subsequently only equalled by Roberto Alagna) and 'Away in a Manger' were stunning, whilst 'It Came Upon the Midnight Clear' was nothing short of a revelation. Some years later, samples from all four sets of Christmas songs (1950, 1951, 1956, 1959) would be issued on compilation albums, and not even the so-called experts would be able to tell which song had come from which particular session: critics, having read the exaggeratedly caustic reviews of former colleagues, would attempt to guess which was which and invariably get it wrong.

In June, Mario finally recorded the album which had been on the cards for years: *Mario Lanza Sings Caruso Favourites*. He had wanted the 12 songs to be arranged and conducted by Costa, who had just returned from Athens, but RCA had already committed the project to Paul Baron. The finished result was still first class: the best-known Caruso songs were all here, along with his part-composition, 'Serenata', and the little-heard 'Musica proibita' and Tosti's 'Ideale'. The voice may be deeper, baritone at times, and with those infamous embellishments restrained or even missing, but Mario gives a polished, solid reading throughout, and the fans were far from disappointed, even if many critics were disapproving. The album was released as part of a 'novelty' package containing two records – the Lanza songs were on one record, whilst the other contained different songs performed by Caruso himself. Many fans confessed to playing the latter only out of curiosity; once they had worked out how much better Mario was than his idol, they were no longer interested.

The album completed, Paul Baron was given his marching orders, and to celebrate his return to the fold, Costa made a final attempt to stop Mario drinking by taking him to the cinema to see the recently released *Voice In A Mirror* – in hindsight, an act not dissimilar to handing a psychopath a loaded automatic. This tells the ubiquitous story of a commercial artist (Richard Egan) who hits the bottle with a vengeance following the death of his small daughter. His long-suffering, hard-working wife (Julie London) watches helplessly as he heads towards self-destruction, but in the end he is saved by helping a fellow alcoholic who is far worse off than himself, and together they found an AA-style organisation and, in true Hollywood fashion, all ends well. Mario confessed that watching the film had given him the creeps, and for the umpteenth time vowed to lay off the booze – a commitment he stuck to for all of 24 hours before going to a night club and getting smashed.

Someone from Mario's entourage must have contacted Toyopa Drive in Los Angeles to explain the situation he was in, well aware that there were probably only two people in the world capable of getting through to him: his mother and Terry Robinson. Whilst Robinson appears to have been unable or unwilling to acquire a passport, Maria Cocozza boarded the first flight for Rome, accompanied by her father, Salvatore, and Betty's mother, May Hicks, whose chief concern, she later said, was the children. Tony Cocozza, who gives every impression of being the archetypal hypochondriac, stayed put, claiming that he was too ill to fly. Mario had not seen his family for over two years, and they were treated like royalty – offered the best suites at the villa, personal assistants, and introduced to Rome society. The day after they arrived, he threw a no-expense-spared party for his mother, where an obligatory guest was Lucky

Luciano. The next day, the party was for Salvatore and May. The old man had expressed a desire to meet Anna Magnani. Italy's greatest actress, however, was not interested in brushing shoulders with 'the Mob'.

At the end of June, Mario's attention was drawn to a profile penned by the *Daily Mirror*'s well-respected entertainments columnist, Donald Zec, which had been syndicated around the world. In his feature, Zec wrote about Lanza the bad boy: the tantrums and problems he had encountered with co-stars and studio executives. It had all been done before, and many times, but for some reason Mario took exception to Zec and arranged for a box of 36 luxury pink toilet rolls to be delivered to his London home. The handwritten note which accompanied it read, 'These foolish things remind me of you.' This harked back to his early days at MGM, his way of dealing with so-called 'asswipes' – yet he very quickly regretted his action and, having obtained Zec's phone number, called him and invited him to spend the weekend with him and the family in Rome.

During the first week of July, Mario entered the Cinecitta Studios to record songs from Friml's *The Vagabond King*, and insisted that his entire family – wife, mother, grandfather, mother-in-law, all four children and his two dogs – be allowed in the listening booth to spur him on. Costa's influence and guiding hand shows in the quality of these recordings: Mario is relaxed and supremely confident, and it comes as no surprise to learn that in such a convivial atmosphere, the whole album was put down in a single evening. The fake element can be detected, however, when listening to the finished product: as had happened with *The Student Prince*, completion of the 'duets' was left to RCA's discretion as they were unable to find a soprano who Mario approved of, and later, when he was no longer around to bawl them out, they added Judith Raskin.

Why Maria Cocozza opted to return home at the end of the month, leaving her father and May Hicks behind, is not known. Maybe by her being in Rome, Mario felt that she was cramping his style, or maybe there was tension between her and Betty, whom she had never made any secret of disliking. Maria had frequently meddled in her son's affairs, and all too often she had persuaded Mario to push his wife into the background so that she could bathe in his reflected glory. She had been able to get away with this in America, but now that Betty had Mario on home territory, so to speak – no longer in a position to run home to his

family when things were not going his way – she had no time for
anybody else interfering in their lives, and in rare moments of lucidity,
she was finally starting to show her authority. It may well be, also, that
Maria did not wish to be around if or when things turned nasty between
Mario and his 'friends' from the Mob. She had already expressed her
concerns to Mario over his involvement with Lucky Luciano, having
witnessed at least two potentially violent slanging matches between the
two. 'Freddie, stay away from people like Luciano,' Terry Robinson
quotes her as telling him before boarding the plane. 'He means no good
and can only cause you problems. You've always said you would never
work with these people. Don't start now.' Whatever the reason for
Maria's sudden departure, she promised to be back – along with Antonio
and Terry Robinson – in time for Christmas.

Mario's behaviour, which during his mother's presence had been
exemplary, reverted to its usual fractious self when he began recording
the first of his operetta projects, *The Desert Song*, with Costa. The first
afternoon they turned up at the Cinecitta Studios, both complained
about the 'shambolic' state of the orchestra – several members had fallen
sick and the studio had, they claimed, replaced them with inferior
musicians. The session was cancelled until the next day, but when
Mario turned up looking very much the worse for wear after a night on
the town, Costa called a halt to the proceedings. When this happened
again the next day, Costa asked Mario to leave the studio. 'He looked
drained, used up, a wasted fat man,' he ungallantly recalled. 'An
unforgettably forlorn sight, Mario sat slumped in a chair at the side of the
stage. He didn't utter a word the whole time.'

It was agreed, with extreme reluctance on Mario's part, that Costa
would stay back at the studio and record just the orchestra. This way,
Mario's vocals could be overdubbed on to the tape when he was feeling
better – in other words, when he was sober. In the late 1950s this was a
blatantly unprofessional practice but, too weak to argue, Mario went
home. Betty as usual offered little comfort, yelling at him that all his
problems were self-inflicted, which was more or less true, so he resorted
to seeking solace elsewhere. For several months the couple had been
sleeping in separate rooms, and at least one Italian tabloid suggested that
they were on the verge of divorcing. Shutting himself in his room, Mario
drank himself into a stupor and collapsed, half-naked, on the cold

marble floor, where he remained all night. One of the children's
nannies found him the next morning, unconscious and soaking wet
from the rain which had blown in through the open window. With a
temperature of 103°F (39.4°C), he was rushed to the Valle Giulia.
During the night he developed double pneumonia, and the clinic's
Doctor Silvestri gave him a 50-50 chance of surviving, telling Betty that
the next 48 hours would prove crucial.

Once this danger point had passed and his temperature was brought
under control, Mario discharged himself – promising that this time he
really would start taking care of himself. One of his first visitors at the
Villa Badoglio was Lucky Luciano. The mobster was promoting and
part-financing a charity concert to take place in Naples on 4 October –
aided by Michael Stern, a journalist friend, and unofficially listed as a
NATO benefit evening – and wanted Mario to top the bill. Mario agreed
wholeheartedly, though Luciano made it clear that his participation
would be mandatory. The *Desert Song* sessions were resumed, with
Costa playing the recorded orchestral tape three times – the first time for
Mario to listen to, the second for him to hum or sing along to and get his
bearings, the third time to capture the take. Such was his professionalism
that all the tracks were laid down without having to repeat the
procedure, and the album remains definitive.

With his weight back up to 260 pounds and advised against strenuous
exercise on account of his phlebitis, Mario consulted a clinical dietician
to help him shed the 60 pounds required by Al Panone's insurance
company to permit him to work on *Laugh, Clown, Laugh*: despite all the
setbacks, shooting was still set for late November to early December.
Panone visited the Villa Badoglio on a daily basis to coach him through
the script, usually accompanied by his publicist, Sam Steinman. Another
frequent visitor was Ricardo Vitale. Since rejecting Cavaradossi, Mario
had shown great interest in singing the role of Canio in *Pagliacci*, which
Vitale considered a better proposition: the opera was much shorter and
almost always presented in tandem with *Cavalleria Rusticana*. Mario also
received a serious offer to sing the same role at San Carlo, Naples.
Considerable support for these projects had come from Peter Herman
Adler, Mario's former mentor from *Winged Victory*. Adler wanted to take
him under his wing once more and groom him for the opera stage: he
sincerely believed that if the process was carried out slowly, beginning

with getting him well again, then teaching him the discipline he had always lacked, there was every chance of Mario making it even at this late stage. For once, his weight was not considered too much of a problem: on stage he could be any size he wanted, though first of all he would have to do something about his phlebitis. Doctors at the Valle Giulia again reassured him that his heart was strong – all they needed to do was bring down his blood pressure so that they could operate and remove the blood clot from his leg.

Another project said to have been discussed at this time was *That's My Man*, co-starring Eve Arden or Dalida, and possibly to be directed by Rudolph Maté. The locations would be filmed around Naples. Dalida, who shared several hits with Mario, including 'Come prima', divulged this in a radio interview with France Inter, shortly before her death in 1987. She also revealed that she had been Maté's original choice for *For the First Time*, but that she had had to turn the part down due to other work commitments. Whether this was a reworking of *Tales of the Vienna Woods* is unclear.

On 10 September, Costa was due to fly to New York to resume working with the City Opera, though like Mario's family he planned on returning to Rome for Christmas. According to him, that same morning he and Mario entered the Cinecitta Studios where they recorded 'The Lord's Prayer' with a simple piano accompaniment – RCA wanted this to be the closing song on the new Christmas album, he said, and he had been instructed to take the tape with him to New York. If the company felt that the song needed full orchestration, this would be overdubbed there, and the album released at the end of October. 'He sang the selection with memorable expansiveness,' Costa recalled. 'This was a voice at its best – after everything and in spite of everything.' The song has never turned up in the 50 years since it was allegedly recorded; RCA archivists know nothing about it. It is possible that Mario taped it and, as had happened so many times when a take displeased him, demanded that the tape be destroyed. Alternatively Costa, wishing to have one final special memory of Mario all to himself, simply invented the story. Officially, the very last song Mario recorded was the perhaps appropriately titled 'One Good Boy Gone Wrong', from *The Desert Song*.

On 27 September, privileged fans saw Mario in public for the last time. The occasion was a special open-air performance of *Aida* at

Rome's ancient Caracella Baths – completed in AD 217, these had been the largest *thermae* in the world. As usual, Mario wore his feeble hat and dark glasses disguise – and as usual he was rumbled, mobbed by so many fans that security men had to spirit him, Betty and the children out of the vast arena during the interval to enable the second act to begin. Once, he had enjoyed such rough-and-tumble adulation, but this singular event now saw him taking to his bed for 24 hours: he was already suffering from a cold, and this now developed into a fever, brought on by nervous exhaustion. He was sufficiently recovered by the evening of the 29th to host a party at the Villa Badoglio for his friend Peter Lind Hayes, who was in Rome to tape an interview with him for an American radio series. In this, Mario spoke of a future he would not see: the new film, the albums already on the cards, the concerts he had lined up. 'This may be the successor to *The Great Caruso*,' he enthused of *Laugh, Clown, Laugh*. The next morning, he was visited by officials from RAI, who were planning a six-part radio series about his life. The group stayed to lunch, where as usual a spread was put on fit to feed a royal deputation. One hour later, Mario summoned his chauffeur, and asked him to drive him to the Valle Giulia.

No specific reason was given for Mario checking himself in to the clinic: some newspapers later claimed that he was suffering from chest pains, others that he had suspected food poisoning, or that he was about to undergo more sleep therapy to lose weight. He was installed in Room 404 on the fourth floor – nothing odd about this, save that the entire level was shut off, which the clinic's director maintained was to keep fans, reporters and unwelcome visitors at bay. He was assigned a private nurse, of whom nothing is known. The chauffeur who had brought him here – a recent employee at the Villa Badoglio, and equally mysterious – was supplied with a truckle-bed so that he could sleep in Mario's room. The mind boggles, in view of what happened, why no one ever questioned this. His specialist, Dr Frank Silvestri, gave explicit instructions that no one but these two and members of Mario's family should be permitted to enter the room under any circumstances. His telephone conversations were also supervised: during his first 24 hours at the clinic he was only allowed to call his parents, Betty, and Terry Robinson. All were informed that his phlebitis had flared up again, and nothing whatsoever was mentioned about any other condition or ailment.

Dr Silvestri and the clinic's administrators were however powerless to bar Lucky Luciano, who according to hospital records is known to have visited Mario with two associates during the afternoon of 3 October, the day before the NATO concert. What was said between these two headstrong individuals is not known, though if their past meetings were anything to go by, this one would have ended with Luciano making his usual threats, and with Mario hurling expletives at him and ordering him out. Some sources maintain that Luciano accused Mario of faking illness to get out of doing the concert. Otherwise, why would he admit himself to the clinic? According to one report, a few weeks earlier Mario had failed to turn up for a rehearsal, feigning illness, only to have been spotted by Luciano's cronies drinking wine in a local café and singing lustily to the other customers. It was also later suggested that Luciano had agreed to pay for Mario's stay at the clinic, hence him being the only occupant of the fourth floor, to facilitate the task of threatening him into submission – or 'taking him out' if need be.

Now, at the eleventh hour, Luciano decreed that Betty should be her husband's replacement at the charity concert. This was the first she had heard of the agreement between Mario and the mobster. 'Are you trying to sign your own death warrant?' Terry Robinson quotes her as yelling at him. 'Mario, these people don't fool around. You should never have agreed to do the concert if you didn't intend to go through with it. This isn't MGM you're walking out on!' Mario's response to this was that he considered himself too important to be seriously harmed by the Mafia: little did he know that Luciano had taken out much bigger men in his time. Later that afternoon, Betty and two helpers returned to the clinic, armed with boxes of albums and photographs for Mario to sign – 500 items in all. The concert itself almost turned into a riot when fans realised that Mario would not be singing. Betty was booed, and some members of the audience threw shoes at the stage when she tried to explain that he was ill: nothing whatsoever had been reported in the press about this latest hospitalisation.

All this changed when the tabloids reported another Lanza no-show and reporters turned up at the Valle Giulia, wanting to know what was happening. Dr Silvestri announced that two other doctors (who never figured in the events of the next few days) had been put at Mario's disposal: Guido Morica, and Loredana Dalla Torre – the latter a heart specialist who diagnosed 'acute hypertensive heart disease and blocked arteries', which just does not make sense. Betty later claimed that she had no idea until now that her husband had a bad heart, and nor did Mario's closest friends, including Terry Robinson: none of his previous very thorough examinations, including the recent one at Walchensee, had detected anything more serious than high blood pressure, and of course phlebitis. Almost certainly, Dalla Torre's diagnosis was pure invention, suggesting that Dr Silvestri and several members of his staff might well have been in Lucky Luciano's pocket. Complete rest was prescribed, along with blood-thinning agents such as warfarin, while tests were supposedly carried out to see if Mario was strong enough to undergo an operation to remove the blood clot in his leg. Some years later (in the television documentary *An American Caruso*) a very shifty-looking Michael Stern claimed that Mario was only here to undergo another sleep cure to lose weight, as had happened at Walchensee. But as Stern was involved with Luciano, at least so far as the NATO concert was concerned, if not more deeply – many believed that he knew a good deal more than he was letting on – anything he says must be taken with a large dose of salt. By this time, Mario was out of bed and impatiently pacing his room, demanding that he be discharged: Betty was visiting him several times a day, but he was missing the children. Again, the question must be posed: why, with his history of discharging himself from hospitals, was he seemingly prevented from doing so now? He was also suffering from alcohol withdrawal symptoms, but most of all he wanted to get back to his projects, particularly to recording the soundtrack for the new film.

During the afternoon of 6 October, Mario called his parents and Terry Robinson, and once more informed them that there was nothing seriously wrong with him, that he would be home in a couple of days, and that he was looking forward to the big Christmas reunion. At the Valle Giulia, doubtless to patronise him, no restrictions had been imposed on Mario should he feel like singing – no matter how loud he let rip, he would disturb no one – which of course only adds weight to the suspicion that the clinic's spokesman had wildly exaggerated his 'deteriorating' condition. One of the staff claimed to have heard him rehearsing an aria during the morning of 7 October, another that she had been in his room when he had called Betty, complaining that he was sick of the place, and planning to discharge himself later that afternoon.

Terry Robinson, who of course was not there, cites second-hand what happened next. He reports how Mario dispatched the mysterious chauffeur to the Villa Badoglio to collect a change of clothes, telling him, 'Don't let anyone know what you're up to. Bring me something to wear, and let's get the hell out of here before they kill me with these injections.' If Robinson's story is to be believed, had the clinic staff therefore taken away Mario's clothes and left him just in his pyjamas? The chauffeur is then alleged by Robinson to have told one of the children's nurses, 'He thinks they're trying to kill him. I've never seen him so upset.' Robinson concludes:

> When he arrived back at the clinic with Lanza's clothes, he found Mario comatose with the intravenous needle still attached to his arm. He yelled for the nurse, who appeared from just outside the room. The chauffeur pointed wildly at the IV jar with the tube running down the needle. There was no fluid in the jar, and only air could be entering Lanza's body.

The official story, given to the Italian press, was that Mario's nurse found him collapsed on his bed shortly after noon, scarcely breathing, his pulse very weak. A crash team was rushed into his room within seconds, the report read, though no one was sure how long they worked on him – anything between 30 minutes and two hours. Their efforts were in vain.

Epilogue: Murdered by the Mob?

I was not there when it happened, but draw your own conclusions.

Mike Stern, journalist friend

Mario was just 38 years old. The official cause of death was listed as a heart attack, brought about by the blood clot in his leg breaking free and travelling to his heart. Doctors at the Valle Giulia claimed that he had been ailing for some time and was 'expected to drop dead at any given minute', therefore they decided that a post-mortem would not be necessary. Neither was there an inquest.

The treatment afforded those he left behind, and Mario's remains, was nothing short of scandalous. He, who had shown little respect to others during his lifetime – and justifiably so, in many instances – was offered none whatsoever in death. The first to be informed of his demise was his grandfather: the news was broken to Salvatore Lanza on the steps of the Villa Badoglio by Mario's chauffeur, and for some reason the old man decided to keep this to himself. Betty only learned what had happened when she called Dr Silvestri and asked to speak to Mario. With his limited English, Silvestri's abrupt response was, 'Not possible, Signora. He just died.' One hour later, he attempted to make up for his gaffe by turning up at the Villa Badoglio to console the by now hysterical widow. No one from the clinic bothered contacting Mario's parents. Terry Robinson, now living with the Cocozzas at Toyopa Drive, was called by a friend just before sitting down to breakfast. Refusing to believe that his friend was dead, he switched on the radio in the kitchen just as Mario was finishing 'Be My Love'. Maria just happened to be entering the kitchen when the record stopped and the announcer said, 'The voice of the late Mario Lanza, whose voice was stilled by heart attack, today in Rome.' Whilst Maria went to pieces and flaked out on the floor, Antonio is reported to have rushed out into the street, screaming his son's name.

Later that afternoon, Maria Cocozza received a call from Dr Silvestri: Betty was in such a state of shock, she could barely function. Someone would have to fly to Rome to help sort out the funeral arrangements and look after the children, who were yet to be informed of their father's death. Salvatore Lanza and May Hicks were still at the villa – the former in no state to care for anyone but himself, while May's priority lay with her daughter. Antonio refused to accompany her, claiming that he was too distraught, so Mario's business manager, Myrt Blum, organised a travelling companion – the soprano Elizabeth Doubleday, who had partnered Mario on *The Student Prince* soundtrack album. The long flight was turned into a nightmare when the pilot announced over the tannoy that Mario Lanza's mother was on board – for 12 hours non-stop she was pestered by the other passengers.

When Maria arrived in Rome, she found herself surrounded by reporters wanting to know if the rumour was true – that Mario's last request was that he should be buried in Naples, near his idol Caruso. This had brought a ferocious response from the tenor's family. Enrico Caruso Jr, who thus far had only admired Mario, and would do so again once the furore had died down, told Reuter's, 'This family has nothing against Mario Lanza, living or dead, but his screen impersonation of my father gives him no more a claim in the family vault than portraying Abraham Lincoln would give Raymond Massey the right to be buried in Arlington.'

With Betty completely out of it, Maria – who had never forgiven her daughter-in-law for taking Mario away from her – believed that it should have been up to her to handle the funeral arrangements, but Mario's lawyers forbade this. Maria therefore suggested a compromise: to placate his grieving Italian fans, her son would have a funeral service in Rome, after which his body would be placed in cold storage until Betty had decided what to do. What no one had reckoned on was the neglected state of his remains, and the sight which awaited Maria when she arrived at the villa where he had been installed in the marble living room. The body had been transferred from the Valle Giulia to an undertaker's, who had neither removed the intestines nor embalmed it, some believed on Lucky Luciano's orders. Mario, 260 pounds at the time of his death, had been shoved into a wooden coffin several sizes too small: to fit him in, his ankles and shoulder-blades had been broken, and the cotton wool used by nurses at the clinic to block his nose and ears was still in place. A piece of elastoplast had been stretched across his mouth, and his eyes had been left open. His severely bloated stomach protruded six inches above the rim of the coffin, so much so that the lid could not be closed.

Because of the body's putrefying state, Mario's obsequies were brought forwards by 24 hours to the afternoon of 10 October. Transferred to a larger, more ornate but still non-leakproof wooden casket, he was transported in a glass-walled hearse drawn by four plumed and liveried black horses to the Church of the Immaculate Heart of Mary, in Rome's opulent Parioli suburb. The hearse, until then used exclusively for the funerals of Italian heads of state, was the personal contribution from President Giovanni Gronchi, 'in appreciation of the great joy that Mario Lanza has brought to the people of this country'. Attached to the back was a huge heart-shaped wreath, bearing the children's names in white carnations. En route to the church, the cortege encountered a repetition, *en miniature*, of what had happened following the death of Valentino, 33 years earlier. An estimated 20,000 people lined the streets, some falling to their knees as the hearse passed by. Fanatics and reporters flung themselves at it: one young man ended up under the wheels and had to be dragged to safety by the police, wielding batons. The pallbearers included actors Rossano Brazzi and Robert Alda, RCA executive Frank Folsom and Mike Stern. These men had great difficulty carrying the casket into the building: at one stage they almost dropped it when fans surged forwards, chanting Mario's name.

Only two celebrities were observed by the press: bandleader Xavier Cugat, and actor Van Johnson, who had happened to be filming in Rome. Betty, who many thought would never make it to the ceremony, stared blankly into space. At one stage she collapsed and had to be supported by her father and Dr Silvestri. She had wanted a recording of Mario singing 'Ave Maria' to be played during the service, which was officiated by Father Paul Maloney – the priest, now resident at the city's Santa Susanna Church, who had baptised her sons in Los Angeles before the family had left for Italy. The request was denied; Betty was accused of 'attempting to commercialise' a solemn occasion, but at the last minute a local baritone stepped in to do the honours. What happened next was very strange indeed. Betty was yet to make up her mind what to do with Mario's body, and asked for the casket to be returned to the funeral home and placed in cold storage. Between the church and the funeral home, however, someone else – it has never been determined who – made up her mind for her. That same evening, without the family's permission, Mario was buried in Rome's Verrano Cemetery.

When Betty and the children returned to the Villa Badoglio after the funeral, a lawyer was waiting: rent was owing on the property, and the owners had given them just seven days to vacate the premises. For two of these days, Betty drank and deliberated, then somehow came to a decision. She would return the family – and Mario – to America, and have him buried where he belonged amongst the other Hollywood superstars. She, the children and their nannies, and two of Mario's dogs would fly to Los Angeles with her mother and Maria: to placate Salvatore, Mario's remains would be flown to New York, then conveyed by train to Philadelphia, where his body would lie in state before being taken to its final resting place. Therefore, during the night of 12 October, having spent 48 hours in the ground, the casket was disinterred.

On 15 October, Mario was put on display – there is no other way of describing what happened – at Leonetti's Funeral Parlour, on South Philadelphia's South Broad Street. He was still in the same casket, and when the lid was removed his stomach was found to have burst. Under pressure from the 2,000 fans queuing outside the building, but fearing a visit from the Public Health Department, the manager announced that Mario could stay on view for a maximum three hours, between 4pm and 7pm. When fans filing past began fainting on account of the stench – one elderly lady suffered a heart attack, and died later in hospital – an undertaker's assistant doused the body with a mixture of perfume and disinfectant, and it was decided to cover it with a thick sheet of plate glass to help conceal the odour. When Leonetti's closed its doors, a riot erupted in the street and Salvatore Lanza persuaded the manager to stay open until everyone had paid their last respects to his grandson. Between now and the early hours of the morning, until hygiene officials ended what had become little more than a circus, over 20,000 fans filed past the catafalque.

Mario's second funeral was celebrated the next morning at St Mary Magdalene de Pazzi, the church where he had been baptised. Later that afternoon, the casket and its contents were placed in a refrigerated room until 18 October, when it was flown to Los Angeles. Here, in what can only be described as an act of sadistic torture, Mario's relatives were told that he would have to be formally identified before permission could be granted to bury him in the city. This was done by Terry Robinson. To his credit, many believed at the time, Robinson had personally bought his friend a leakproof copper casket, the cost of which he subsequently reclaimed from the state, along with $2,300 in unpaid salary. First of all, however, Mario's body was taken to a public chapel of rest, where it was stripped and dressed in clean clothes which Robinson had also provided. What a gruesome task this must have been, squeezing his rotting remains into a suit which was two sizes too small.

The Lanza family's ordeal finally ended on 21 October, 14 days after Mario's death, at the Blessed Sacrament Church on Sunset Boulevard. Here, Antonio Cocozza was seen in public for the first time since his son's death, scarcly able to function and screaming to the casket that it should have been him. Betty was also reunited with Terry Robinson, telling him, 'I think the Mafia had something to do with it. I think they murdered Mario.' The ceremony was officiated by Reverend Harold Ring, but aside from the 1,500 fans there were considerably fewer people here than there had been in Rome and Philadelphia: Lanza had left Los Angeles under a dark cloud, and would never be forgiven by colleagues and peers for the way he had behaved. Amongst the handful of celebrity mourners were actress Dolores Hart (Betty's niece, and here by way of family duty), Zsa Zsa Gabor and George Stoll. There was not a single studio executive, and MGM's technicians – Mario's 'little people' – had been given a stern warning that they would be fired, should any of them defy their bosses by showing up. Kathryn Grayson stayed away too. However, despite her apparent dislike for Mario, she kindly asked Betty and the children to move in with her until they had found a place of their own. After the brief ceremony, the casket was placed in the Calvary Museum, from which it would later be taken for private burial at the Holy Cross Cemetery. Mario's was Hollywood's second important funeral that week: Errol Flynn had died on 14 October, seven days after Mario.

Because there was no autopsy, as had happened with Valentino – and as would later happen with Marilyn Monroe – there have always been rumours that Mario did not die from natural causes. In his case, however, this seems a foregone conclusion. In her memoirs, Zsa Zsa Gabor, who would have made a better gossip columnist than she ever was an actress, observed, 'The rumour was that a gang of Philadelphian gangsters had ordered him to sing at one of their gala evenings, that Mario had refused and that, in revenge, they had hired a nurse at the fat farm to inject air into Mario's veins one night while he was sleeping and kill him.' Many fans and at least two biographers – the same group of people who refuse to believe how truly detested Mario was in some Hollywood circles – have dismissed such a claim as nonsense, largely because they did not want to believe that some had found their idol so positively loathsome that they had taken the ultimate step to get rid of him. Yet the following facts must be taken into consideration:

1) Whilst those denouncing the murder theory have maintained that the Mafia would have exacted their revenge on Mario by menacing him, roughing him up, or at the very worst by kidnapping one of his family, such was Lucky Luciano's very well-publicised sadistic streak that he would have been more than capable of taking his revenge to the extreme. Mario may have been many things, but he was never a coward, and never afraid of speaking his mind. All too frequently he would open his mouth and let rip, without first weighing his words. There are too many reported incidents of him directing vociferous, vulgar insults and threats of his own, not just to Luciano's cronies, but to the mobster himself. Rocky Marciano, who knew many of the day's underworld figures but vigorously denied ever being involved with any of them, supported the Mafia 'hit-man' theory. So too did Betty Lanza. Both Maria Cocozza and Terry Robinson had witnessed Mario arguing with various Mob members. Tommy Lucchese's warning, 'Keep your big mouth shut, or I'll shut it permanently,' does not exactly rule out a Mafia hit.

2) That Mario owed Luciano some kind of debt cannot be denied, whether this was a financial or a moral obligation. On the face

of it, execution following a failed concert seems extreme unless principle was a deciding factor. There is no evidence that Mario was at any time financially supported by the Mafia; then again, neither party would have advertised the fact. Yet his income to support himself and a relatively large household at an expensive villa in one of Rome's most exclusive districts must have come from a source other than his movie salaries and record royalties. RCA had negotiated a new contract which guaranteed Mario a minimum annual income of $200,000. This deal had been signed in October 1958, and Mario was paid a substantial advance which he very quickly spent. This advance was deducted from his first half-yearly payment in April 1959, along with all dues and demands owed to the tax-man and various agents and lawyers. His second half-yearly payment would have been due at around the time of his death. The down payment, if any, for *Laugh, Clown, Laugh* would also have been spent long since. This leaves the percentages from Mario's previous films made exclusively with MGM, which would not have supported his extravagant lifestyle during the last six months of his life. Therefore his income must have come from somewhere else. The fact that he checked himself into the Valle Giulia during his final illness, if indeed he was ill at all, could have been interpreted by Luciano as Mario bottling out of an obligation he is very definitely known to have made.

3) Why was Mario afforded the entire fourth floor at Valle Giulia, unless it was to be out of sight and earshot of everyone in the building? During previous stays here he had always been given a private suite, and there had been absolutely no problems with security, intrusive fans or the press. Why were his calls supervised? When calling his family in Los Angeles and persistently informing them that there was nothing wrong with him, was he doing this because he was seriously ill and did not wish to worry them? Or was he hoping that they would read between the lines and interpret his calls as some sort of cry for help; that he really was a prisoner at the clinic? In Rome, Mario

was lonelier than he had ever been in his life. He had the children and Betty, of course, but she had more than her share of personal demons; most of the time she could not cope and needed help herself. Almost certainly, had Mario's mother and/or Terry Robinson been in Rome, the tragedy would have been averted.

4) Who was the private nurse assigned to caring for Mario – and indeed, was she a nurse at all? Similarly, who was the chauffeur, and why did he sleep in Mario's room? Was he effectively Mario's jailer, appointed to prevent him from escaping until Luciano had decided what course of action to take? Were this pair the only ones at the clinic on Luciano's payroll? Why did they suddenly disappear, and why were no questions asked at the time unless those 'in the know' already knew the answers? Were Dr Frank Silvestri and/or any of the clinic's administrative staff also in Luciano's employ? And why did they insist that there was no need for a post-mortem? What would they have had to lose, unless someone had something to hide?

5) What part, if any, did journalist Michael Stern play in the cover-up? Having previously confessed to his 'involvement' with Luciano, leaving us to speculate in what capacity, in *An American Caruso* he refuses to commit himself any further, saying of Mario's death, 'I was not there when it happened, but draw your own conclusions.'

6) Why, whilst Betty was deliberating over Mario's final resting place, were his remains interred in a cemetery when she had specifically requested that they be placed in cold storage? Were those responsible for this hoping that she would change her mind and leave him where he was, effectively getting rid of any evidence?

Fifty years on, we are no further towards knowing the truth.

Mario had died relatively poor, though not penniless as some of the tabloids proclaimed. Shortly after his death, his estate received

$325,000, his second half-yearly record royalties from RCA. An investigation launched by Myrt Blum also brought in another $25,000, money which Mario had overpaid to the IRS. The claims made against the estate were, however, astronomical, ranging from $1,200 for 'destenching processes' at various funeral homes, to a $1,500 final telephone bill for the Villa Badoglio. The bill for funeral expenses came to over $8,000, with half of this paid to Transworld Airlines for 'hygienic transportation' of Mario's casket. The first claims tally, calculated at the end of October 1959, was just over $30,000, but this mounted almost daily as those who had worked with Mario in the past, including coach Giacomo Spadoni, suddenly remembered that he had not paid them. Over each of the next seven years, his estate would earn in excess of $1 million, of which two-thirds would be recovered by the various agents and lawyers that had represented him, including of course Sam Weiler.

That Betty would never cope on her own came as no surprise. After spending just two weeks with Kathryn Grayson, she moved her family into a rented house in Beverly Hills. Fearful that her daughter might have been neglecting the children, May Hicks turned up there four weeks after Mario's death, obviously disapproved of what she saw, and returned with them to Chicago. Today, with her history of drug and alcohol dependence, Betty would almost certainly have been deemed an unfit mother and her children taken into care, but in those days things were done differently. The police questioned May, but no charges were filed when she stressed that she had been acting purely in the children's interests, of which there can be no doubt. Betty never got over her loss. On the morning of 11 March 1960, having been alerted by her maid, Terry Robinson broke down the locked door of her room and found her dead in bed. The coroner's report stated that in addition to having a blood-alcohol level of .24, Betty had swallowed 'a more than substantial quantity' of Seconal pills. The official verdict was, 'Death from asphyxiation brought about by a self-destructive regimen of alcohol and prescription narcotics.' She was just 36. Close friends such as Robinson maintained that she had died of a broken heart, but there is very little doubt that, at the extreme end of her tether, she had taken her own life. The insurance company believed so, too, for they refused to settle the $200,000 claim made on behalf of her children. Three years later, after a great deal of legal wrangling, they would receive just $35,000.

Betty was buried next to Mario at Holy Cross, and there followed a custody battle for the children between Maria Cocozza and May Hicks. Using May's earlier 'abduction' incident as a weapon, Maria won the case and the children were raised, almost jointly, by the Cocozzas and Terry Robinson.

The friends, loved ones and retainers are mostly gone. Maria Cocozza died of a stroke in July 1970, aged 68. Shortly afterwards, Terry Robinson was appointed the children's legal guardian. Antonio died five years later, aged 81. Costa died in 1986, and Sam Weiler lived on until 1995, earning a fortune in royalties from the legacy of a man who had ended up despising him. Under the terms of the contract drawn up after his court case with Mario, upon his death Weiler's royalty rights were passed on to the surviving Lanza children.

For a while, Marc Lanza shared the house on Toyopa Drive with his brother Damon. Following a failed business venture, the house was repossessed, sending Marc into a downward spiral of drink, drugs and depression. Believed to be also HIV-positive, he died in 1991, aged 37, of an opiate-induced heart attack. Mario's daughter, Colleen, had inherited his drink problem. In August 1997, blind drunk, she wandered into the road without looking, was struck by a car, and managed to stagger away from the scene only to be struck by a second car. She died soon afterwards, aged 48. She had attempted a show-business career under the watchful eye of singer-songwriter-producer Lee Hazlewood, the man who had launched Nancy Sinatra, but nothing much had come of this. Damon Lanza died of a heart attack in August 2008, aged 53.

Perhaps the last word should be left to Placido Domingo, one of the many tenors whom Mario inspired:

> The successes and tragedies of his life will be forgotten, but his glorious voice will not be.

Appendix I: Filmography

That Midnight Kiss   MGM, 1949
Director: Norman Taurog. Script: Bruce Manning, Tamara Hovey. Cinematographer: Robert Surtees. Musical director: Charles Previn. Costumes: Helen Rose, Valles. With Kathryn Grayson, José Iturbi, Ethel Barrymore, Keenan Wynn, J. Carol Naish, Thomas Gomez, Marjorie Reynolds. Mario (as Johnny Donetti) was second billing. 97 minutes.

The Toast of New Orleans   MGM, 1950
Director: Norman Taurog. Script: Sy Gomberg, George Wells. Cinematographer: William Snyder. Music: George Stoll, Johnny Green. Choreography: Eugene Loring. Costumes: Helen Rose, Walter Plunkett. With Kathryn Grayson, David Niven, J. Carol Naish, Rita Moreno, James Mitchell. Mario (as Pepe Duvalle) was second billing. 95 minutes.

The Great Caruso   MGM,1951
Director: Richard Thorpe. Script: Sonya Levien, William Ludwig, very loosely based on the biography by Dorothy Caruso. Cinematographer: Joseph Ruttenberg. Music: Peter Herman Adler, Johnny Green. Costumes: Helen Rose, Gile Steele. With Ann Blyth, Jarmila Novotná, Dorothy Kirsten, Carl Benton Reid, Eduard Franz, Blanche Thebom, George Chakiris, Alan Napier, Ludwig Donath. Mario (as Enrico Caruso) was top billing. 106 minutes.

Because You're Mine   MGM, 1952
Director: Alexander Hall. Script: Leonard Spiegelgass. Cinematographer: Joseph Ruttenberg. Music: Johnny Green. Costumes: Helen Rose. With Doretta Morrow, James Whitmore, Paula Corday, Bobby Van, Jeff Donnell, Spring Byington. Mario (as Renaldo Rossano) was top billing. 101 minutes.

The Student Prince   MGM, 1954
Director: Richard Thorpe. Script: William Ludwig, Sonya Levien.
Music: George Stoll. Cinematography: Paul Vogel. Costumes: Helen
Rose, Walter Plunkett. With Ann Blyth, Edmund Purdom, S.Z. Sakall,
Edmund Gwenn, John Williams, Louis Calhern, John Erickson.
Mario (singing the Purdom role of the Prince) did not appear in the
film. 106 minutes.

Serenade   Warner Brothers, 1956
Director: Anthony Mann. Script: Ivan Goff, Ben Roberts, based on the
novel by James M. Cain. Cinematographer: J. Peverell Marley. Music:
Ray Heindorf. Costumes: Howard Shoup. With Joan Fontaine, Sarita
Montiel, Vincent Price, Joseph Calleia, Vince Edwards, Licia Albanese,
Jean Fenn. Mario (as Damon Vincenti) was top billing. 96 minutes

Seven Hills of Rome   MGM/LeCloud-Titanus, 1958
  (Arrivederci Roma)
Director: Roy Rowland. Script: Art Cohn, Giorgio Prosperi. Cinema-
tographer: Tonino Delli Colli. Music: George Stoll. Costumes: Maria
Baroni. With Renato Rascel, Marisa Allasio, Peggy Castle, Luisa Di
Meo. Mario (as Marc Revere) was top billing. 102 minutes.

For the First Time   MGM/Corona, 1959
Director: Rudolph Maté. Script: Andrew Solt. Cinematography: Aldo
Tonti. Music: George Stoll. Costumes: Alfred and Charlotte Bucken.
With Johanna von Koczian, Kurt Kaznar, Zsa Zsa Gabor, Walter Rilla,
Nico. Mario (as Tony Costa) was top billing. 96 minutes.

and also...

Heavenly Creatures   MIRAMAX (New Zealand), 1994
Director: Peter Jackson. Script: Peter Jackson, Fran Walsh. Cinema-
tography: Alun Bollinger. With Kate Winslet, Melanie Lynskey, Diana
Kent. Mario (portrayed by Stephen Reilly) sang 'Be My Love', 'The
Donkey Serenade', 'Funiculi, funicula', 'The Loveliest Night of the Year',
'You'll Never Walk Alone'. 107 minutes.

Appendix II: Studio Recordings

Pre-RCA Victor

16 December 1940
La Fanciulla del West: Ch'ella mi creda, Torna a surriento; *La Traviata*: Dei miei bollenti spiriti; Pecche? (part only)
Private recordings, New York, accompanist unknown.

September 1942
La Bohème: O soave fanciulla*, Marcello finalmente**
*With Lois MacMahon; **with Lois MacMahon and Robert Weede
Private recordings, piano Dora Reinhardt, studio unknown.

22 May 1944
Andrea Chénier: Un di all'azzurro spazio, Come un bel di di maggio; *Cavalleria Rusticana*: Addio alla madre; *Tosca*: E lucevan le stelle
Melotone Studios, New York, accompanist unknown.

RCA Victor

June 1945
Tosca: E lucevan le stelle; *La Bohème*: Che gelida manina; *Carmen*: La fleur que tu m'avais jetée; *Pagliacci*: Vesti la giubba; Mattinata; I'm Falling in Love with Someone
Test recordings, accompanist unknown.

5 May 1949
Aida: Celeste Aida; *La Bohème*: Che gelida manina; Mama mia, che vo' sape; Core 'ngrato
Orchestra with Constantine Callinicos, New York.

23 August 1949
They Didn't Believe Me; Mattinata; I Know, I Know, I Know
Orchestra with Ray Sinatra.

28 October 1949
O sole mio; Lolita; Granada; Granada (alternative take)
Orchestra with Ray Sinatra.

8 April 1950
L'Africana: O paradiso; *Carmen*: La fleur que tu m'avais jetée (two
takes); *Martha*: M'appari tutt' amor
Orchestra with Constantine Callinicos.

11 April 1950
Madama Butterfly: Stolta paura l'amor (takes 1 and 2); *La Traviata*:
Libiamo, libiamo, ne' lieti calici (takes 1, 2 and 3) All with Elaine
Malbrin
Orchestra with Constantine Callinicos.

11 May 1950
Ave Maria (Bach–Gounod)
Violin solo, Eudice Shapiro
Orchestra with Constantine Callinicos.

15 May 1950
L'Elisir D'Amore: Una furtiva lagrima; *Pagliacci*: Vesti la giubba (takes
1, 2 and 3); *Rigoletto*: Questa o quella, La donna e mobile
Orchestra with Constantine Callinicos.

18 May 1950
Andrea Chénier: Un di all'azzurro spazio, Come un bel di di maggio;
Tosca: Recondita armonia, E lucevan le stelle
Orchestra with Constantine Callinicos.

29 May 1950
Cavalleria Rusticana: Addio alla madre (takes 1 and 2); The Virgin's
Slumber Song; O Holy Night; *Rigoletto*: Parmi veder le lagrime (takes
1 and 2); *La Gioconda*: Cielo e mar
Orchestra with Constantine Callinicos.

6 June 1950
La Forza Del Destino: O tu che in seno agli angeli; Serenade (Toselli);
Serenade (Drigo)
Orchestra with Constantine Callinicos.

27 June 1950
Be My Love; The Tina-Lina
Orchestra with Ray Sinatra, the Jeff Alexander Choir.

29 June 1950
Toast of New Orleans; The Bayou Lullaby; Boom-Biddy-Boom-Boom;
I'll Never Love You
Orchestra with Ray Sinatra, the Jeff Alexander Choir.

26 August 1950
My Song, My Love; I Love Thee; Because*; For You Alone*
*Acetates presumed destroyed
Orchestra with Ray Sinatra.

19 February 1951
Because; For You Alone
Orchestra with Constantine Callinicos.

23 February 1951
The Loveliest Night of the Year; A vucchella; Marechiare
Orchestra with Constantine Callinicos.

28 September 1951
Silent Night; Away in a Manger: Guardian Angels; O Little Town of
Bethlehem; The First Nowell; O Come All Ye Faithful
Orchestra with Ray Sinatra, the Jeff Alexander Choir.

29 September 1951
The Lord's Prayer; We Three Kings of Orient Are
Orchestra with Ray Sinatra, the Jeff Alexander Choir.

24 July 1952
You Do Something to Me; Lee-Ah-Loo
Orchestra with Constantine Callinicos.

1 August 1952
The Song Angels Sing; Because You're Mine
Orchestra with Constantine Callinicos.

17 June 1953
Song of India; Call Me Fool; If You Were Mine (takes 1 and 2); You
Are My Love (takes 1 and 2)
Orchestra with Constantine Callinicos.

28 December 1953
I'll Walk with God (takes 1 and 2, rejected); Summertime in
Heidelberg (with Gale Sherwood, rejected)
Orchestra with Constantine Callinicos.

14 May 1956
More than You Know; Falling in Love with Love; Why was I Born;
This Nearly Was Mine
Orchestra with Irving Aaronson, the Jeff Alexander Choir.

15 May 1956
Speak Low; September Song; So In Love; My Romance
Orchestra with Irving Aaronson, the Jeff Alexander Choir.

17 May 1956
On the Street Where You Live; You'll Never Walk Alone; And This is
My Beloved; Younger than Springtime
Orchestra with Irving Aaronson, the Jeff Alexander Choir.

10 August 1956
Hark the Herald Angels Sing; This Land; Deck the Halls; Joy to the
World; God Rest Ye Merry Gentlemen; Earthbound
Orchestra with Henri René, the Jeff Alexander Choir.

15 August 1956
Do You Wonder; I Saw Three Ships; O Christmas Tree; It Came
Upon the Midnight Clear; Love in a Home
Orchestra with Henri René, the Jeff Alexander Choir.

27 August 1956
Only a Rose; I've Told Every Little Star; Will You Remember; Yours is

My Heart Alone (take 1)
Orchestra with Henri René, the Jeff Alexander Choir.

31 August 1956
The Donkey Serenade; Gypsy Love Song; Rose Marie; All the Things You Are
Orchestra with Henri René, the Jeff Alexander Choir.

6 September 1956
Lover Come Back to Me; Giannina mia; Yours is My Heart Alone (take 2); Thine Alone; Tramp! Tramp! Tramp!
Orchestra with Henri René, the Jeff Alexander Choir.

15 April 1957
Come Dance with Me; A Night to Remember; Behold!
Orchestra with Henri René, the Jeff Alexander Choir.

7 November 1957
The Loveliest Night of the Year; Never Till Now; Arrivederci, Roma; Younger than Springtime
Orchestra with George Stoll.

16 January 1958
Lamento di Federico; Lasciatemi morire (Monteverdi); Gia il sole dal Gange; Pieta, Signore; Tell Me O Blue, Blue Sky; Bonjour, ma belle; The House on the Hill; E lucevan le stelle; Mama mia, che vo' sape; A vucchella; Marechiare; Seven Hills of Rome; Softly as in a Morning Sunrise; I'm Falling in Love with Someone; Because You're Mine: La donna e mobile
Live recording, Royal Albert Hall, London; piano, Constantine Callinicos.

24 November–24 December 1958
Neapolitan Songs: Passione; Santa Lucia luntana; Funiculi, funicula; Tu ca nun chiagne; Voce 'e notte; Maria Mari; O surdato 'namurato; Dicitencello vuie; Canta pe' me; Comme facette mammeta; Fenesta che lucive; Na sera 'e maggio
Orchestra with Franco Ferrara, Chorus Franco Potenza.

April 1959

The Student Prince: Summertime in Heidelberg*; Just We Two*;
Deep in My Heart, Dear*; Gaudeamus igitur; Beloved; Drink, Drink,
Drink; I'll Walk with God; Golden Days; Serenade; Thoughts Will
Come Back to Me
*Lanza solo, with the voice of soprano Norma Giusta probably added
later on 24 September, when chorus was overdubbed in New York
Orchestra with Paul Baron.

May 1959

Joy to the World; Deck the Halls; O Come All Ye Faithful; I Saw
Three Ships; The First Nowell; Guardian Angels; God Rest Ye Merry
Gentlemen; Silent Night; O Little Town of Bethlehem; Away in a
Manger; Hark the Herald Angels Sing; It Came Upon the Midnight
Clear; O Christmas Tree; We Three Kings of Orient Are
Choir overdubbed New York, 16–17 September
Orchestra with Paul Baron.

June 1959

Lolita; Pour un baiser; Santa Lucia; L'alba separa dalla luce l'ombra;
Vieni sulmar; Ideale; Senza nisciuno; Musica proibita; Vaghissima
sembianza; Serenata; Luna d'estate; La mia canzone
Orchestra with Paul Baron.

July 1959

The Vagabond King: Nocturne (takes 1 and 2); Song of the Vagabonds;
Drinking Song; Love Me Tonight; Only a Rose*; Someday*;
Tomorrow*; Finale*
*With Judith Raskin (voice and chorus added March 1960)
Orchestra with Paul Baron.

August 1959

The Desert Song: Riff Song; My Margo (not used); One Alone (takes 1
and 2); Azuri's Dance; Then You Will Know*; The Desert Song*;
One Good Boy Gone Wrong*; One Flower in Your Garden**; I Want
a Kiss***
*With Judith Raskin; **with Donald Arthur; ***with Judith Raskin
and Raymond Murcell (voices and chorus added April 1960)
Orchestra with Constantine Callinicos.

10 September 1959
The Lord's Prayer
Piano, Constantine Callinicos.

MGM Studios Soundtracks

8 September 1947
La Bohème: Che gelida manina; *Pagliacci*: Vesti la giubba
Test recordings, piano André Previn.

1 December 1948
Mama mia, che vo' sape?*; I Know, I Know, I Know**; They Didn't
Believe Me (with Kathryn Grayson)**
*Piano, Giacomo Spadoni; **orchestra with Charles Previn
Soundtrack for *That Midnight Kiss*.

9 December 1948
Aida: Celeste Aida*; *L'Elisor D'Amore*: Una furtiva lagrima**
*Orchestra with José Iturbi; **piano, José Iturbi
Soundtrack for *That Midnight Kiss*.

30 December 1948
Love is Music (with Kathryn Grayson)
Orchestra with José Iturbi
Soundtrack for *That Midnight Kiss*.

31 December 1948
One Love of Mine (with Kathryn Grayson) (not used)
Orchestra with José Iturbi
Soundtrack for *That Midnight Kiss*.

14 January 1949
L'Africana: O paradiso (not used)
Piano, Irving Aaronson
Soundtrack for *That Midnight Kiss*.

5 December 1949
Madama Butterfly: Stolta paura l'amor (with Kathryn Grayson)
Orchestra with Johnny Green
Soundtrack for *The Toast of New Orleans*.

6 December 1949
I'll Never Love You*; *La Traviata*: Libiamo, libiamo, ne' lieti calici
(with Kathryn Grayson)**
*Orchestra with George Stoll; **orchestra with Johnny Green
Soundtrack for *The Toast of New Orleans*.

7 December 1949
Martha: M'appari tutt' amor; *L'Africana*: O paradiso (montage);
Carmen: La fleur que tu m'avais jetée
Piano, Joseph Gimpel
Soundtrack for *The Toast of New Orleans*.

15 December 1949
Bayou Lullaby; Be My Love (both with Kathryn Grayson)
Orchestra with George Stoll
Soundtrack for *The Toast of New Orleans*.

27 December 1949
The Tina-Lina
Orchestra with George Stoll
Soundtrack for *The Toast of New Orleans*.

28 December 1949
I'll Never Love You (retake); Be My Love
Orchestra with George Stoll
Soundtrack for *The Toast of New Orleans*.

25 January 1950
The Tina-Lina (with J. Carol Naish and chorus)
Orchestra with George Stoll
Soundtrack for *The Toast of New Orleans*.

17 February 1950
Boom-Biddy-Boom-Boom
Orchestra with George Stoll
Soundtrack for *The Toast of New Orleans*.

17 July 1950
Pagliacci: Vesti la giubba (takes 1 and 2)
Orchestra with Peter Herman Adler
Soundtrack for *The Great Caruso*.

22 July 1950
Tosca: E lucevan le stelle; *La Gioconda*: Cielo e mar*; *La Bohème*:
Che gelida manina*
*Outtakes thought to have been destroyed
Orchestra with Peter Herman Adler
Soundtrack for *The Great Caruso*.

7 August 1950
Mattinata (*a cappella*); La danza*; Torna a Surriento (takes 1 and 2)*
*Piano, Irving Aaronson
Soundtrack for *The Great Caruso*.

9 August 1950
Because*; Marechiare**; Santa Lucia* (outtake)
*Orchestra with Peter Herman Adler; **piano, Irving Aaronson
Soundtrack for *The Great Caruso*.

11 August 1950
Ave Maria (Bach–Gounod) (with Jacqueline Allen and St Luke's
Choristers)
Organ, Wesley Tourtelot
Soundtrack for *The Great Caruso*.

18 August 1950
Aida: O terra, addio (with Dorothy Kirsten and Blanche Thebom);
Tosca: Torture scene (with Teresa Celli and Giuseppe Valdengo);
Andrea Chénier: Un di all'azzurro spazio (outtake)
Orchestra with Peter Herman Adler
Soundtrack for *The Great Caruso*.

19 August 1950
Il Trovatore: Miserere (with Lucine Amara); *Aida*: Celeste Aida*
*Lanza is thought to have re-recorded the last note of this on 29 August
Orchestra with Peter Herman Adler
Soundtrack for *The Great Caruso*.

22 August 1950
Martha: Finale – The Last Rose of Summer (with Dorothy Kirsten and
Nicola Moscona); *Rigoletto*: Bella figlia dell'amore (with Blanche
Thebom, Olive May Beach and Giuseppe Valdengo)

Orchestra with Peter Herman Adler
Soundtrack for *The Great Caruso*.

23 August 1950
Lucia di Lammermoor: Sextet (with Dorothy Kirsten, Blanche
Thebom, Giuseppe Valdengo, Gilbert Russell and Nicola Moscona);
Cavalleria Rusticana: Vivo il vino spumeggiante
Orchestra with Peter Herman Adler
Soundtrack for *The Great Caruso*.

28 August 1950
Rigoletto: E il sol dell'anima (with Jarmila Novotná, outtake)
Orchestra with Peter Herman Adler
Soundtrack for *The Great Caruso*.

29 August 1950
Martha: M'appari tutt' amor (part only); *La Gioconda*: Cielo e mar
(part only); *La Bohème*: Che gelida manina (outtake); *Rigoletto*: La
donna e mobile (takes 1 and 2)
Orchestra with Peter Herman Adler
Soundtrack for *The Great Caruso*.

17 October 1950
Cavalleria Rusticana: No, Turiddo, rimani (with Marina Koshetz)
Orchestra with Johnny Green
Soundtrack for *The Great Caruso*.

18 December 1950
A vucchella; *Aida*: Nume, custode e vindice (with Nicola Moscona
and Bob Ebright)
Orchestra with Johnny Green
Soundtrack for *The Great Caruso*.

12 July 1951
L'Africana: O paradiso; Mama mia, che vo' sape; All the Things You
Are (outtake)
Orchestra with Johnny Green
Soundtrack for *Because You're Mine*.

2 August 1951
The Lord's Prayer
Organ, Wesley Tourtelot
Orchestra with Johnny Green
Soundtrack for *Because You're Mine*.

19 October 1951
Lee-Ah-Loo; All the Things You Are (outtake)
Orchestra with Johnny Green
Soundtrack for *Because You're Mine*.

21 October 1951
The Song Angels Sing
Orchestra with Johnny Green
Soundtrack for *Because You're Mine*.

30 October 1951
Granada
Orchestra with Johnny Green
Soundtrack for *Because You're Mine*.

1 November 1951
Il Trovatore: Miserere (excerpt)*; The Lord's Prayer (outtake)**
*Piano, Irving Aaronson; **organ, Wesley Tourtelot
Soundtrack for *Because You're Mine*.

10 November 1951
Cavalleria Rusticana: Addio alla madre
Orchestra with Johnny Green
Soundtrack for *Because You're Mine*.

24 November 1951
Rigoletto: Addio, addio (solo version: Peggi Bonini's vocals were added
28 November 1951)
Orchestra with Johnny Green
Soundtrack for *Because You're Mine*.

1 December 1951
Because You're Mine (reprise, takes 1 and 2) (with Doretta Morrow)
Orchestra with Johnny Green
Soundtrack for *Because You're Mine*.

20 June 1952
A Mighty Fortress (takes 1 and 2); I'll Walk with God
Organ, Wesley Tourtelot
Soundtrack for *The Student Prince*

29 July 1952
Serenade; Summertime in Heidelberg (with Ann Blyth); Beloved
Orchestra with Constantine Callinicos
Soundtrack for *The Student Prince*.

31 July 1952
Golden Days; What's to Be
Orchestra with Constantine Callinicos
Soundtrack for *The Student Prince*.

5 August 1952
Drink, Drink, Drink
Orchestra with Constantine Callinicos
Soundtrack for *The Student Prince*.

7 August 1952
Gaudeamus igitur (takes 1 and 2 with chorus, rejected)*; Ergo
bibamus**
*Orchestra with Constantine Callinicos; **piano, Constantine
Callinicos
Soundtrack for *The Student Prince*.

12 August 1952
Deep in My Heart (takes 1 and 2 with Ann Blyth)
Orchestra with Constantine Callinicos
Soundtrack for *The Student Prince*.

20 May 1953
Beloved
Orchestra with Constantine Callinicos
Soundtrack for *The Student Prince*.

June 1957
Seven Hills of Rome (version 1); Seven Hills of Rome (version 2,
rejected); All the Things You Are; There's Gonna be a Party Tonight;

Come Dance with Me; Lolita; Arrivederci Roma (with Luisa Di Meo);
Imitation Sequence (Temptation; Jezebel; Memories are Made of
This; When the Saints Go Marching In); Ay-Ay-Ay; Be My Love ('joke'
version); The Loveliest Night of the Year
Orchestra and chorus with George Stoll
Soundtrack for *Seven Hills of Rome*
Recorded at the Auditorium Angelico Studios, Rome.

July 1957
Rigoletto: Questa o quella
Orchestra with Silvio Clementelli
Soundtrack for *Seven Hills of Rome*
Recorded at the Auditorium Angelico Studios, Rome.

28 August 1958
Aida: Grand March; I Love Thee; *Cosi fan tutte*: E voi ridete (bass and
baritone names missing); *Pagliacci*: Vesti la giubba; *Otello*: Niun mi tema
Rome Opera House Orchestra and Chorus with Constantine
Callinicos
Soundtrack for *For the First Time*.

September 1958
Come prima; Ave Maria (Schubert) (takes 1 and 2)*; Je n'en connais
pas la fin**; O sole mio**; *Rigoletto*: La donna e mobile (accordionist
unknown)
*Orchestra with George Stoll; **orchestra with Carlo Savina
Soundtrack for *For the First Time*.

October 1958
Pineapple Pickers; The Hofbrauhaus Song
Accompanied by Johannes Rediske and his Band
Soundtrack for *For the First Time*.

Warner Brothers Studios

28 June 1955
La danza
Jazz-accordion, Dominic Frontiere
Soundtrack for *Serenade*.

30 June 1955
Torna a Surriento
Piano, Jacob Gimpel
Soundtrack for *Serenade*.

5 July 1955
La Bohème: O soave fanciulla (solo version)*
*Soprano section, Jean Fenn, recorded 23 August 1955
Piano, Jacob Gimpel
Soundtrack for *Serenade*.

7 July 1955
Serenade (take 1, test-recording); My Destiny (take 1)
Piano, Jacob Gimpel
Soundtrack for *Serenade*.

11 July 1955
My Destiny (take 2); *Der Rosenkavalier*: Di rigori armato
Piano, Jacob Gimpel
Soundtrack for *Serenade*.

13 July 1955
Fedora: Amor ti vieta; *L'Arlesiana*: Lamento di Federico; *Tosca*: Qual
occhio al mondo (rejected); *Il Trovatore*: Di quella pira; *La Bohème*:
Ti lasciaremo all stagion fiori (solo version)*
*Soprano section, Jean Fenn, recorded 23 August 1955
Orchestra with Ray Heindorf
Soundtrack for *Serenade*.

15 July 1955
Serenade (take 2); Serenade (alternative title track); *L'Africana*: O
paradiso
Piano, Jacob Gimpel
Soundtrack for *Serenade*.

19 July 1955
Turandot: Nessun dorma (rejected); *Otello*: Dio ti giocondi (take 1
with Gloria Boh) (rejected, but Lanza end monologue retained for
soundtrack)

Orchestra with Ray Heindorf
Soundtrack for *Serenade*.

21 July 1955
Turandot: Nessun dorma; My Destiny; Serenade; *Otello*: Dio ti
giocondi (take 2 with Gloria Boh, rejected)
Orchestra with Ray Heindorf
Soundtrack for *Serenade*.

18 August 1955
Ave Maria
Piano, Jacob Gimpel, overdubbed by Eugene Le Pique, organ, 23
August 1955
Soundtrack for *Serenade*.

25 August 1955
Serenade (takes 3 and 4)
Orchestra with Ray Heindorf
Soundtrack for *Serenade*.

26 August 1955
Serenade (take 5)*; *Don Giovanni*: Il mio tesoro (takes 1 and 2,
rejected)
*Accordion, Dominic Frontiere; piano, Jacob Gimpel, with unnamed
accompanists on bass, guitar and marimba
Soundtrack for *Serenade*.

22 November 1955
Otello: Dio ti giocondi (with Licia Albanese)
Orchestra with Ray Heindorf
Soundtrack for *Serenade*.

Appendix III: The Coca-Cola Shows

The so-called Coca-Cola Shows, sponsored by this company, were broadcast 'live' between 10 June 1951 and 5 September 1952, initially on Sunday evenings before moving to a regular Friday evening slot. The tracks were put down in the Los Angeles Radio Recorder Studios; the applause and introductions by MC Bill Baldwin were added to the tapes by the studio technician. As such, they compare well with Lanza's other studio work – indeed, many of these recordings are superior to the ones he made for RCA Victor, whilst others are unique only to the shows, and thus doubly important from the fans' perspective, even though (with a 30-minute time limit for each show) some of the operatic items were performed faster than the composer intended. Almost all of these items have at some time been released on vinyl album or CD. The exact dates they were recorded is unclear: the following represent the dates the shows were aired. The orchestra is conducted by Ray Sinatra, save for items marked * when the conductor is Constantine Callinicos.

10 June 1951
Granada; Toselli's Serenade; Because; Be My Love.

17 June 1951
Tra-la-la; Ah, Vucallo; I'm Falling in Love with Someone; Come Back to Sorrento.

24 June 1951
My Song, My Love; Drigo's Serenade; I'll Never Love You; *Pagliacci*:
Vesti la giubba.

1 July 1951
Funiculi, funicula (English); Mama mia, che vo' sape; Someday;
Thine Alone.

8 July 1951
For You Alone; La danza; I'm Falling in Love with Someone; Torna
a Surriento.

15 July 1951
The Tina-Lina; Lolita; *Rigoletto*: La donna e mobile (English); If.

22 July 1951
The World is Mine Tonight; Yours is My Heart Alone; Oh, Nights of
Splendour; *Tosca*: Recondita Armonia.

29 July 1951
Jerome Kern Special: All the Things You Are; Long Ago and Far Away;
The Touch of Your Hand; The Song is You.

5 August 1951
Cosi, cosa; Softly as in a Morning Sunrise; Diane.

12 August 1951
The Loveliest Night of the Year; A vucchella; Wanting You; Ave Maria
(Bach–Gounod).

19 August 1951
I've Got You Under My Skin; Marechiare; My Heart Stood Still;
L'Africana: O paradiso.

26 August 1951
Ah, Sweet Mystery of Life; If You are But a Dream; Time on
My Hands.

2 September 1951
Without a Song; Wonder Why; They Didn't Believe Me; The Lord's Prayer.

9 September 1951
Night and Day; The Desert Song; *Tosca*: E lucevan le stelle.

16 September 1951
Song of Songs; Strange Music; The Rosary.

3 December 1951
Valencia; Through the Years; Where or When; None but the Lonely Heart.

10 December 1951
Ay-Ay-Ay; Look for the Silver Lining; Your Eyes have Told Me So; Guardian Angels.

17 December 1951
Ciribiribin; Only Make Believe; Sylvia; You and the Night and the Music.

24 December 1951
O Come All Ye Faithful; Silent Night; O Little Town of Bethlehem; The First Nowell.

31 December 1951
Siboney; Neapolitan Love Song (Victor Herbert); When Day is Done.

7 January 1952
The Best Things in Life are Free; Temptation; Trees.

14 January 1952
The Donkey Serenade; The Thrill is Gone; *Rigoletto*: Questo o quella.

21 January 1952
Lygia; My Romance; The Hills of Home; One Night of Love.

25 January 1952
The Night is Young and You're So Beautiful; Somewhere a Voice is
Calling; Roses of Picardy; Begin the Beguine.

1 February 1952
Lady of Spain; Charmaine; What is This Thing Called Love; I'll See
You Again.

8 February 1952
Romance; Tell Me That You Love Me Tonight; Among My Souvenirs;
L'Elisir D'Amore: Una furtiva lagrima.

15 February 1952
I'll See You in my Dreams; Memories; I Never Knew; My Buddy.

22 February 1952
If I Loved You; Fools Rush In; Someday I'll Find You; Tell
Me Tonight.

7 March 1952
Yesterdays; Day In, Day Out; *Carmen*: La fleur que tu m'avais jetée.

14 March 1952
Danny Boy; A Kiss in the Dark; The Trembling of a Leaf; My Wild
Irish Rose.

21 March 1952
A Little Love, a Little Kiss; Santa Lucia*; *Cavalleria Rusticana*: Addio
alla madre*.

28 March 1952
The Moon was Yellow; Marcheta; Core 'ngrato*; *Rigoletto*: La donna
e mobile*.

4 April 1952
April in Paris; And You are Here; Fenesta che lucive*; *La Bohème*:
Che gelida manina*.

11 April 1952
Deep in My Heart, Dear; You Are Love; Dicitencello vuie*.

18 April 1952
Play Gypsies, Dance Gypsies; When You're In Love; Maria Mari*; *La Gioconda*: Cielo e mar*.

25 April 1952
Alone Together; Non ti scordar di me*; *Rigoletto*: Parmi veder le lagrime*.

2 May 1952
Beautiful Love; I'll Be Seeing You; Santa Lucia luntana*; *Aida*: Celeste Aida*.

9 May 1952
Love is the Sweetest Thing; *Andrea Chénier*: Come un bel di di maggio*.

16 May 1952
You'll Never Walk Alone; Na sera 'e maggio*; *L'Arlesiana*: Lamento di Federico*.

23 May 1952
Somebody Bigger than You and I; *Andrea Chénier*: Un di all'azzurro spazio*; Tu ca nun chiagne*.

30 May 1952
One Alone; Canta pe' me*; *La Forza Del Destino*: O tu che in seno agli angeli*.

6 June 1952
Besame mucho; Senza nisciuno*; *Fedora*: Amor ti vieta*.

13 June 1952
A Kiss; Parlami d'amore Mariu*.

20 June 1952
Musica proibita*; *Pagliacci*: Un tal gioco*.

27 June 1952
La Spagnola*; *La Bohème* (Leoncavallo): Testa adorata*.

The following were alternative takes recorded for *The Mario Lanza Show*, but not broadcast; the recording dates are unknown.

a) With Ray Sinatra
Day In, Day Out; Deep in my Heart, Dear; The Hills of Home; I'm Falling in Love with Someone; Look For the Silver Lining; Love is the Sweetest Thing; My Romance; Oh, Nights of Splendour; One Night of Love; Serenade (*The Student Prince*); Someday I'll Find You; Wanting You; You are Love; You'll Never Walk Alone; Your Eyes have Told Me So.

b) With Constantine Callinicos
Na sera 'e maggio; Santa Lucia luntana.

Appendix IV: Selected Albums

Pre-1960 RCA Red Label Vinyl Albums

Love Songs and Neapolitan Serenade (LM 1188)
Because; For You Alone; Marechiare; A vucchella; Serenade (Toselli); Serenade (Drigo); I Love Thee; Mattinata; O sole mio; My Song, My Love; Be My Love; I'll Never Love You.

A *Kiss and Other Love Songs* (LM 1860)
A Kiss; Begin the Beguine; Long Ago and Far Away; The Night is Yours and You're So Beautiful; My Heart Stood Still; Sylvia; The Moon was Yellow; Night and Day; My Romance; Siboney; The Thrill is Gone; Valencia; Beautiful Love; Yesterdays; Besame mucho; Without a Song.

Magic Mario (LM 1943)
The World is Mine Tonight; Wanting You; When You're In Love; Parlami d'amore Mariu; Tell Me Tonight; Softly as in a Morning Sunrise; Fools Rush In; One Alone; None but the Lonely Heart; Ay-Ay-Ay; The Trembling of a Leaf; Make Believe; Roses of Picardy.

Mario Lanza in Serenade (LM 1996)
Serenade; La danza; Torna a Surriento; O soave fanciulla (with Jean Fenn); Di rigori armato; Di quella pira; Amor ti vieta; O paradiso; Dio ti gioconda (excerpt with Licia Albanese); Dio! mi potevi scagliar; Ave Maria; Lamento di Federico; Nessun dorma; My Destiny.

The Touch of Your Hand (LM 1927)
The Touch of Your Hand; The Song is You; Oh, Nights of Splendour;

Someday I'll Find You; Your Eyes have Told Me So; Strange Music;
The Desert Song; You Are Love; Day In, Day Out; Love is the
Sweetest Thing; I'm Falling in Love with Someone; Look For the
Silver Lining; I've Got You Under My Skin; The Hills of Home.

Lanza on Broadway (LM 2070)
On the Street Where You Live; Younger than Springtime; Speak Low;
More than You Know; Falling in Love with Love; Why was I Born;
And This is My Beloved; So In Love with You am I; September Song;
My Romance; This Nearly was Mine; You'll Never Walk Alone.

Seven Hills of Rome (LM 2211)
Seven Hills of Rome; There's Gonna be a Party Tonight; Lolita;
Questa o quella; Arrivederci Roma; Temptation/Jezebel/Memories are
Made of This/When the Saints Go Marching In; Come Dance with
Me; Never Till Now; Do You Wonder; Earthbound; Love in a Home;
Serenade; My Destiny.

Mario Lanza in A Cavalcade Of Show Tunes (LM 2090)
Lover Come Back to Me; I've Told Every Little Star; Donkey
Serenade; All the Things You Are; Giannina mia; Rose Marie; Yours is
My Heart Alone; Thine Alone; Will You Remember; Gypsy Love
Song; Only a Rose; Tramp! Tramp! Tramp!

Mario! (LM 2331)
Funiculi, funicula; Dicitencello vuie; Maria Mari; Voce 'e notte; Canta
pe' me; O surdato 'namurato; Come facette mammeta; Santa Lucia
luntana; Fene che lucive; Tu ca nun chiagne; Na sera 'e maggio;
Passione.

Lanza Sings Christmas Carols (LM 2333)
The First Nowell; O Come All Ye Faithful; Away in a Manger; We
Three Kings of Orient Are; O Little Town of Bethlehem; Silent Night;
Deck the Halls; Hark the Herald Angels Sing; God Rest Ye Merry
Gentlemen; Joy to the World; O Christmas Tree; I Saw Three Ships; It
Came Upon the Midnight Clear; Guardian Angels.

For the First Time (LM 2338)
Come prima; Tarantella; O sole mio; Neapolitan Dance; Je n'en
connais pas la fin; Mazurka; Vesti la giubba; *Otello*: Finale; *Aida*: Act
I; Ich liebe dich; Ave Maria; Wer einmal nur in München war;
Pineapple Pickers.

The Student Prince (LM 2339)
Overture; Golden Days; Thoughts will Come Back to Me; Beloved;
Serenade; Drink, Drink, Drink; I'll Walk with God; Student Life;
Gaudeamus igitur; Summertime in Heidelberg; Just We Two; Deep in
my Heart, Dear.

Mario Lanza Sings Caruso Favourites (LM 2393)
Vieni sul mar; Senza nisciuno; Musica proibita; Vaghissima sembianza;
Serenata; Lolita; Luna d'estate; L'alba separa dalla luce l'ombra; Pour un
baiser; La mia canzone; Ideale; Santa Lucia.

The Desert Song (LM 2440)
Overture; Riff Song; Azuri's Dance; One Alone; The Desert Song;
French Military Marching Song; Then You will Know; Romance; One
Good Boy Gone Wrong; I Want a Kiss; Let Love Go; One Flower in
Your Garden.

The Mario Lanza Program (Recital, Royal Albert Hall, London)
(LM 2454)
L'Arlesiana; Lamento di Federico; Gia il sole dal Gange; Pieta
Signore; Tell Me, Oh Blue, Blue Sky; Bonjour, ma belle; The House
on the Hill; E lucevan le stelle; Mama mia, che vo' sape; A vucchella;
Marechiare; I'm Falling in Love with Someone; Because You're Mine;
Seven Hills of Rome.

The Vagabond King (LM 2509)
Overture; Opening Chorus; Someday; Drinking Song; Love Me
Tonight; Only a Rose; Tomorrow; Love For Sale; Hunting; Nocturne;
Huguette Waltz; Song of theVagabonds; Finale.

I'll Walk with God (LM 2607)
Ave Maria; Addio alla madre; I'll Walk with God; The Virgin's
Slumber Song; O Holy Night; Somebody Bigger than You and I;
Because; The Trembling of a Leaf; None but the Lonely Heart;
Through the Years; I Love Thee; Trees; The Lord's Prayer;
Guardian Angels.

I'll See You In My Dreams (LM 2720)
Spring is Here; With a Song in my Heart; Among my Souvenirs;
Marchetta; Memories; Naughty Marietta; Ah! Sweet Mystery of Life;
I'll Be Seeing You; Cosi, cosa; Lady of Spain; La Spagnola; When Day
is Done; Good News; The Best Things in Life are Free; I'll See You in
my Dreams.

If You are But a Dream (LM 2790)
April in Paris; Time on my Hands; What is This Thing Called Love;
Charmaine; A Little Love, a Little Kiss; If You are But a Dream; Play
Gypsies, Dance Gypsies; Where or When; A Kiss in the Dark; My Buddy;
You and the Night and the Music; Alone Together.

Appendix V: Television Appearances

30 September 1954
The Shower of Stars, USA
Sponsored by Chrysler Motors
Mario mimed 'Be My Love', 'Vesti la giubba' and 'Marechiare'.

28 October 1954
The Shower of Stars, USA
Sponsored by Chrysler Motors
Mario sang 'E lucevan le stelle' and 'Someday'.

31 October 1957
The Christophers Show, Italy
Sponsored by The Christophers religious movement, New York, and
filmed at the Vatican
Introduced by Father Keller
Mario sang 'Ave Maria' (Schubert), 'Because You're Mine' and
'Santa Lucia'.

24 November 1957
Sunday Night at the London Palladium, UK
Introduced by Hughie Green
Mario repeated his *Royal Variety Show* programme of 18 November:
'Because You're Mine', 'E lucevan le stelle' and 'The Loveliest Night of
the Year'.

18 January 1958
Saturday Night Spectacular, UK
Introduced by David Jacobs
Mario sang 'Softly as a Morning Sunrise', 'Marechiare' and 'I'm Falling in Love with Someone'.

18 January 1958
The Tonight Show, USA
Introduced by Ed Sullivan
A short film of Mario showed him at the Villa Badoglio, Rome, but he was not asked to sing.

Bibliography: Primary and Secondary Sources

Anger, Kenneth, *Hollywood Babylon I & II*, Arrow, 1986.

Anonymous, 'Million Dollar Voice', *Time*, August 1951.

Bernard, Matt, *Mario Lanza*, McFadden-Bartell, 1971.

Bessette, Roland L., *Mario Lanza: Tenor In Exile*, Amadeus Press, 1999.

Bret, David, 'Interviews With Marlene Dietrich', 1989.

Bret, David: *Maria Callas: The Tigress and The Lamb*, Robson Books, 1997.

Callinicos, Constantine, with Ray Robinson, *The Mario Lanza Story*, Coward-McCann, 1960.

Charles, Arthur, 'Return Engagement', *Modern Screen*, March 1953.

Cocozza, Maria, 'Mario Lanza Lives', *Photoplay*, December 1962.

Dalida, Interview with France Inter, 1986.

Eames, John Douglas, *The MGM Story*, Octopus, 1979.

Gabor, Zsa Zsa, *One Lifetime Is Not Enough*, Delacorte, 1991.

Gould, Helen, 'Is Lanza A Changed Man?', *Movieland*, April 1956.

Green, Isadore, 'The Nervous Mario Lanza', *Record Mirror*, December 1957.

Henaghan, Jim, 'Wonderful Madman', *Modern Screen*, June 1950.

Hopper, Hedda, 'Lanza Talks', *Photoplay*, November 1953.

Hopper, Hedda, *The Whole Truth and Nothing But*, Doubleday, 1963.

Lanza, Betty, 'My Heart Sings', *Motion Picture*, November 1950.

Lanza, Betty, 'My Husband's First Love', *Movie Stars Parade*, November 1951.

Lanza, Mario, 'My Home Town', *Modern Screen*, September 1950.

Maddox, Ben, 'Lanza: My Personal Plans', *Movieland*, May 1953.

Newton, Jim, 'He Knows What He Wants', *Modern Screen*, June 1953.

Parish, James Robert, *The Hollywood Book of Death*, McGraw-Hill, 2001.

Parsons, Louella, *Tell It To Louella*, Putnam, 1961.

Peterson, Marva, 'Lanza Lives Big', *Modern Screen*, November 1953.

Quinlan, David, *Quinlan's Film Stars: Film Character Actors*, Batsford, 1981, 1986.

Robinson, Terry and Strait, Raymond, *Lanza: His Tragic Life*, Prentice-Hall, 1980.

The Royal Variety Performance: London Palladium Archives.

Toby, Henry, 'Lanza Speaks', *Picturegoer*, September 1957.

Various, *The Mario Lanza Story*, BBC Radio, 1974.

Wade, Jack, 'They're Talking About Lanza', *Modern Screen*, October 1951.

Wallace, Leonard, 'The Golden Voice', *Picturegoer*, June 1957.

Whitney, Dwight, 'Handsome Mario Lanza...Celluloid Caruso?', *Collier's*, September 1949.

Zec, Donald, *Put The Knife In Gently*, Robson Books, 2003.

Zeitlin, Ida, 'The Mario Lanza Story', *Photoplay*, August 1951.

Zeitlin, Ida, 'In The Name Of Love', *Photoplay*, June 1952.

Index